# Cybersecurity Threats with New Perspectives

*Edited by Muhammad Sarfraz*

Published in London, United Kingdom

IntechOpen

*Supporting open minds since 2005*

Cybersecurity Threats with New Perspectives
http://dx.doi.org/10.5772/intechopen.92535
Edited by Muhammad Sarfraz

Contributors
Mohammed Ibrahim Alghamdi, Prasanta Kumar Sahoo, Rodolfo Augusto Melo Ward de Oliveira, Borka Jerman Blažič, Rebecca Parry, Davi Alves, Manfred Sneps-Sneppe, Francisco José Cesteros García, Nazahah Rahim, Joshua Ojo Nehinbe



First published in London, United Kingdom, 2021 by IntechOpen
IntechOpen is the global imprint of INTECHOPEN LIMITED, registered in England and Wales, registration number: 11086078, 5 Princes Gate Court, London, SW7 2QJ, United Kingdom
Printed in Croatia

British Library Cataloguing-in-Publication Data
A catalogue record for this book is available from the British Library

Additional hard and PDF copies can be obtained from orders@intechopen.com

Cybersecurity Threats with New Perspectives
Edited by Muhammad Sarfraz
p. cm.
Print ISBN 978-1-83968-852-2
Online ISBN 978-1-83968-853-9
eBook (PDF) ISBN 978-1-83968-854-6

For EU product safety concerns:
IN TECH d.o.o., Prolaz Marije Krucifikse Kozulić 3, 51000 Rijeka, Croatia, info@intechopen.com or visit our website at intechopen.com.

# Meet the editor

Muhammad Sarfraz is a professor in the Department of Information Science, Kuwait University, Kuwait. His research interests include optimization, computer graphics, computer vision, image processing, machine learning, pattern recognition, soft computing, data science, and intelligent systems. Prof. Sarfraz has been a keynote/invited speaker at various platforms around the globe. He has advised/supervised more than 110 students for their MSc and Ph.D. theses. He has published more than 400 publications as books, journal articles, and conference papers. He has authored and/or edited around seventy books. Prof. Sarfraz is a member of various professional societies. He is a chair and member of international advisory committees and organizing committees of numerous international conferences. He is also an editor and editor in chief for various international journals.

# Contents

# Preface

Cyber threats and security are active and important areas of study, practice, and research today. This book compiles original and innovative findings on ethical, political, legal, and social issues relating to cyber security and threats. The ten chapters in this comprehensive reference explore the developments, methods, approaches, and surveys of cyber security and threats in a wide variety of fields and endeavors. It covers technical aspects as well as management, social, and government issues. The book has been compiled with views to provide researchers, practitioners, academicians, military professionals, government officials, and other industry professionals with an in-depth discussion of the latest advances in the field.

Mohammed I. Alghamdi starts the book with Chapter 1, "Digital Forensics in Cyber Security—Recent Trends, Threats, and Opportunities" which examines the use of digital forensics in countering cybercrimes, a critical breakthrough in cybersecurity. The chapter analyzes the most recent trends in digital forensics, including cloud forensics, social media forensics, and the Internet of Things (IoT) forensics. The research presented relates to specific threats to digital forensics, including technical, operational, and personnel-related challenges. Additionally, the chapter examines the use of USB forensics, intrusion detection, and artificial intelligence as major opportunities for digital forensics that can make the processes easy, efficient, and safe.

Chapter 2, "An Assessment of the Risk of Service Supplier Bankruptcies as a Cybersecurity Threat" by Rebecca Parry, states that behind technology service suppliers lie companies that are subject to the risk of business failure due to market conditions and trading risks. Such failures could suddenly stop customers from accessing services or content, with potentially devastating business and personal impacts, given the rising importance of digital economies. The risk can be illustrated by reference to cloud computing insolvencies. This cybersecurity risk has barely been touched upon in the literature, since it lies at the intersection between law and computer science, both areas requiring high levels of specialist understanding. This chapter is part of initial attempts to identify the threats presented.

In Chapter 3, "Cybersecurity Skills in EU: New Educational Concept for Closing the Missing Workforce Gap," Borka Jerman Blažič emphasizes that recruiting, retaining, and maintaining a validated number of cybersecurity professionals in the workplace is a constant battle, not only for the technical side of cybersecurity but also for the overlooked area of non-technical, managerial-related jobs in the cyber sector. This chapter presents and discusses the actions and developments in the education concept of cybersecurity knowledge and skills intended to meet the needs of the labor market in the European Union. It also presents and discusses changes in the education prepared by higher-education institutions and professional training providers.

Chapter 4, "An Emerging Solution for Detection of Phishing Attacks," by Prasanta Kumar Sahoo discusses how more and more people are using the Internet to carry out their daily work and how hackers are orchestrating security attacks on web browsers and servers to steal vital data. This chapter uses machine learning algorithms to classify between phishing e-mails and genuine e-mails and help the user detect attacks. The architectural model proposed in this chapter is to identify phishing and use a J48 decision tree classifier to distinguish fake e-mail from real e-mail. The algorithm presented advances through several stages to identify phishing attacks and helps users protect their vital information.

In Chapter 5, "A Model for Auditing Smart Intrusion Detection Systems (IDSs) and Log Analyzers in Cyber Physical Systems (CPSs)," NehinbeJoshua Ojo Nehinbe discusses how one can hardly find suitable models that can be adopted by auditors to concurrently audit smart IDSs and log analyzers in CPSs that are also founded on sound empirical claims. This chapter uses alerts from Snort and the C++ programming language to practically explore the issues related to cyber threats and propose a feasible model for operators and researchers to lessen problems. Evaluation with real and synthetic datasets demonstrates that the capabilities and resilience of smart IDSs to safeguard CPSs can be improved given a framework to facilitate auditing of smart IDSs and log analyzers in cyberspaces and knowledge of the variability in lengths and components of alerts warned by smart IDSs.

In Chapter 6, "Digital Culture: Control and Domination of Technical Images in the Era of Psychocapitalism," Rodolfo Augusto Melo Ward de Oliveira presents a theoretical study to understand the transmutation of modern culture into digital culture, which is intrinsically linked to technological, political, economic, artistic, and cultural advances. The goal of this chapter is to unite components of the visual culture and the culture of convergence to explain how new realities and new forms of control and domination are created through images and used on a large scale by the neoliberalist system in the network society, inaugurating the new phase of capitalism, that is, psychocapitalism. The chapter uses the disciplines of art, sociology, philosophy, anthropology, and social as a basis.

Chapter 7, "The Impact of Denial-of-Service Attack for Bitcoin Miners, Lisk Forgers, and a Mitigation Strategy for Lisk Forgers" by Davi Alves, states that bandwidth-depleting Denial-of-Service (DoS) attacks can impact the propagation of a mined block in the Bitcoin blockchain network. On Bitcoin Proof-of-Work (PoW) consensus, several machines try to resolve an expensive cryptographic puzzle faster than anyone else and succeed to mine a valid block. Despite a DoS attack impeding one's machine to propagate its mined block allowing it to become valid for most peers, there are several other peers to resolve the puzzle in time, hence the blockchain will continue to grow. However, from the perspective of the owner of the attacked machine, this can be critical because it will not receive a mining reward. This chapter covers such an attack in the Lisk blockchain that utilizes the Delegated Proof of Stake (DPoS) consensus mechanism. A mitigation strategy has been created, based on two tools allowing a delegate account to be configured in more than one node, allowing to forge a block even when one of its nodes is under DoS attack. The chapter also explores the transaction flood DoS attack and presents a mitigation strategy created for a specific sidechain in the Lisk ecosystem. Finally, the chapter evaluates scenarios and mitigation strategies created for each attack demonstrating solutions for several scenarios.

Chapter 8, "On Telecommunications Thorn Path to the IP World: From Cybersecurity to Artificial Intelligence" by Manfred Sneps-Sneppe, is devoted to discussion of the telecommunications development strategy. This chapter discusses the Defense

Information System Network move from circuits to packets, namely, the Joint Vision 2010 doctrine, which is the implementation of signaling protocol #7 and Advanced Intelligent Network, and Joint Vision 2020, which is the network transformation by the transition to Assured Services Session Initiation Protocol and Multifunctional Soft Switches. It describes some packet-switching shortcomings during the implementation of Joint Vision 2020, namely, the failed GSM-O contract and joint regional security stacks failures. The US Department of Defense (DoD) newly released cloud strategy positions the general-purpose Joint Enterprise Defense Infrastructure (JEDI) cloud initiative as the foundation. The strategy emphasizes a cloud hierarchy at the DoD, but JEDI cloud strategy leaves a series of unanswered questions relating to the interoperability of clouds. The chapter concludes that long-term channel–packet coexistence seems inevitable, especially in the face of growing cyber threats.

In Chapter 9, “Private Investigation and Open Source INTelligence (OSINT),” Francisco José Cesteros García explains how to use the Open Source INTelligence (OSINT) methodology to legally become part of the steps in a private investigation.

The amount of personal information available online is growing, due to it being willingly exposed and published via data sharing by users. This has the effect of facilitating investigations, i.e. increases the rate of driving them to their conclusions. OSINT is the first step that private investigation must consider and this chapter covers and explains why and how to do this.

The book closes with Chapter 10, “Bibliometric Analysis of Cyber Threat and Cyber Attack Literature: Exploring the Higher Education Context” by Nazahah Rahim. This chapter examines the trends of literature on cyber threats and cyber attacks with a focus on higher education. It employs a bibliometric analysis through the Scopus database to offer research ideas and trigger debates. Analyzed parameters include the number of document types, publications, authorship, citation, and subject areas, as well as the topographical dispersion of published research. As many as 606 papers were published since 2003. The results indicate that publications hit a plateau in 2018, with English becoming the main publication language. The most prominent country that has contributed to the literature is the United States. Nonetheless, most of the publications were contained by the subject area of “Computer Science”, hence it is relatively challenging to track progress in the education context. This chapter presents a groundwork providing insights for others to probe into the topic further.

**Muhammad Sarfraz**
Department of Information Science,
College of Life Sciences,
Kuwait University,
Kuwait

Chapter 1

# Digital Forensics in Cyber Security—Recent Trends, Threats, and Opportunities

*Mohammed I. Alghamdi*

## Abstract

The rapid technological advancement has led the entire world to shift towards digital domain. However, this transition has also result in the emergence of cybercrimes and security breach incidents that threatens the privacy and security of the users. Therefore, this chapter aimed at examining the use of digital forensics in countering cybercrimes, which has been a critical breakthrough in cybersecurity. The chapter has analyzed the most recent trends in digital forensics, which include cloud forensics, social media forensics, and IoT forensics. These technologies are helping the cybersecurity professionals to use the digital traces left by the data storage and processing to keep data safe, while identifying the cybercriminals. However, the research has also observed specific threats to digital forensics, which include technical, operational and personnel-related challenges. The high complexity of these systems, large volume of data, chain of custody, the integrity of personnel, and the validity and accuracy of digital forensics are major threats to its large-scale use. Nevertheless, the chapter has also observed the use of USB forensics, intrusion detection and artificial intelligence as major opportunities for digital forensics that can make the processes easier, efficient, and safe.

**Keywords:** digital forensics, data security, cybercrime, data theft, security attack

## 1. Introduction

The introduction of Web 2.0 technologies and the significant development in the digital hemisphere has notably changed the paradigm of the entire world. Nowadays, people are increasingly engaged in web-based interactions, contribute to open projects, and share their Chapter online. However, the anonymity and ease with which all of these can be executed raise distress about trust and verifiability [1]. In particular, the evolution of digital technologies has resulted in the emergence of new ways of conducting computer crimes. Besides, the availability of networks, along with highly optimized data transfer, has raised security concerns. Malicious methodologies, tools, and software are implemented and designed every day to pose a threat to public and private networks while simultaneously exploiting data storage, for extracting useful information [2]. To counter this emerging threat, digital forensics has gained major attention in resolving cybersecurity threats. As discussed by [3], digital forensics is the science of presenting, documenting, analyzing, preserving, and identifying information and evidence from electronic and digital devices while safeguarding the privacy of users. Furthermore, it also makes use of scientific techniques to recreate and explain the sequence of the events. By evaluating, reviewing, and recording these sequences, digital forensics aims at presenting such illegal artifacts as evidence in the court of law.

The modern world is undoubtedly driven by social networks and the evolution in digital technologies have further evolved cyber-crimes that significantly contributed in the development of new techniques, tools, and attacks that enable attackers to penetrate even in the well-controlled environment [4]. With that said, security experts, academics, and law enforcement agencies use digital forensics to tackle the increasing number of cyber anomalies. Such experts deploy scientific methods, such as identification, validation, interpretation, and documentation on digital devices like RAM, phones, memory cards, floppy disks, and flash drives to collect digital evidence. However, with the advancement in digital forensics techniques, hackers are equally exploiting anti-forensics technology to either produce delay or completely erase digital evidence [5]. Moreover, albeit the digital forensics framework is designed to ensure users privacy, the availability of ubiquitous internet access, the internet of things (IoT), and cloud computing has inspired new cybercrime waves. Furthermore, digital forensics is expected to face unique and new challenges because cyber threats and malware are being equipped with highly sophisticated and powerful anti-forensics techniques. Thus, it is important to investigate those challenges while simultaneously discovering recent digital forensics trends. In this account, the present study is dedicated to analyzing threats, opportunities, and recent trends of digital forensics in cybersecurity.

## 2. Recent digital forensic trends

### 2.1 Cloud forensics

Cloud forensics has recently immense much attention by forensics experts due to the fact that cloud computing offers massive resource pool, cost-effective solution, dynamicity, and wide access for storage. Hybrid, private, and public models of cloud computing exists, in addition to multiple services, such as security as service, database as service, integration as service, and software as service [5]. Furthermore, most companies and organizations transfer their products and services across the cloud every day due to multiple benefits, including high scalability, reduced cost of IT infrastructure, business continuity, and access to automatic updates. As a result, cloud computing has been widely accepted in multiple governments and private companies. Likewise, Communication Service Providers have established data centers across the globe in various jurisdictions that provide cloud services for ensuring value-effectiveness and service availability [4]. However, the rise in the number of cybercrimes and security in the cloud environment are the major hurdles for organizations to transfer their systems to this platform. Moreover, since forensics investigation in a cloud computing environment is complex, security analysts see cloud computing as a potential area of concern. Therefore, cloud forensics has gained major attention by forensics investigators to resolve cloud computing issues. Cloud forensics can be described as the potential application of digital forensics in a cloud-based environment [6]. This field utilizes scientific principles, proven methods, and technological practices to process events in cloud environment via reporting, examination, preservation, collection, and identification of digital data, so that events can be reconstructed.

The default characteristics of cloud computing, which includes a high degree of virtualization, data duplication, jurisdiction, and multi-tenancy add various complexity layers in cloud forensics. Besides, the procedures involved in cloud forensics depends on the deployment and service model of cloud computing [7]. For PaaS and SaaS, there is very limited control over the network or process monitoring. In contrast, IaaS not only offers a higher degree of control (DOC), but it also supports friendly forensic mechanism (See **Figure 1**). Despite the complexity involved in cloud forensics, it is undeniable that the evolution of cloud computing has raised privacy and security concerns. This has significantly increased the interest of digital forensics officers in the cloud forensics as it emphasizes on authentication, authorization, and accounting (AAA) protocol while simultaneously reconstructing, investigating, and analyzing a cloud attack event so that cloud system can be quickly recovered from it [8]. This is highly effective and stark in contrast with traditional forensics techniques that utilizes log files to isolate the system in the hope of extracting useful information. Still, it blurs the view of the event. Cloud forensics can be categorized into three categories: Legal, Organizational, and Technical [9]. The legal dimension takes care of the development of agreements and regulations to ascertain that digital forensics methods do not breach regulations and laws. On the contrary, the organizational dimension encompasses organizational factors of the digital forensics [10]. Finally, the technical dimension covers the procedures and tools that are essential to execute forensic investigation in a cloud computing domain. Thus, it can be established that cloud forensics is one of the most prominent trends in the digital forensic domain. It is because, it enables forensics investigators to take full advantage of cloud computing characteristics, such as distributed forensic processing, computing power, reporting, and scalability.

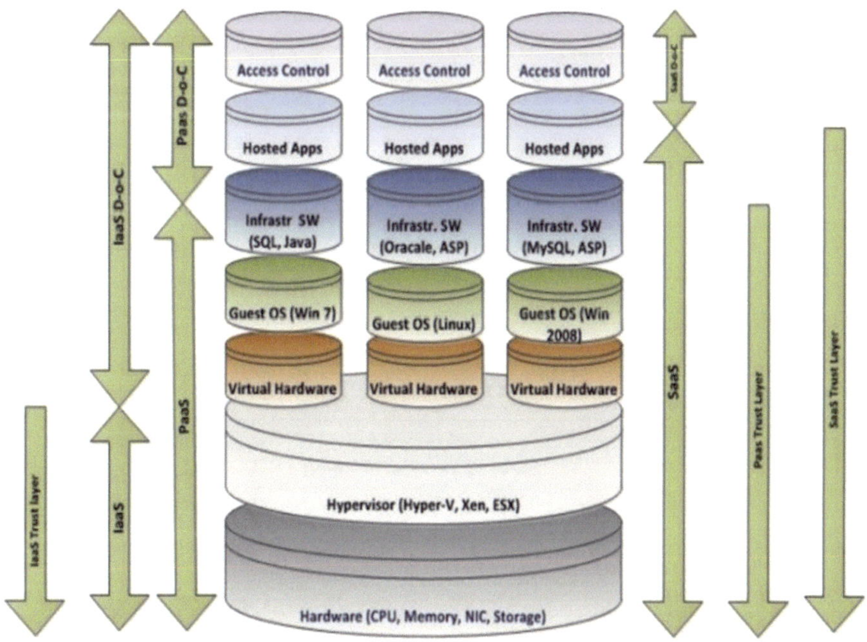


**Figure 1.**
*Trust layer, degree of control, cloud model [6].*

## 2.2 Social media forensics

The advancement in Industry 4.0 and Web 2.0 technologies has significantly increased the acceptance of social media platforms and it has become a primary source of socialization. Users actively share their information, create accounts, and get engage in social forms through these sites. As a result, hackers are exposed to various opportunities to exploit user's account [5]. In addition, different social media applications like LinkedIn, Instagram, Facebook, and Twitter have been exposed to multiple cyber threats and malware. Attacks on social media platforms can take place outside the system/network or within the network. Outside systems attack usually include DDoS, or DoS, while attacks within the network include retrieving cookies data [4]. Besides, it is established that the database of these social media applications is most vulnerable to such attacks. Considering this situation, digital investigators have shifted their interest towards social media forensics. Social media forensics assist experts in carrying out a criminal investigation, where social media posts serve as excellent evidence to investigators (See **Figure 2**). Likewise, social media platforms are a perfect source of information regarding potential offenders, suspects, and witnesses, and it is considered supreme for profiling [11]. In addition, by combining social media with digital forensics, investigators can gain access to a modern and diverse subset of sources of data, including demographic location, photographs, contact lists, geo-location, and text messages. This network data, combined with the metadata, has the potential to assist digital forensics investigations. Furthermore, the metadata can also be used to authenticate online social networking facts. Thus, it can be contended that social media forensics is a rising trend in the digital forensics' domain due to its ability to efficiently providing adequate digital evidence.

The advent of social media apps on a mass of platforms has enabled these networking domains to leave digital forensic trace or artifacts that can be of a valuable asset in an investigation. For instance, research like [12] discovered that the chat logs could be extracted from social media applications like Facebook and a huge amount of digital forensic artifacts, such as pictures, location data, friends, posts,

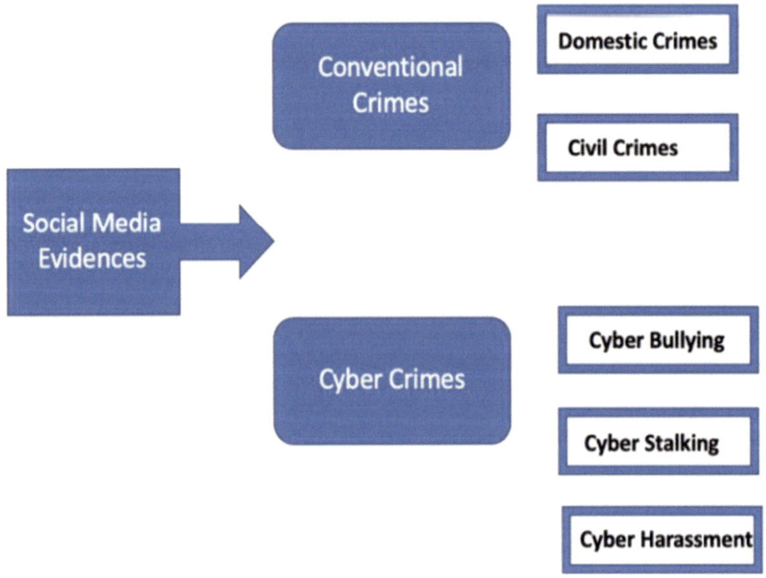


**Figure 2.**
*Use of social media forensics in criminal investigation [4].*

passwords, and usernames are left behind as potential evidence. These artifacts are essential evidence, which makes social media forensics as one of the most prominent digital forensic trends. Studies like [13] forensically examined social media applications, including MySpace, Twitter, and Facebook on Androids, iPhones, and Blackberries. The study proclaimed that they were successful in extracting digital forensic artifacts like comments posted, timestamps, passwords, URLs, pictures, and user data in text format. This indicates that social media forensics is not only a powerful tool to trace digital evidence spread across social media, but it also highly efficient in analyzing, authenticating, and acquiring digital evidence. In addition, social media forensics provide three dimensions of functionalities, namely reverse search integration, tempering localization analysis, and metadata visualization and extraction [14]. The first take advantage of Google Image Search is that it provides results in a web browser tab. Secondly, it incorporates six different tampering localization maps that are generated through forensic algorithms, which is further aimed at acquiring different tempering traces on social media. Thirdly, it fully supports metadata listing and displays any potential embedded thumbnails. With the help of these functionalities, forensic experts can further examine the information to extract useful evidence. This has made social media forensics a rising trend in the digital forensic domain.

### 2.3 IoT forensics

IoT is the latest paradigm that has notably changed the way mobile communication works. Conceptually, IoT can be defined as the interconnectivity of electronic devices that combines situational knowledge and sensing powers to execute tasks, intelligently [15]. Major IoT devices include smartphones, tablets, laptops, personal computers (PCs), and other various embedded portable devices. The continuous growth in the area of IoT has enabled users to share their data across different platforms. Besides, IoT systems can communicate with each other either via internet application programming interface or directly. In addition to this, they can also be controlled through computing devices, like cloud servers. The networking capabilities and smartness of IoT systems provide significant benefits for both business and domestic applications [16]. However, despite its tremendous advantages, IoT systems are subjected to several security threats and attacks, such as mass monitoring, destruction of IoT networks, Denial of Service (DoS), and ransomware. Therefore, digital forensic experts have developed a keen interest in IoT forensics to carry out the digital investigation. The rise of IoT forensics trend is due to the fact that IoT systems present multiple complex and unique challenges in the digital forensics field [4]. Moreover, IoT-based applications contain a huge number of resources and distinct devices that generates a tremendous amount of data, which is known as Big IoT data. This data, combined with digital forensics tools and techniques, provide investigators with an opportunity to trace cybercrimes that further help them in preventing cyber-attacks.

Despite the growing benefits of IoT forensics, it cannot be denied that it produces a massive amount of data and acquiring this data significantly increases the workload on data centers [17]. As a result, forensic investigators are forced to face additional analytics, security, and capacity challenges. Furthermore, the preservation and extraction of data from IoT-enabled services and devices present protocol, data formats, and physical interface challenges which further complicate evidence extraction process. However, regardless of several limitations, IoT forensics offers a richer and authentic source of evidence, as compared to conventional computer systems [18]. IoT forensics react to the requirements of users without requiring users' conscious interaction. As a result, the IoT forensics environment provides contextual evidence that helps digital forensic investigators to analyze physical world events. Thus, IoT forensics is one of the prominent trends of digital forensics domain, not only because of its ability to provide contextual and digital evidence but also due to various challenges faced by this domain.

## 3. Threats faced by digital forensics

### 3.1 Technical challenges

The advancement in digital technology has opened doors to various opportunities; however, it has also caused the digital forensics domain to face various challenges. Although different digital forensic experts and researchers have been analyzing and studying numerous known digital forensic issues, there is still a requirement to classify these challenges [19]. In this account, it has been discovered that digital forensic systems are exposed to technical challenges that threaten the integrity of these systems. Technical challenges are those potential threats that can be addressed using existing operations, protocols, and expertise. Understanding that digital forensics demands an optimum combination of ethical conduct and technical skills. Some of the major technical challenges, associated with digital forensics are encryption, a huge volume of data, and incompatibility among diverse forensic tools [20]. The advancement in communication technology has made sophisticated encryption products and services easy and widely accessible. Due to this, encryption algorithms and standards are becoming more complex, which further increases the time and difficulty of conducting cryptanalysis. This technique joins encrypted files together to extract meaningful information. In addition, encryption makes electronic data unreadable, which further enable criminals to camouflage their criminal activities [21]. For a digital forensic officer, this can negatively affect their investigation process. It has been discovered that around 60% of cases - involving some type of encryption - goes unprocessed because it significantly limits the ability of the investigator to extract information from the evidence [22]. Thus, the easy implementation, low cost, and the availability of encryption tools greatly pose a threat to the integrity and credibility of the digital forensics process.

In addition to encryption, huge volumes of data that exist within numerous applications- like enterprise resource planning-also poses a great threat to digital forensic operations. The substantial increase in data volumes significantly reduces the capability of legal systems and forensic investigators to keep up with the digital threats [23]. Likewise, with the introduction of cloud computing, much IT-related hardware, such as network switches, racks, and servers have been replaced with remote-on-demand, virtualized software that are configured according to business needs. Besides, these services and data can be managed and hosted by a third-party or the user from any place. Thus, the data and software have the possibility that it is stored physically across multiple geographic locations [22]. This distributive nature of data substantially lowers the control and visibility of forensic experts over digital forensic artifacts. Similarly, digital forensic tools and techniques commonly differ in cost, complexity, and functionality. Due to this, most of the digital forensic tools contain heterogeneous parts or elements, which increases their incompatibility to work together [20]. Moreover, some forensic tools are not able to handle the ever-increasing storage capacity of target devices. This means that vast targets constitute a major technical challenge to digital forensic operations because they demand more complex analysis techniques. Thus, it is affirmed that different technical challenges pose a great threat to the performance and integrity of digital forensic operations.

### 3.2 Operational challenges

It is a known fact that digital crimes are intentional in their scope of operation. Due to this, digital forensics is exposed to various operational challenges. Among such challenges, incidence prevention, response, and detection have gained much attention. Traditional IT environments that have on-premises data processing have integrated internal incident management process for ensuring utmost security [20]. This process utilizes intrusion detection systems, log file analysis, and monitoring, in addition to data loss prevention systems that identify and detect data loss, attackers, and intruders. For cloud users, these security incidents can often prove to be challenging. This is because, these security incidents compromise business and personal data and since they are equipped with anti-forensics technology, attackers can steal or destroy potential evidence [24]. Likewise, the lack of standardized procedures and processes in digital forensics alarmingly endangers the evidence extraction and investigation process. It is established that currently, digital forensic models lack standardization that has further increased the complexity of the process. Besides, studies like [22] argue that the lack of universal standards makes it quite tough to assess the competency of forensic experts. The absence of standardized procedures was acceptable when digital forensics was considered a mysterious investigation process that enabled experts to discover hidden pieces of evidence and information that further provided useful insights regarding criminal behaviors. However, with the increase in the development of digital technologies, digital forensic investigation is no longer limited to small computer systems rather a virtualized environment that consists of non-standard interfaces and different storage devices.

In addition to above-discussed threats, digital forensics is also exposed to forensics readiness problem. Forensic readiness can be understood as the capability of computer networks or computer systems to record data and activities in such a way that it can be perceived as authentic and are sufficient enough for forensics purposes [25]. However, the rapid development in cloud computing has forced organizations to dynamically change how they enact, develop, and plan IT strategies. Besides, cloud computing lacks forensic readiness aspect, which further threatens digital forensic operations. Similarly, manual analysis and intervention of physical hard drives is another potential operational challenge that is faced by digital forensics. Albeit, it is simple and straightforward in a single drive, or a single partition, the process becomes much more complicated when RAID configurations are involved [20]. Also, due to the complex nature of digital forensics, manual inspection of hard drive images can potentially risk the digital artifacts. Likewise, it is believed that forensic analysis should be valid, accurate, complete, and reliable. However, balancing between user privacy and retrieving key digital evidence is a major threat to digital forensics. Due to the increase in the storage capacity, often a small portion of the information is used for investigation and a larger amount of information is discarded [26]. This can lead to a breach of the user's privacy, which poses an additional challenge to digital forensic operations. Thus, in light of the evidence, it can be affirmed that operational challenges can notably endanger digital forensic analysis.

### 3.3 Personnel related challenges

Personnel related challenges endanger the integrity of digital evidence. Among various personnel-related challenges, lack of well-trained forensic staff is the most prominent one [20]. Despite the overwhelming significance of the digital forensics field because of cyber-crimes, the lack of qualified forensic officers threatens the process of digital forensics. The shortage of well-trained forensic investigators is due to the fierce competition in law enforcement as well as high requirements since digital forensics require technically proficient personnel that are certified and trained to deliver scientifically valid evidence [22]. Likewise, it cannot be denied that digital forensics has gained major importance among forensic practitioners, law enforcement agencies, and computer professionals. Unfortunately, the advancement in this field has encouraged an environment that is threatened by semantic disparities. Another potential personnel-related challenge is a chain of custody. Chain of custody refers to the location log that defines the collection point of the evidence. In digital forensic analysis, it is one of the most crucial issues because it requires physical control of the evidence that is not possible in a digital environment [7]. In addition, due to proprietary technology, procedures, and multi-jurisdictional laws, effectively managing the chain of custody is a major challenge that is faced by digital forensics. Hence, it can be established that personnel-related challenges pose a great challenge to traditional forensic operations.

In addition to the discussed challenges, it is undeniable that digital forensics lack a unified formal representation of standardized procedures and knowledge for analyzing and gathering digital artifacts. This inevitably causes incompatibility and conflict within various digital forensics tools [27]. Errors in the interpretation and analysis of digital artifacts occur when the standardized or formalized procedure for analyzing, preserving, and collecting digital evidence is absent. Likewise, when forensic experts manage a vast amount of data while simultaneously performing forensic investigation, they utilize specialized skills and digital technologies. However, these experts often fail to record their work, which further hampers training and external reviews [22]. Past knowledge and experience should be utilized to further train new digital forensic personnel while fostering knowledge sharing among detective communities. Unfortunately, digital forensic officers either fail to record their work or simply do not follow legal practices that further poses a great threat to digital forensic investigation.

## 4. Opportunities

### 4.1 USB forensics

Universal Serial Bus (USB) is a widely used storage device and it is considered very effective for their mobility and capacity. Normally, USB uses USB controller command to ensure security within the USB drive. However, due to its easy accessibility, it is often used in conducting cyber-crimes. The controller command in the USB increases the vulnerabilities when users are undergoing user certification process, which makes it susceptible to cyber-attacks [3]. Fortunately, since USB generates an IP address, it can be used to track USB bypassing attempts. This means that as USB grow in capability and capacity, it has the potential to offer more information in digital forensics analysis. Despite its growing significance in the digital forensics domain, it is undeniable that USB drives pose a great risk to both systems and sensitive data. The easy accessibility, cheap, and small form factor makes USB ideal for theft and destroying potential digital evidence [28]. Malicious software and viruses can be installed in networked or stand-alone computer systems through USB, either inadvertently or deliberately. As a result, potential hackers can completely wipe or cover up their malicious activities. For this reason, USB forensics has become a vital component in computer investigations that allow digital forensic experts to trace USB connection activities in PreFetch, Shortcuts, and Link file folders [29]. Such traces can assist forensic investigators in identifying various file-related operations, including copying pictures or opening documents. Thus, it is apparent that USB forensics is a rising area of interest for digital forensic analysts and it has the ability to assist them in analyzing and identifying potential digital evidence.

Digital evidence is usually stored on a wide range of media devices, usually, the storage devices having removable or internal memory that contains digital artifacts which are usually discovered at a crime scene. These devices often include cellular phones, laptops, portable media players, and digital cameras that use magnetic, electrical, or optical storage media, among which USB flash drives are the most popular ones [22]. Metadata stored in USB flash drives can assist digital forensic experts in identifying detailed information about digital data. This information includes copyright information, geospatial information, or even timestamps that are vital in examining digital forensic evidence. Besides, it is undeniable that USB storage device is considered as the standard for transfer and backup of data files, due to this, potential hackers use USB devices to conduct data theft [30]. Hence, by comprehending the diversity and complexity involved in analyzing USB devices, digital forensic operations can greatly benefit in terms of tracking traces that could lead forensic analysts to potential wrongdoers.

Moreover, in terms of forensics, USB devices contain significant footprints in a various digital environment that are vital in forensic examination [31]. In addition, in USB specification, MSC is considered as a standard for establishing a connection between removable drives. MSC can be defined as a protocol set that takes care of communication between operating systems and USB devices [30]. From a digital forensic standpoint, the MSC protocol gives the digital forensic officer direct access to file systems, clusters, and sectors. Having full control over such file systems, digital forensic experts can easily identify, extract, and thoroughly analyze digital evidence. As a result, USB forensics cannot only reduce the complexity of the digital forensic investigation, but it can also ascertain that the extracted evidence is authentic.

### 4.2 Intrusion detection

Due to recent development in information systems and rapidly increasing network attacks, intrusion detection systems (IDSs) have become a crucial area of interest in digital forensics field. According to [32], IDS has the capability to detect intrusion attempt that can either render a system unreliable, or unusable, gain access to critical digital evidence, or manipulate information. Such systems are ideal for digital forensic investigators as they reveal suspicious behavior within the network. Likewise, with efficient IDS in place, forensic analysts can easily determine whether the security of the computer system is compromised or the data is being accessed from an unauthorized location [33]. This information is critical in forensic investigations; as forensic experts can use this information to extract useful data which can be presented as potential evidence in the court of law. Besides, if an attacker attempts to sabotage a public or private network, IDS will identify and activate incident response (IR). The digital forensic investigation - combined with IR protocols - would allow investigators to preserve, gather, and identify live data [34]. Further, digital forensic methodologies, combined with IDS, will ascertain that no changes are made to the seized content and evidence. IDS systems can also help in detecting hostile and malicious network activities, specifically by analyzing the acquired packets, blocking attack connections, and by alarming the system administrator for limiting the potential damages. These functionalities are crucial in case of digital forensic investigation, as the attacker would always attempt to erase potential digital evidence.

Albeit digital forensic has made it easy to analyze and detect cyber-crimes, the fact remains that it cannot provide fool-proof security to the network or online storage. In this case, IDS has opened doors to various opportunities for digital forensics, as it not only detects malicious activities, it also monitors traffic data to determine the nature of the attack [35]. Moreover, IDS also possess the ability to warn the system administrator - in case the system has been compromised. Once the event has been detected, the digital forensic process can be conducted for discovering the damage and the extent of the intrusion. Although the primary objective of IDS is to identify potential malicious attempts to prompt evasive measures, with the help of digital forensics, it can be used to extract useful digital evidence for civil, legal, and criminal proceedings [36]. The ultimate goal of IDS is efficiently detecting misuse or unauthorized use of computer networks and systems by both external penetrations and insiders. With digital forensics, investigators can trace criminal, intrusive, or illegal activity back to the criminal while simultaneously obtaining sufficient evidence. Thus, it can be established that IDS provide various opportunities and have the ability to assist in digital forensic investigation. Moreover, IDS systems can ensure that the obtained evidence is safe and it can detect and effectively respond to cybersecurity threats.

### 4.3 Artificial intelligence

With the rapid rise in the volumes of digital data, digital forensics often struggles to analyze a complex and large amount of information that requires intelligent analysis and computing. For this purpose, artificial intelligence (AI) has become a well-established and crucial domain of latest computer science, which has the ability to tackle sophisticated and computationally large problems in real-time [37]. The complexities and growth in cyber-crime combined with limited resources and time, both human and computational, in addressing cyber-crime significantly limits the capabilities of the digital forensic investigators to apply digital forensic operations and obtain results in a realistic time-frame. This problem can be resolved by combining digital forensic methods, tools, and techniques with AI. The combination of these dynamic domains gives rise to intelligent forensics that can be considered as an interdisciplinary approach that not only uses resources more intelligently and efficiently but also utilizes technological advances to solve digital forensic investigation [38]. Intelligent forensics incorporates a wide range of techniques and tools from social network analysis, computational modeling, and AI for improving the efficiency and overall credibility of digital investigations while simultaneously lowering the time required to extract digital evidence. What makes intelligent forensics unique is its ability to conduct a digital forensic investigation- both before and after the incident. Besides, since intelligent forensics make use of AI technologies like machine learning, it can assist digital forensic investigators in resolving specificity and generality problems by considering cyber-crime patterns.

In addition, by combining digital forensics with AI, forensic experts can effectively apply digital forensic operations both reactively – after cyber-crime has taken place - and proactively – before cyber-crime has occurred. The reactive ability of intelligent forensics can be considered as a part of digital forensic investigation that helps in gaining in-depth insight into the incident, which can further assist the digital forensic officer in examining data sources for potential evidence [38]. For this purpose, intelligent forensics make use of various techniques, including AI and social network analysis. Likewise, intelligent forensics can also be used proactively, where numerous state-of-the-art techniques like machine learning and deep learning predict future threats, specifically by assessing past trends. This can be very valuable for digital forensic investigators, as they will be able to predict what digital resources have to be preserved for digital evidence. Moreover, with the help of computational intelligence and AI, forensic investigators can employ digital forensic methods more efficiently while ensuring the credibility and reliability of the results [39]. AI also helps in handling large datasets, while collecting digital evidence for forensics [40]. Thus, it can be established that AI has the capability to dynamically transform the way digital forensic works while increasing the accuracy of the results and lowering the time needed to extract useful digital evidence.

## 5. Conclusion

Digital forensics has gained notable attention due to the increase in cyber-crimes. Albeit the rise in digital technology has benefited various fields, the fact remains that it has presented new ways of conducting cyber-crimes. Besides, malicious software, methodologies, and tools are being designed and implemented every day to pose a threat to public and private networks and simultaneously exploiting data storage, in hope of extracting and exploiting the useful information. These security vulnerabilities and breaches have inspired the developments in digital forensics domain so that digital evidence can be extracted from digital devices and can be used in criminal and civil legal proceedings. For understanding the importance of digital forensics, the present study has thoroughly discussed the recent trends, potential threats, and opportunities of digital forensics in cybersecurity.

## Author details

Mohammed I. Alghamdi
Department of Computer Science, Al-Baha University, Al-Baha City, Kingdom of Saudi Arabia

*Address all correspondence to: mialmushilah@bu.edu.sa

## References

[1] E. A. Gollub, "Recent trends in digital text forensics and its evaluation," *In International Conference of the Cross-Language Evaluation Forum for European Languages,* pp. 282-302, (2013), September.

[2] A. Aminnezhad and A. Dehghantanha, "A survey on privacy issues in digital forensics," *nternational Journal of Cyber-Security and Digital Forensics (IJCSDF),* vol. 3, no. 4, pp. 183-199, (2014).

[3] F. Dezfouli and A. Dehghantanha, "Digital forensics trends and future," *International Journal of Cyber-Security and Digital Forensics (IJCSDF),* vol. 3, no. 4, pp. 183-199, (2014).

[4] B. K. Sharma, M. A. Joseph, B. Jacob and L. C. B. Miranda, "Emerging trends in Digital Forensic and Cyber security-An Overview," *In 2019 Sixth HCT Information Technology Trends (ITT),* pp. 309-313, (2019), November.

[5] M. Wazid, A. Katal, R. H. Goudar and S. Rao, "Hacktivism trends, digital forensic tools and challenges: A survey.," *n 2013 IEEE Conference on Information & Communication Technologies,* pp. 138-144, (2013), April.

[6] A. Pichan, M. Lazarescu and S. T. Soh, " Cloud forensics: Technical challenges, solutions and comparative analysis.," *Digital investigation,* vol. 13, pp. 38-57, (2015).

[7] S. Zawoad and R. Hasan, "Cloud forensics: a meta-study of challenges, approaches, and open problems," *arXiv preprint arXiv,* p. 1302.6312., (2013).

[8] A. Aminnezhad, A. Dehghantanha, M. T. Abdullah and M. Damshenas, "Cloud forensics issues and opportunities.," *International Journal of Information Processing and Management,* vol. 4, no. 4, p. 76, (2013).

[9] K. Ruan, J. Carthy, T. Kechadi and I. Baggili, "Cloud forensics definitions and critical criteria for cloud forensic capability: An overview of survey results," *Digital Investigation,* vol. 10, no. 1, pp. 34-43, (2013).

[10] K. Ruan, J. Carthy, T. Kechadi and M. Crosbie, "Cloud forensics," *In IFIP International Conference on Digital Forensics. Springer, Berlin, Heidelberg. ,* pp. 35-46, (2011), January.

[11] A. E. A. Rocha, "Authorship attribution for social media forensics.," *IEEE Transactions on Information Forensics and Security,* vol. 12, no. 1, pp. 5-33, (2016).

[12] I. Baggili and F. Breitinger, "Data sources for advancing cyber forensics: what the social world has to offer.," *n 2015 AAAI Spring Symposium Series.,* (2015), March.

[13] N. Al Mutawa, I. Baggili and A. Marrington, "Forensic analysis of social networking applications on mobile devices.," *Digital Investigation,* vol. 9, pp. S24-S33, (2012).

[14] M. Zampoglou, S. Papadopoulos, Y. Kompatsiaris, R. Bouwmeester and J. Spangenberg, "Web and social media image forensics for news professionals.," *In Tenth international AAAI conference on web and social media,* (2016), April.

[15] A. Zanella, N. Bui, A. Castellani, L. Vangelista and M. Zorzi, "Internet of things for smart cities," *IEEE Internet of Things journal,* vol. 1, no. 1, pp. 22-32, (2014).

[16] M. Vangeti, S. K. Yadav and V. Pinnti, "Advantages of Internet of Things (Iot) For Developing Smart Services in Manufacturing Business," *Purakala with ISSN 0971-2143 is an UGC CARE Journal,* vol. 31, no. 25, pp. 62-68, (2020).

[17] A. MacDermott, T. Baker and Q. Shi, "Iot forensics: Challenges for the ioa era.," *In 2018 9th IFIP International Conference on New Technologies, Mobility and Security (NTMS),* pp. 1-5, (2018), February.

[18] R. Hegarty, D. J. Lamb and A. Attwood, "Digital Evidence Challenges in the Internet of Things," *In INC,* pp. 163-172, (2014).

[19] M. Al Fahdi, N. L. Clarke and S. M. Furnell, "Challenges to digital forensics: A survey of researchers & practitioners attitudes and opinions.," *In 2013 Information Security for South Africa, IEEE,* pp. 1-8, (2013).

[20] N. M. Karie and H. S. Venter, "Taxonomy of challenges for digital forensics.," *Journal of forensic sciences,* vol. 60, no. 4, pp. 885-893, (2015).

[21] A. M. Balogun and S. Y. Zhu, "Privacy impacts of data encryption on the efficiency of digital forensics technology.," *arXiv preprint arXiv:1312.3183.,* (2013).

[22] E. A. Vincze, "Challenges in digital forensics. Police Practice and Research," vol. 17, no. 2, pp. 183-194, (2016).

[23] S. Raghavan, "Digital forensic research: current state of the art.," *CSI Transactions on ICT,* vol. 1, no. 1, pp. 91-114, (2013).

[24] P. Cichonski, T. Millar, T. Grance and K. Scarfone, "Computer security incident handling guide.," *International Journal of Computer Research,,* vol. 20, no. 4, p. 459, (2013).

[25] Z. Baig, P. Szewczyk, C. Valli, P. Rabadia, P. Hannay, M. Chernyshev, M. Johnstone, P. Kerai, A. Ibrahim, K. Sansurooah and N. Syed, "Future challenges for smart cities: Cyber-security and digital forensics.," *Digital Investigation,* vol. 22, pp. 3-13, (2017).

[26] I. Hong, H. Yu, S. Lee and K. Lee, "A new triage model conforming to the needs of selective search and seizure of electronic evidence.," *Digital Investigation,* vol. 10, no. 2, pp. 175-192, (2013).

[27] N. Rahim, W. A. Wahab, Y. I. Idris and L. M. Kiah, "Digital Forensics: An Overview of the Current Trends.," (2014).

[28] J. Collie, "The windows IconCache. db: A resource for forensic artifacts from USB connectable devices," *Digital investigation,* vol. 9, no. 3-4, pp. 200-210, (2013).

[29] T. Roy and A. Jain, "Windows registry forensics: an imperative step in tracking data theft via USB devices.," *International Journal of Computer Science and Information Technologies,* vol. 3, no. 3, p. International Journal of Computer Science and Information Technologies, (2012).

[30] S. B. Deb and A. Chetry, "USB Device Forensics: Insertion and removal timestamps of USB devices in Windows 8.," *In 2015 International Symposium on Advanced Computing and Communication (ISACC),* pp. 364-371, (2015).

[31] S. Verma, A. Singh, D. Singh and V. Laxmi, "Computer forensics in IT audit and credit card fraud investigation-for USB devices," *In 2014 International Conference on Computing for Sustainable Global Development (INDIACom),* pp. 730-733, (2014).

[32] S. Agrawal and J. Agrawal, "Survey on anomaly detection using data mining techniques.," *Procedia Computer Science,* vol. 60, pp. 708-713, (2015).

[33] M. Ahmed, A. N. Mahmood and J. Hu, "A survey of network anomaly detection techniques.," *Journal of Network and Computer Applications,* vol. 60, pp. 19-31., (2016).

[34] C. P. Grobler, C. P. Louwrens and S. H. von Solms, "A multi-component view of digital forensics.," *In 2010 International Conference on Availability, Reliability and Security, IEEE.*, pp. 647-652, (2012).

[35] P. K. Khobragade and L. G. Malik, "Data generation and analysis for digital forensic application using data mining.," *In 2014 Fourth International Conference on Communication Systems and Network Technologies, IEEE.*, pp. 458-462, (2014).

[36] M. Kumar, M. Hanumanthappa and T. S. Kumar, "Network Intrusion Forensic Analysis Using Intrusion Detection System.," *Int. J. Comp. Tech. Appl,*, vol. 2, no. 3, pp. 612-618, (2011).

[37] F. Mitchell, "The use of Artificial Intelligence in digital forensics: An introduction.," *Digital Evidence & Elec. Signature L. Rev,* (2010).

[38] A. Irons and H. S. Lallie, "Digital forensics to intelligent forensics.," *Future Internet,* vol. 6, no. 3, pp. 584-596, (2014).

[39] A. K. Muda, Y. H. Choo, A. Abraham and S. N. Srihari, "Computational intelligence in digital forensics: forensic investigation and applications.," *Springer International Publishing.,* (2014).

[40] O. M. Adedayo, "Big data and digital forensics.," *In 2016 IEEE International Conference on Cybercrime and Computer Forensic (ICCCF). IEEE.*, pp. 1-7, (2016).

Chapter 2

# An Assessment of the Risk of Service Supplier Bankruptcies as a Cybersecurity Threat

*Rebecca Parry*


## Abstract

Behind technology service suppliers lie companies that are subject to the risk of business failure due to market conditions and trading risks. Such failures could suddenly stop customers accessing services or content, with potentially devastating business and personal impacts, given the rising importance of digital economies. The risk can be illustrated by reference to cloud computing insolvencies but similar issues may affect other service providers. The insolvency of a cloud service provider would be likely to present problems of access to infrastructure, platforms, services and data and insolvency laws are not always designed to enable a managed close-down of a business, which would be needed to enable replacement services to be sourced and data recovered. This cybersecurity risk has barely been touched upon in literature, since it lies at the intersection between law and computer science, both areas requiring high levels of specialist understanding, and this chapter is part of initial attempts to identify the threats presented.


**Keywords:** cloud computing, bankruptcy law, impact on service supply, downtime

## 1. Introduction

Recent years have seen increasing reliance on digital economies to support ways of working and yet the prospect of business failures in this context have not yet received detailed attention as potential cybersecurity risks. An example of a technology which is of growing significance in this environment is cloud computing, which has revolutionised professional activities, through facilitating home working as well as significantly cutting costs for businesses, financial institutions, healthcare providers and government departments. It is easy to see why cloud services have grown in popularity, as cloud computing offers significant benefits. For example, major recent usage has widely arisen in the context of home working in the wake of the Covid-19 pandemic. One way in which the cloud has been important in this context is through virtualized desktops, which can seamlessly enable an employee to work on a project both at home and in the office. Even before the pandemic, cloud computing services were increasing in importance, given their adaptability and scalability as well as other benefits, for example that software and artificial intelligence functions can be accessed more cheaply. The scalable nature of cloud services can also for example enable big data analytics to be carried out much more cheaply than was previously possible. Cloud storage also offers greater security in some ways: a lost datastick or stolen laptop no longer entails an expensive loss of data, since the content is now securely stored in the cloud servers [1]. As a result of these and other attractions the public cloud sector has been forecast to grow by 6.3% worldwide in 2020 [2].

In spite of its considerable benefits and wide usage, the cloud computing sector is not always properly understood by those using it. Indeed, users may often not always realise that the service that they are using is provided via the cloud. Rather than consisting of anything as ethereal as storage in a cloud in the sky, as some users might envisage, cloud computing simply means that services are provided and accessed on offsite machines, rather than on a local machine. These services are operated by companies, which can get into difficulties and become insolvent and this cybersecurity risk that has barely received attention before now [3, 4].

Possible reasons why a service provider can get into difficulties include a downturn in economic conditions, mismanagement, reputational damage, hacking, terrorism and natural disasters leading to financial difficulties and insolvency. Further problems may arise if there is disruption to the services or property that the cloud service provider relies upon. A service provider which is insolvent will not be able to pay its creditors in full and bankruptcy laws provide rules to address this in a fair way, as discussed in Part 5 below. Bankruptcy proceedings are typically designed to enable creditors to be repaid efficiently and at a limited cost, yet cloud computing insolvencies present challenging difficulties of complexity from a customer perspective, since customers will want to recover their content and source alternative providers before the service is shut down. Keeping the business running while this is done will be potentially costly in a circumstance where there will be limited funds. These bankruptcies therefore present a tension between the interests of creditors, who already face the loss of most, or all, of what they are owed, and the interests of cloud computing customers who will expect that the cloud service provider continues to operate temporarily while their content is recovered.

This Chapter will first provide some background regarding cloud service provision. This will be presented in part 2, followed by a more detailed examination of the cybersecurity risk of insolvencies in this sector in part 3. Part 4 will discuss risk mitigation and then the complexities of insolvencies in this area will be discussed in Part 5. Part 6 will look at whether the law may be developed to offer more help to customers of insolvent cloud computing providers, before some conclusions are offered.

## 2. Concise overview of cloud service provision

The main forms of cloud service are termed IAAS, SAAS and PAAS. “IAAS” is infrastructure as a service, “SAAS” is software as a service and “PAAS” is platform as a service. IAAS primarily enables hardware provision for processing or storage, such as servers and real or virtual machines, together with virtualisation software to allocate hardware to particular customers. Examples are Rackspace and IBM Bluemix. Examples of SAAS arrangement are customers who access software such as Microsoft 365 and movies from Netflix via the cloud, rather than software on their machine. PaaS is often used for application development and deployment and an example provider is Heroku. See also **Table 1**, below.

Cloud services can be offered via a public cloud, a private cloud or a hybrid. Public clouds are operated by third parties for a variety of users on a pay as you go basis and hosted on the premises of the third party and, due to their nature, may be unsuitable for business critical or security sensitive information. Private clouds are operated by a single organisation for its exclusive use and are therefore low risk,

| Type of Service | Example usage | Example providers | What is provided | Problem in the event of provider insolvency | Possible safeguards |
|---|---|---|---|---|---|
| Platform as a service, "PAAS" | Provision of platform e.g. for the development of software applications. | Heroku, Salesforce's Force.com | Operating system, middleware, virtualisation and hardware | Loss of platform | Contingency planning, identification of potential alternative platform supplier |
| Software as a service, "SAAS" | Provision of software enabling e.g. project management, collaboration, management tools and business processes | Microsoft 365, Apple iCloud, Gmail, Basecamp, Trello, Netflix, Spotify, Dropbox | Underlying infrastructure, middleware, software application and application data | Loss of software and uploaded content. Potential loss of readability of data | Software escrow, copyright splitting, step-in rights. Contingency planning e.g. indentification of potential alternative providers (if any). |
| Infrastructure as a service, "IAAS" | Instant access to infrasctructure, useful for unpredictable or increased demand e.g. for big data analytics, complex website hosting | Rackspace, IBM Bluemix, Microsoft Azure, Amazon Web Services | Hardware provision for processing or storage, such as servers and real or virtual machines, together with virtualisation software to allocate hardware to particular customers | Loss of infrastructure | Contingency planning e.g. identification of alternative provider. |

**Table 1.**
*Overview of cloud services and insolvency risks and safeguards.*

although potentially used by many employees, provided that the private cloud is hosted by the organisation on its own premises. Risks are presented where a private cloud is operated by a third party and off-premises. Hybrid clouds allow data and applications to be used across public and private clouds and commonly they will deploy the private cloud for business critical or commercially sensitive information and other data will use the public cloud. Provider failures in the cases of hybrid and public clouds and third-party provided private clouds will then give rise to problems for large numbers of users.

## 3. Identification of the cybersecurity risk presented by cloud computing insolvencies

It is often unappreciated by users that cloud service providers are operated by companies and they carry risks of failure, for example due to market conditions or cyber-attacks. Insolvency risks have however been identified in technology literature [5], by Lloyd's of London [6] and by research organisations [7]. Lloyd's, an insurance provider, identified the potential risk most plainly: 'reliance on a relatively small number of companies has resulted in systemic risk for businesses using their services'. Most obviously the failure of one of the leading service providers would present problems but cloud services can be provided by complex arrangements of companies and risk are presented by smaller companies also. The European Telecommunications Standards Institute considered that the bankruptcy of a cloud service provider would be 'hard to deal with'.

Yet it is clear that there is potential for a cloud service provider to become bankrupt [8]. For example, Fusion Connect Inc. filed for Chapter 11 bankruptcy protection in the US in 2020. There have been other previous examples. Nirvanix filed for US Chapter 11 bankruptcy protection in 2013 and gave customers two weeks' notice before closing down [9]. Other cloud providers which have gone out of business are Megaupload and MegaCloud, and the UK example of 2e2, a data centre, which failed, leaving customers with expensive costs for the recovery of their content (around £1 million or $1.3 million) [10].

In the event of bankruptcy of a cloud service provider, a customer will be faced with the need to recover their content and to source an alternative provider of infrastructure, software or platform.

There may be considerable practical difficulties both in relation to recovery of content and the sourcing of an alternative provider. The recovery of large volumes of data is a slow process. It may be that an alternative service is unavailable. This may render content unreadable. It may be that the business is closed before customers can recover their content and make alternative arrangements. The insolvency office holder may require funding from customers to keep the business running while content is recovered. However, in an extreme case a business may simply shut down and content will be lost. Problems for customers can stem from difficulties not just of the cloud service provider itself - the service provider may have outsourced services to a third party which shuts down. Business arrangements such as these will add levels of complexity to the recovery of content from the cloud.

The potential difficulties for customers in recovering content from a cloud service provider insolvency will be considered in more detail in part 5 below.

## 4. Mitigation of the risk

The main steps that customers can take relate to diligence in selecting a cloud service provider and, where possible, the inclusion of terms in the agreement with the service provider to protect the customer's content in the event of insolvency. However, customers would also be wise to have an alternative plan in the event of a loss of content or access to software. Regular backups with a third-party provider would be one option, although not perfect, since any backup will be a snapshot of the content at the time of the most recent backup.

### 4.1 Assessment of supplier viability

Given the potential risk, what can customers do to protect themselves from the risk of cloud service provider insolvencies? Users would be wise to consider the potential long-term viability of cloud service providers before entering into a contract with them [11], in particular if the provider will be storing or processing data, or supplying access to important software. Large market players in the cloud service industry may offer greater prospects of longevity of supply but fewer prospects of a bespoke service. Not all customers will realistically be able to bargain with cloud service providers, as discussed below. However, some sectors such as banking [12, 13] may place pre-conditions on eligibility for cloud service providers and large customers for example [14] may also have specifications for eligible suppliers.

It would be prudent as well to identify potential alternative service providers in the event that the worst happens and selected provider can no longer offer the contracted service, denying access to data or to critical software.

### 4.2 Contractual bargaining

Cloud computing customers may try to address the risks of insolvency contractually [15, 16] however there are limitations to the effectiveness of this. For many customers, service will be on standard terms that will contain no provision for insolvency [17]. Large companies may have more negotiating power. In the event that a customer can bargain to obtain contractual protection, it will be important to clarify that there is a distinction between the ownership of the cloud infrastructure and the ownership of content in the cloud, such as data, so that the data does not form part of the bankruptcy estate [18], as discussed in the next section. Other options would be to include:

1. Step-in rights: entitlements that are common in outsourcing contracts and enable control to be taken of the service provider. In the cloud computing context difficulties in exercising such powers would arise where there is shared infrastructure, staff and technology.

2. Software escrow is another approach, which can be of benefit to customers who access software via the cloud. Under such an arrangement a third party would hold the software source code under a software escrow arrangement and release it upon the occurrence of a triggering event, which could include the insolvency of the service provider [19].

3. A further example is copyright splitting [20], but this might be practicably difficult to implement in the event that there are numerous users of the software.

These approaches can potentially provide workable approaches in the event of a cloud service provider insolvency.

## 5. A concise overview of bankruptcy possibilities and their consequences

In the event that a cloud service provider gets into financial difficulties there are normally two main formal insolvency possibilities that can be used to address the company's inability to pay its debts. Most simply, the cloud service provider may be liquidated or it may be reorganised, both of which procedures will be explained below. It must be added, however that the procedures that apply in the event of insolvency are not international and they will vary depending on the country in which the proceedings are opened. This presents a complication in the case of cloud service providers, which may have supranational affairs. The proper venue in which to open insolvency proceedings may be unclear, although both the US and UK are jurisdictions with well-developed insolvency frameworks, and which both take fairly expansive approaches to jurisdiction to open insolvency proceedings [21, 22] and it may be that these will be favoured as venues in cases where there is some connection with the cloud service provider.

We can illustrate the main likely insolvency procedures and issues that may arise in this context by reference to those which operate in the US and UK. As noted, both of these countries have well-developed insolvency laws. However, insolvency laws in other countries may be more limited and so may the infrastructure to deal with proceedings in respect of insolvent cloud service providers, since courts may be over-burdened and lacking in specialist expertise and insolvency professionals may lack experience and sometimes integrity. Again, these factors may hamper efforts to recover content from the cloud since there may not be a vehicle to support a managed closedown of the company's affairs. Indeed, the sophistication of the US and UK systems does not guarantee this steady closure and customers may lose their cloud content, infrastructure, platform or software.

### 5.1 Liquidation

The process of liquidation is normally used to bring the affairs of an insolvent company to an end, with an impartial trustee (in the UK a liquidator) being appointed to do this according to detailed procedures set out in laws. Examples are the United States Chapter 7 and the UK Insolvency Act 1986, Part IV. This section will initially consider the United States position before briefly examining the position in the UK. Claims by customers of cloud computing services can potentially give rise to complexities in both jurisdictions that can only be briefly touched upon.

The opening of Chapter 7 liquidation proceedings, an accessible introduction to which can be found at [23], will give rise to an automatic stay under 11 United States Code § 362 (hereafter "USC") to prevent creditors from taking action to enforce their claims and this gives temporary protection to the debtor while the liquidation is carried out. This is however a time of vulnerability for customers since the trustee, when appointed, may not realise that the company operates a cloud service on which customers depend and may fail to take steps to ensure continuity of service, in particular since funds to do so may be lacking. Even where the trustee takes steps to continue service, s/he may lack specialist skills and experience to operate a cloud service business and may face a steep learning curve in relation to the business, combined with a lean staffing structure and high volume of communications from concerned customers. Moreover, liquidation is not primarily a vehicle to enable ongoing trading. In the US, the business may continue to operate if it is in "the best interest of the estate and consistent with the orderly liquidation of the estate" under 11 USC §721 and this might feasibly enable a temporary operation of the company to enable customer needs to be attended to. There is a risk however that there may be insufficient funds to enable the trustee to continue to operate the business for long enough to enable customers to recover their content and it may be necessary for customers to provide funds if this is to be done.

The main role of the trustee will be to take steps to bring the company's affairs to an end by selling the company's assets and using the proceeds to pay off creditors, as far as possible, according to a system of priorities and customers claims will be dealt with as part of this. Since the trustee is dealing with the debtor's property it will be important for customers to establish their entitlement to the content that they have uploaded, so that it is not included in the estate that the trustee will be looking to sell. Preferably the customer's ownership of content should have been agreed in any contract with the cloud service provider, although the customer's ownership of the content is likely to be implied even if the contract does not address the point.

As to the distribution of assets in the liquidation, there is a distinction to be drawn between creditors with claims to specific property, such as items covered by a lien, and those without. The former are known as secured creditors and the latter as unsecured creditors. Unsecured creditors are further divided into those with priority and nonpriority status. In view of the secured creditors' claims to specific assets, or classes of assets, these assets do not form part of the estate for distribution to creditors. Similarly, customers with ownership of the content uploaded to the cloud are entitled to recover the content, since it does not form part of the estate, but this may be more difficult in practical terms, as discussed elsewhere in this Chapter. Unsecured creditors, in contrast, typically occupy a low level of priority.

As previously noted, there are two types: priority unsecured and nonpriority unsecured. The priority claims, such as the costs of running the bankruptcy, are to be paid first, so that nonpriority claims may have limited prospects for payment. The class of nonpriority unsecured creditors would be those with claims to damages. These might include cloud service customers whose service contracts have been prematurely discontinued, or who have other claims to damages as a result of breaches of the service contract. These claims are unsecured and are not therefore claims to specific assets and so they do not have priority and will have a low ranking in the scheme of priority for payment, as nonpriority unsecured claims.

It is important to look in a little more detail at the claims that customers may have based on service agreements and how they will fare in the bankruptcy. In the liquidation these will be regarded as executory contracts [24] under 11 USC § 365(a), since both parties have ongoing performance obligations at the time of the bankruptcy filing and, as such, the trustee can choose whether or not to continue performance. If the trustee elects to discontinue performance the customer will have merely a claim to damages, which, as discussed in the previous paragraph, is likely to be worthless in the liquidation, and their access to content may be lost. Similar considerations apply in relation to software licences that customers hold, however there are additional protections under 11 USC §365(n) for customers in this instance, since customers can elect to retain rights under the contract to the software and its embodiments, including source code. This does not however require the liquidator to perform any of the licensor's obligations, such as updating the software, which can present problems for customers unless and until a replacement provider can be found, or unless the liquidator assigns the software to a third party capable of continuing service. Nor are all cloud computing services necessarily protected by this provision, since not all will have the character of software licences, even SAAS contracts, since the customer does not necessarily obtain a copy of the software, s/he merely accesses it online.

Ongoing trading in liquidation is also potentially difficult in the UK as similar issues will arise. Under the legislation, the liquidator of a company may continue to carry on business "so far as may be necessary for its beneficial winding up", according to Insolvency Act 1986, Sch 4, para 5, but this does not guarantee that there will be ongoing trading or that any period of ongoing trading will again be long enough to enable customers to recover their content and make alternative arrangements. In addition to the practical problems noted in the US context, the liquidator is not obliged to honour customers' service agreements and the liquidator has powers under Insolvency Act 1986, s 178 to disclaim unprofitable contracts, which could include cloud service agreements. Where the customer benefits from a software licence one possibility is that the liquidator will prefer to assign the software to a third party, in which case this third party will normally be subject to the licence, see further [25].

### 5.2 Reorganisation

Reorganisation, on the other hand, is designed to enable ongoing trading, through the restructuring of the debtor's financial obligations. Notable examples are the US Chapter 11 and the UK administration. There are great variations in reorganisation laws globally and some jurisdictions as yet lack suitable procedures. The main objective of reorganisation proceedings is to enable struggling but viable companies to recover from their difficulties, although these procedures are not always used to achieved this. Often reorganisation is used to enable the sale of the company's underlying business, prior to a liquidation of the company, or to otherwise enable greater returns to be made to creditors in liquidation.

Taking the US Chapter 11 as a well-developed system of reorganisation proceedings, the company's management will become what is termed a "debtor in possession", under 11 USC §1101(1), unless a trustee is appointed. Briefly, this means that the company's pre-Chapter 11 management will remain in control, with or without personnel changes. The debtor in possession will formulate a plan of reorganisation, which must be approved by creditors and by the court, and this can enable the debtor to continue trading. The debtor in possession has the power to reject contracts, as discussed in relation to liquidation. A valuable feature of Chapter 11, which also applies in Chapter 7, is the automatic stay in 11 USC § 362 and this will protect the cloud service provider from debt collection efforts by creditors, including lawsuits. Chapter 11 therefore may offer better prospects of continue trading but it is also a relatively expensive process that is used in only a small minority of insolvencies in the US.

A new UK procedure, the restructuring plan, is similar to Chapter 11 and would be suitable for larger companies which have viable prospects of recovery from their difficulties. In the UK there is also a more simple option, the company voluntary arrangement in Insolvency Act 1986, Part 1, which enables a company to reach agreement with creditors or members and does not need to be presented to a court for approval. However, the company voluntary arrangement does not provide the company with a moratorium/automatic stay on creditor claims.

Moratorium protection can be obtained if the company is first put into administration under Insolvency Act 1986, Sch B1, whether or not the plan is to introduce a company voluntary arrangement or restructuring plan. This is a relatively expensive procedure where an administrator is appointed by the company or a major creditor to take control of the company in circumstances where the company cannot pay its debts, or where it is reasonably likely to become unable to pay its debts. Administration, as it was originally designed, can be used to manage the company with a view to presenting to creditors proposals for how the company can be saved, however it is more often used to achieve greater returns to creditors than would be possible in an immediate liquidation. Administration is not particularly well suited to a managed closedown of a cloud service provider since an appointment must be reasonably likely to achieve the purpose of administration, set out in Insolvency Act 1986, Sch B1, para 3. The primary purpose of administration is to save the company but if this is not reasonably practicable efforts can be focused on achieving a better return for creditors than would be likely if it was closed down without first going into administration, or if that is not reasonably practicable to make a distribution to one or more secured or preferential creditors. Since the managed closedown of a cloud service provider would be likely to add costs without benefit to creditors it is this latter objective that would need to be relied on but there is a difficulty that the administrator must 'perform his functions in the interests of the company's creditors as a whole' and the costs of a managed closedown may reduce the sums available for creditors.

Protection can alternatively be obtained via a new procedure, the restructuring moratorium, under Insolvency Act 1986, Part 1A, which offers a cheaper option than administration but potentially a shorter duration of protection. The restructuring moratorium was introduced as part of package of reforms in the wake of the Covid-19 crisis. It enables an eligible company to enjoy the benefit of a holiday from creditor claims while under the supervision of a monitor. The protection offered will be relatively brief, lasting for an initial 20 business days, although this period can be extended. Under the process for obtaining a moratorium where the cloud service provider is not subject to a winding up petition the directors are required to file documents that indicate that the company is insolvent or approaching insolvency and that the company has likely prospects of being rescued as a going concern. It is this latter requirement that would prevent this route being used for a managed closedown of a cloud service provider. A cloud service provider which is subject to a winding up petition will only be able to obtain a moratorium following an order from the court in circumstances where this will provide a better result for the company's creditors as a whole than would be possible if the company were to be wound up without an initial period of moratorium protection. Since a managed closedown primarily is required for the benefit of customers it may be difficult to argue that it would be for the benefit of creditors as a whole.

It is a weakness that there is arguably a present lack of a reorganisation procedure in the UK that can be used to temporarily facilitate ongoing trading for the managed closedown of a cloud service provider, enabling customers to recover data and source alternative services [26]. None of the many UK procedures is particularly designed for this scenario, since returns to creditors are the priorities.

## 6. How can legislation do more assist customers of insolvent cloud service providers?

The provision of protections for users of cloud services is something that can potentially be better addressed by different jurisdictions. Digital economies can offer significant benefits and many countries, including developing countries, are building on this. A legislative framework that can provide security of data and continuity of service in the event of insolvency can support the development of such economies, as it can attract cloud service providers which can then offer confidence to customers that there will not be a sudden and catastrophic loss of services and content. A special procedure for cloud service providers, enabling a managed closedown, would be one possibility.

An example of existing provision for cloud computing insolvencies is Art 567 of the Luxembourg Code de Commerce [27]. As originally enacted this law enabled the recovery of goods entrusted to debtors upon the debtor's insolvency and in 2012 it was extended to include intangible property such as software in recognition of the growing importance of cloud computing. Such a law would not suffice in itself, since having an entitlement to recover content in the event of the insolvency of a cloud service provider is only one problem and temporary continuity of service to enable recovery of the content is also needed.

Funding to enable temporary continuity of service by an insolvent cloud service provider would be a challenge and in the longer-term consideration might be given as to whether a fund can be established to cover the running costs of a cloud service managed closedown. The fund might be created if, for example, service providers are charged a levy, although it is also notable that cloud service providers are supranational in nature and they might be able to avoid any efforts of any one country to charge a levy, similar to the problems that countries face in taxation. Given these practical difficulties it would likely be preferred that customers should pay, although this may give rise to collective action problems, such as holdouts.

## 7. Conclusion

This Chapter has provided a brief introduction to a threat to cybersecurity that has as yet received only limited attention. The potential for cloud computing insolvencies is globally significant, given the rapidly rising usage and value of content that is stored in the cloud. Importance also arises from the growth of digital economies in many countries, including developing countries, and it would be desirable for domestic laws to pay attention to this matter. The Chapter has discussed in brief how insolvencies in this sector might be handled in the US and UK and has highlighted problems that would be faced by customers of insolvent cloud service providers. Even these sophisticated jurisdictions do not presently provide effective protection for cloud service customers. It is moreover doubtful that domestic insolvency procedures alone will ever be adequate to address failures in this sector, which is supranational in nature. There is arguably a need for discussion at a global level of how cloud computing insolvencies can be addressed, and how improvements can be made to the infrastructure to support this. There is also a need to identify if there are any other complex areas of supranational technology that will have potential for significant impact of insolvencies, since similar issues are likely to arise in other cases of service supply. This Chapter has focused on cloud computing as there is here a clearly identified risk of insolvency having a significant impact and a need for legislative attention to be paid. In the longer term the development of robust laws to handle cloud computing insolvencies requires collaboration between data scientists and insolvency lawyers and attention on a global scale.

## Acknowledgements

I am grateful to Roger Bisson, who first brought the risk of cloud computing insolvencies to my attention and was my co-author on a longer version article, Rebecca Parry & Roger Bisson (2020): Legal approaches to management of the risk of cloud computing insolvencies, Journal of Corporate Law Studies, DOI: 10.1080/14735970.2020.1724504. I am also grateful to Adrian Walters who provided a helpful review of that article when it was at a draft stage.

## Conflict of interest

The author declares no conflict of interest.

## Author details

Rebecca Parry
Nottingham Law School, Nottingham Trent University, UK

*Address all correspondence to: rebeccca.parry@ntu.ac.uk

## References

[1] Ryan P, Falvey S. Trust in the Clouds. Computer Law & Security Review 2012;28:513.

[2] Gartner. Gartner Forecasts Worldwide Public Cloud Revenue to Grow 6.3% in 2020 [Internet]. 2020. Available from: https://www.gartner.com/en/newsroom/press-releases/2020-07-23-gartner-forecasts-worldwide-public-cloud-revenue-to-grow-6point3-percent-in-2020 [Accessed: 2020-12-07].

[3] Parry R, Bisson R. Legal approaches to management of the risk of cloud computing insolvencies. Journal of Corporate Law Studies 2020;20:421-451. DOI: 10.1080/14735970.2020.1724504.

[4] Caplan, DS. Effects of bankruptcy of a cloud services provider. [Report]. San Francisco; 2010. Available from: https://ftp.documation.com:8443/references/ABA10a/PDfs/3_3.pdf [Accessed: 2020-12-07].

[5] Brodkin J. Gartner: Seven Cloud-Computing Security Risks. InfoWorld (Internet) 2008 Jul 3. Available from: www.infoworld.com/d/securitycentral/gartner-seven-cloud-computing-security-risks853 [Accessed: 2020-12-07] .

[6] Lloyd's. Cloud Down, Impacts on the US Economy, Emerging Risk Report 2018. (Internet) 2018, Available from: https://www.lloyds.com/news-and-insight/risk-insight/library/technology/cloud-down [Accessed: 2020-12-07].

[7] European Telecommunications Standards Institute. Special Report: Cloud Standards Coordination Phase 2; Interoperability and Security in Cloud Computing. Sophia Antipolis Cedex, France; 2016.

[8] Morrow T, Pender K, Lee C, Faatz D. Overview of Risks, Threats, and Vulnerabilities Faced in Moving to the Cloud. [Technical Report CMU/SEI-2019-TR-004] Carnegie Mellon University; 2019), 14.

[9] Kepes B. A Nirvanix Post Mortem - Why There's No Replacement For Due Diligence. Forbes (Internet) 2013 Sep 28. Available from: https://www.forbes.com/sites/benkepes/2013/09/28/a-nirvanix-post-mortem-why-theres-no-replacement-for-due-diligence/?sh=3cba13c72556.

[10] Computer Weekly, 2e2 datacentre administrators hold customers' data to £1m ransom. Computer Weekly (Internet) 2013 Feb 8. Available from: https://www.computerweekly.com/news/2240177744/2e2-datacentre-administrators-hold-customers-data-to-1m-ransom [Accessed: 2020-12-07]

[11] Bartolini C, El Kateb, D, Le Traon, Y. et al. Cloud providers viability. Electron Markets 2018;28:53-75. DOI: 10.1007/s12525-018-0284-7

[12] Financial Conduct Authority. Guidance for Firms Outsourcing to the 'Cloud' and other Third Party IT Services. (2019). FG16/5. Available at: https://www.fca.org.uk/publication/finalised-guidance/fg16-5.pdf [Accessed: 2020-12-07]

[13] European Banking Authority, Guidelines on Outsourcing Arrangements. (2019). Available at: https://eba.europa.eu/sites/default/documents/files/documents/10180/2551996/38c80601-f5d7-4855-8ba3-702423665479/EBA%20revised%20Guidelines%20on%20outsourcing%20arrangements.pdf [Accessed: 2020-12-07].

[14] Geant. GN3plus Support to Clouds Terms & Conditions Requirements for Cloud Service Providers, Draft #3.2, 2.iv. Available at: https://www.

geant.org/Services/Connectivity_and_network/GTS/Documents/GN3Plus_SA7_Requirements%20DRAFT.pdf [Accessed 2020-12-07]

[15] Lifshitz L, Rothchild J, editors. Cloud 3.0: Drafting and Negotiating Cloud Computing Agreements. Chicago: ABA Publishing; 2019.

[16] European Commission. Cloud Computing Contracts [Internet]. Available from: https://ec.europa.eu/info/business-economy-euro/doing-business-eu/contract-rules/cloud-computing/cloud-computing-contracts_en [Accessed: 2020-12-07]

[17] Michels JD, Millard C, Turton F. Contracts for Clouds, Revisited: An Analysis of the Standard Contracts for 40 Cloud Computing Services (June 11, 2020). Queen Mary School of Law Legal Studies Research Paper No. 334/2020, Available at SSRN: <ssrn.com/abstract=3624712>

[18] Bartolini C, Santos C and Ullrich C. Property and the Cloud. Computer Law & Security Review 2018;34:358

[19] Tasevski I. Business Continuity in Cloud Computing [thesis]. Tilburg University; 2014, 50-51.

[20] Louwers E-J. Continuity in the Cloud: New Practical Solutions Required, an Inventory from a Dutch Perspective [Internet]. 2013. Available from: https://louwersadvocaten.nl/app/uploads/2016/08/louwers__ernst-jan_continuity_cloud.pptx.pdf [Accessed: 2020-12-07]

[21] R3. Insolvency Forum Shopping [Internet]. 2015. Available from: https://www.r3.org.uk/stream.asp?stream=true&eid=22120&node=194&checksum=D92AFA5847F6F1EBE7FEDB3476A797DC [Accessed: 2020-12-07]

[22] Green, DM, Benzija, W. Spanning the Globe: The Intended Extraterritorial Reach of the Bankruptcy Code. American Bankruptcy Institute Law Review 2002;10:85-110

[23] US Courts. Chapter 7 Bankruptcy Basics [Internet]. Available from: https://www.uscourts.gov/services-forms/bankruptcy/bankruptcy-basics/chapter-7-bankruptcy-basics [Accessed: 2020-12-07]

[24] Countryman V, Executory Contracts in Bankruptcy: Part I. (Minn.L.Rev. 1973;57: 439, 460

[25] Toutoungi A, Adams C. Intellectual Property Licenses and Insolvency [Internet]. 2020. Available from: https://www.taylorwessing.com/en/insights-and-events/insights/2020/07/intellectual-property-licences-and-insolvency [Accessed: 2020-12-07].

[26] Parry, R. An assessment of UK insolvency laws in the light of new ways of working in the era of Covid-19. International Corporate Rescue (Forthcoming)

[27] Wellens, V. New Right to Reclaim Data from Bankrupt Cloud Computing Providers. International Law Office (Internet) 2013 Jun 28. Available from: https://www.internationallawoffice.com/Newsletters/Insolvency-Restructuring/Luxembourg/NautaDutilh-Avocats-Luxembourg/New-right-to-reclaim-data-from-bankrupt-cloud-computing-providers [Accessed: 2020-12-07]

Chapter 3

# Cybersecurity Skills in EU: New Educational Concept for Closing the Missing Workforce Gap

*Borka Jerman Blažič*

## Abstract

Recruiting, retaining and maintaining a validated number of cybersecurity professionals in the workplace is a constant battle, not only for the technical side of cybersecurity, but also for the overlooked area of non-technical, managerial-related jobs in the cyber sector. For years, much of the focus within cyberspace has been on the technical needs of the underlying networks and services. Very little emphasis has been placed on the human dimension of cybersecurity. This lack of cybersecurity professionals is a major problem all over the world. To overcome it, current educational systems need to be re-shaped and cooperation introduced between the different stakeholders. This chapter presents and discusses the actions and the developments in the education concept of cybersecurity knowledge and skills intended to meet the needs of the labour market in the EU. The changes in the education prepared by the higher-education institutions and by professional training providers are presented and discussed.

**Keywords:** Cybersecurity skills, cybersecurity knowledge, market skill shortage, cybersecurity labour gap, cybersecurity educational ecosystem in EU

## 1. Introduction

Cybersecurity has increasingly been a headline feature in news media in recent years, generally prompted by spectacular breaches of various information systems, including airlines, health organizations, credit agencies, administrations, financial institutions, telecoms and many others [1]. Until recently, cybersecurity was viewed as an ICT challenge, rather than a business risk. Despite the warnings by cybersecurity professionals, it has taken many years of cyber-attacks and losses caused too many kinds of enterprises in different sectors for there to be a change in this view. Several large, reputable companies have several times announced huge losses arising from different incidents in various economies, including infrastructure sectors like traffic, health, energy and water supply British Airways [2]. Although smaller companies (SMEs) have not reported such incidents regularly, they are also frequently victims of cyber-attacks. From being mainly a problem for ICT professionals, cybersecurity has today become an acknowledged business risk. This finding is now driving long-term changes in the approach to how cybersecurity risk should be managed and by whom, especially within SMEs. The importance of cybersecurity knowledge is now recognized widely, but the need for its widespread application depends on the cybersecurity skills possessed by the work force [3]. The main problem is the lack of cybersecurity skills among this work force, which is estimated globally to be about 3 million workers, according to cybersecurity workforce studies for the years 2018 and 2019 [4]. In that context, skills are understood to represent a combination of abilities, knowledge, and experience that enable an individual to complete a task well [5]. The identified extreme skills shortage in cybersecurity has had an impact on market distortions that started to occur in the past decade with intensive digitalization, with larger, wealthier organizations and service providers being able to attract talent and pay for external professional security support and purchase the appropriate technology for protection. This left the smaller companies and non-profit organizations struggling to attract the knowledge and skills that would allow them to run their businesses safely. These needs and findings are backed by the results of a large workforce study by the ISC organization [6]. Failure to address this problem impacts negatively on the capacity of the business sector and other parts of the modern, digitized society. Cybersecurity skills are becoming very important as the digital economy's winners and losers will be determined by who has these skills. The EU General Data Protection Regulation (GDPR) that came into effect in May 2018 requires much more attention to be paid to data security in every data-processing or information system, but due to the skills shortage many organizations find themselves unprepared for compliance. Several GDPR webinars conducted in the EU in 2019 have shown that 60% of businesses are underprepared for GDPR, a figure which is low in comparison to research conducted in 2020 by computerweekly.com [7] which put the figure as high as 90%.Another problem in this area is that the skills required for security professionals are changing at a faster pace than usual within advanced-technology fields, due to the changes introduced by the new digital technology. The research into ICT skills conducted annually by the Enterprise Strategy Group [7], has revealed that the skills gap in cybersecurity continues to widen and has doubled in the past 5 years. The percentage of answers where organizations reported a shortage of skills rose from 23–51% in just 2 years. This issue is being felt across many industries and organizations, and concern extends much beyond regular ICT education and skills building. What appears to be of even greater concern was revealed in a survey carried out by Tripware in 2020 [8]. This survey not only revealed that the skills gap is growing, but that it is getting harder for industry to find and then hire skilled security professionals Cybersecurity Ventures [9] has also reviewed and synthesized dozens of employment figures from the media, analysts, job boards, vendors, governments, and organizations around the world, with the aim to predict the number of cybersecurity job openings over the next 5 years. Their prediction for 2021 is that there will be 3.5 million unfilled cybersecurity positions on the world labour market. These numbers indicate that cybersecurity job forecasts have been unable to keep pace with the dramatic rise in cybercrime and the need for more cybersecurity professionals. Cybersecurity Ventures predicted they would cost $6 trillion annually by 2021, up from $3 trillion in 2015. Similar numbers relating to the world's cybersecurity skills gap were reported by many familiar ICT industries, including Intel, Symantec and others. The problem is wide-ranging and clear, and it needs to be addressed. Both the higher-education institutions (HEIs) and the professional trainers are working to address the increased skills shortage. But as reported by the European Cybersecurity Organization paper [10] and by other others [11] cybersecurity should be viewed as an emerging meta-discipline that is not simply academic, because the content of HEI programmes are focused mainly on the traditional cybersecurity topics and learning methodology has been left behind. The demand for cybersecurity skills in industry also makes it difficult for academia to attract academics with knowledge, practical experience, a research background and academic aspirations. Another problem to be addressed in combating the current cybersecurity skills shortage is an understanding of the diverse needs in this field, which should be used to shape the curriculum of cybersecurity educational programmes. The rapid evolution of cybersecurity attacks coupled with the static nature of academia has contributed to the emerging discrepancies between the knowledge taught in educational programmes and the skills expected by employers, thereby contributing to the growing gap in the skills of cybersecurity professionals [12, 13]. The need to build and upgrade the knowledge, skills and capacity in the area of cybersecurity has led to the establishment of a number of strategic policy initiatives by several governments [14] along with the setting up of cybersecurity competence centres at the European level. Other international initiatives, such as the Information Assurance and Security Program [15] the USA's National Initiatives for Cybersecurity Education [16] and the ENISA (The European Agency for Network and Information Security) [17] actions were launched with the task of collecting data about cybersecurity educational offers and to propose appropriate changes. This chapter presents and discusses the actions and the development of the new cybersecurity educational landscape in the EU and aims to find out whether there is an answer to the shortage of cybersecurity skills in the EU labour market. This chapter is organized as follows. The efforts put into setting up the educational ecosystem supported by EU industry are presented in Section 3.1. The results of a survey about the current programmes offered by EU HEIs in the area of cybersecurity and the recommendations are presented in Section 3.2. A discussion about both approaches and their envisaged cooperation follows in Section 4. The process of building new cybersecurity ecosystem is discussed in Section 5. The chapter ends with a concluding section.

## 2. The workforce market and the European cybersecurity education ecosystem

In answer to the need to build knowledge, skills and capacity, as required by European employers in the area of cyber security, four competence centers were established. Two of them have specific tasks that address the development of cybersecurity education in the EU. The Concordia competence center is developing a new cybersecurity educational ecosystem that offers training by industry, while Cybersecurity4Europe [18] is focusing on the EU's HEI programmes. Both approaches are intended to contribute to the development of the new cybersecurity education landscape in Europe with the main goal being to narrow the cybersecurity skills gap and answer the needs of the overall digitized society.

### 2.1 Providing cybersecurity education and training that are shaped by industry needs

The need to match the cybersecurity candidates with the requirements for available jobs was put on the table by leading European industry. An investigation by PriceWaterhouseCoopers disclosed that failed hires for cybersecurity jobs lowered the workforce's moral and lengthened the hiring time lines, thereby introducing additional costs [6]. One-third of surveyed executives revealed that the inefficient skills-matching among the candidates was the leading cause of failed hires. A pilot study carried out by the European Cybersecurity Organization [11] and the competence center in cybersecurity ECHO [19] intended to discover what kinds of competence and skills development are required by industry [20] and whether these competences can be acquired through exercise and cybersecurity range, offering a simulation of the real environment.

The responses showed that cybersecurity is understood as an important part of the business. In addition, they pointed out several gaps in the organizational capabilities and the missing employee skills required for implementing cybersecurity rules and tools in everyday life. In general, the preparedness and mitigation with respect to cybersecurity threats were estimated to be as low as 39%, with most of the responders have forms of insurance to cover the losses in the case of cyber-attacks. The survey confirmed that the required skills are not uniform, as the responders reported different skill requirements and, as a consequence, different approaches by the participating organizations to tackle them were expected. One common feature was that the competence and skills development can be achieved with use of cyber range services. Some of them are offered by the European Cybersecurity Hub and the use of the Cyber Range Market Place, which was assessed as a potential trusted solution that connects supply and demand for an applicable cyber-threat intelligence solution.

The Concordia the cybersecurity competence center [21] has started to develop the European Eco-Education System by building a portfolio of cybersecurity courses that are offered by different categories of industry addressing the education of cybersecurity professionals, such as technologists, mid-level managers, and executives. The final goal of these activities was to prepare a cybersecurity-specific methodology for the creation of new courses with a broad range of content as an answer to the various industrial needs. The methodology for developing courses is a tool that enables a specific cybersecurity module with typical cybersecurity topics and skills to be created. These modules can be combined in a course for different types of employees. For example, for middle-managers leading ICT departments that need to know about the new practical techniques for attack prevention, and in the case of an attack, to get the capacity to react quickly and enable a rapid recovery are allocated in the module prepared for them. Middle managers that are not leading ICT departments need to understand the general risks and methods that protect the company's ICT and other facilities, so the module dedicated to them is to teach how to recognize the risk and act in the case of an incident. Executives are another group that should have a general understanding of the cybersecurity area and its impact on business, investment and insurance. Investors should be made aware of the various cybersecurity protective solutions. Non-ICT employees are not very interested in developing cybersecurity skills, but they are frequently asked by the company to have basic knowledge in the area in order to be able to understand the challenges and to react properly in the case of an incident and therefore they also need to attend specific courses that address cybersecurity.

On the other hand, it was found that there are a plethora of courses addressing the cybersecurity professional. For employees these are attractive, especially the on-line courses, as they offer control over the time spent studying the material and make it possible to accommodate it according a professional business engagement. However, face-to face courses for middle and senior managers or executives, or specific training within the cyber ranges for technical experts, have been found to be popular and frequently attended. The study by the same team also revealed several learning platforms with cybersecurity content. Among them, the following are very popular:

- Coursera[1] – has 33 million users and has in its portfolio about 50 courses on cybersecurity, with most of them addressing introductory topics.

- edX[2] platform – has 14 million users, who are offered only around 30 cybersecurity-related courses

[1] https://www.coursera.org/

[2] http://www.edx.org/

- LinkedIn Learning[3] - a learning platform with 9.5 million users, hosts around 120 courses on cybersecurity, with half of them addressing an intermediate skill level, closely followed by courses aimed at developing basic skills

- Cybrary platform[4] offers to its 2 million users about 500 cyber-specific video courses for professionals to develop their careers, but also for businesses in view of workforce development.

- IASACA[5] (Information Systems Audit and Control Association) provides online, offline and mixed courses at different levels (foundation, practitioner) for both information security and cybersecurity, including courses for cybersecurity auditors. The courses are sanctioned by certifications.

- Udacity platform[6] – has 8 million users, but has only a small number of security/cybersecurity courses.

- Cyberwiser[7] is offering the "Civil Cyber Range Platform as a novel approach to Cybersecurity threats simulation and professional training". It was launched at the end of 2018 and benefited from H2020 funding. The platform aims to provide a set of innovative tools for highly detailed exercise scenarios, simulating ICT infrastructures intended for use in cybersecurity professional training, together with tools and solutions that simulate cyberattacks and defensive countermeasures.

Although the existing cybersecurity educational platforms in EU are addressing the same market, it should be noted that each platform is structuring the content based on its own model, and without making reference to any common competence framework. Having this in mind, a comparison of the different offers and their attractiveness becomes difficult. Some common content could be identified and is presented in the form of five cybersecurity pillars that emerged from the analysis of the skills that specific courses are providing. The pillar content development has its source in the 60 courses collected during the two-month study carried out in 2019. The identified five pillars are presented in **Figure 1**. The pillars address the skills related to software, networks, data application, devices and user behavior.

The software content is centered on topics such as middleware, secure OSs and security by design, malware analysis, system-security validation, detection of zero-days and recognizing service dependencies. The network-security content refers to the transportation of data as well as data within the networking and security issues. Data-application security addresses issues like data visualization, while other topics range from DDoS protection, to software-defined networking (SDN), and to encrypted-traffic analyses. The data-application content addresses issues like data visualization and the security of applications like cloud services. The device security deals mainly with data acquisition and the devices that produce raw data in embedded systems, by sensors, IoT devices, drones and other security-centric issues, such as IoT security. User behavior is the least-addressed topic that includes privacy, social networks, fake news, and identity management.

Most of the content was designed and selected to meet the needs of a corporate audience, mainly for the technical team members, but also the managers of the

[3] https://www.lynda.com/
[4] https://www.cybrary.it/
[5] https://www.isaca.org/pages/default.aspx
[6] https://www.udemy.com/
[7] htttps://www.dpoconsultancy.com/

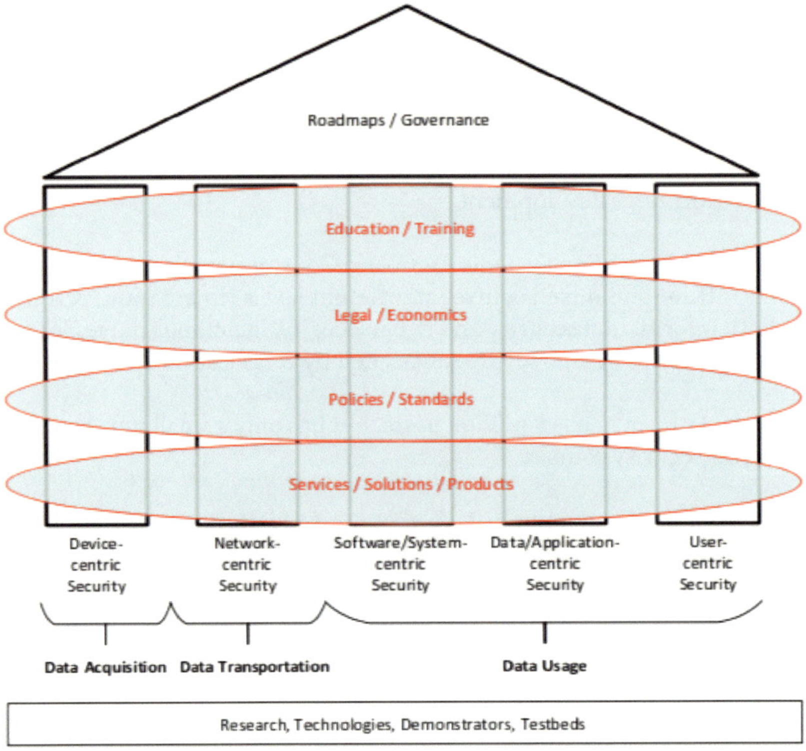


**Figure 1.**
*The five pillars as identified by Concordia cybersecurity competence center.*

non-IT departments and the senior management group. The courses are usually offered as a face-to-face model, but some time is also dedicated to on-line delivery and as a blended format. Altogether, 70+ courses have been collected and published on the Concordia interactive map, which is available on the Concordia website. The proposed roadmap for cybersecurity education addressing industrial needs is presented on **Figure 2**.

## 2.2 Cybersecurity education and training within the European higher-level educational programmes

According to ENISA and others, Europe needs to ensure a sufficient number of skilled engineers, scientist and practitioners in all areas of cybersecurity. Most of these groups have to be educated to support and lead solutions to current and future industrial, scientific, societal and political challenges in the area of cybersecurity. The question that arose was: is the current educational system capable of doing this? The answer to the question was to look at the study and the kind of content that is available in EU HEIs and whether the content was aligned with the much-needed skills [21]. Two studies were carried out to find answers: one from the competence center Cybersecurity4Europe [18] and the other by the ENISA in 2019 [17].

The competence center launched its survey within the project task "University Education" with the aim to investigate the level of tertiary education in cybersecurity that awards master degrees and to find out whether the necessary skills are present in the inspected curricula. More than one hundred MSc programmes were surveyed, accompanied by an information interchange with highly relevant experts such as the heads of the HEI study programmes. The terminology used in the study was based on the ACM Cybersecurity Curricula [15] and the one suggested by the

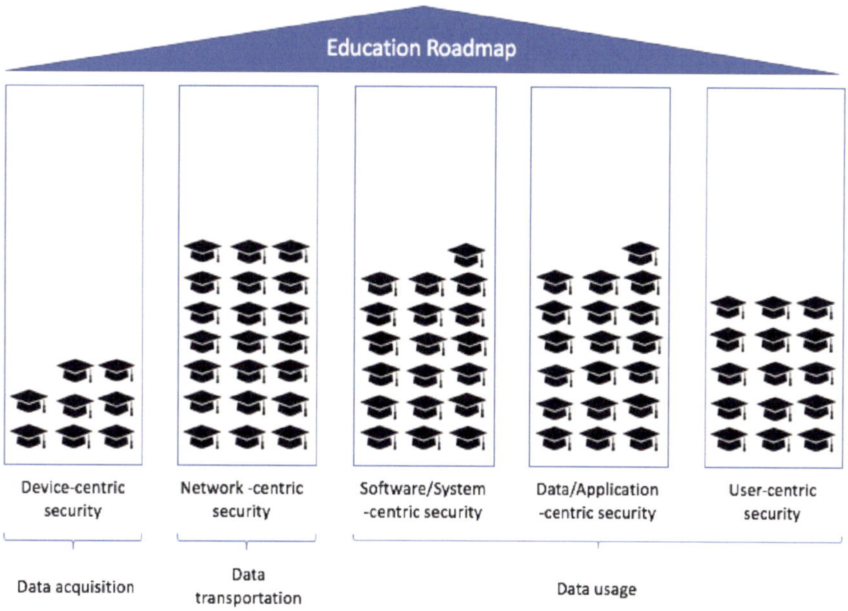


**Figure 2.**
*The roadmap for the evolving cybersecurity education ecosystem as proposed by Concordia center.*

National Initiative for Cybersecurity Education within the Cybersecurity Workforce Framework [18] but missing items were also included from the NICE framework [16]. The collected data from 104 educational programmes were analyzed to find out whether the required cybersecurity skills [18], are sufficiently well or are not covered in a particular EU Member State. Both mandatory and optional courses were analyzed, as well as subtopics that belong to the area of cybersecurity, but are taught in other courses, e.g., in computer science. Several channels were used for the collection data, including the data from the ENISA map of cybersecurity educational programmes [20]. The study resulted in the coverage of 100% of the university MSc programmes in most EU countries. However, it should be noted that the coverage of large countries was smaller due to the presence of a large number and different types of higher-level educational organizations. It should also be noted that the lower-level programmes like BSc programmes where cybersecurity topics are taught were found to be mandatory subjects for the cybersecurity courses at the MSc level and thus the content of the BSc courses was considered as being part of the content survey. The final content of the used framework of knowledge units is based on the ACM definitions of knowledge units that overlap with the NICE framework, but is extended with the knowledge area named "Customer Service and Technical Support" that was found to be missing from the ACM framework.

In general, the data analysis shows that all the knowledge units are covered in the mandatory courses that were provided by the HEIs participating in the survey. The higher frequency of topics was shown by the knowledge units belonging to data security (cryptography and system security). These topics are present in 80% of the studied programmes. Another area that is well covered is connection security. The main lack of sufficient coverage within the studied programmes relates to the area of organizational security and the system-retirement knowledge unit, as their coverage in the studied programmes is close to 20%. However, the study found that there are several knowledge units that are not sufficiently present in most of the programmes. They are Social Security (Customer Service and Technical Support), Organizational Security (Security Operation and Personal security), Component

Security (Component Procurement) and Connection Security (Physical Interface and Connectors). The same applies to some topics of utmost importance in areas like security and privacy by design, which was found in only 30% of the mandatory courses. Usable Security, System Testing, Cybercrime, Social and Behavior Privacy, Security Programme for Management, Documentation and Operation are topics that are not well covered in the optional and mandatory courses. They are present in only 15% of the courses. The national coverage is also not very homogenous, as large countries have many more programmes and have shown greater coverage of the framework knowledge units. For example, Spain, France, Germany and Italy cover 75% of the knowledge units in their mandatory courses. Countries with better coverage of the topics tend to have a more uniform distribution of each knowledge area, whereas countries with lower coverage of the knowledge areas exhibit a more unbalanced distribution. For more details please refer to Cybersec4Europe Report [18].

ENISA produced the EU Cybersecurity Educational Map [17]. The first version of the HEI map was renewed in 2020 with a description of the new user interface and new content was added. The main goal of the map was to become the premiere source of information for EU citizens looking to update their cybersecurity knowledge and skills. In following this goal, the map is designed to serve as a tool providing links to qualitative educational programmes with degrees in cybersecurity and therefore enabling better access to the knowledge and skills for reducing the identified skills shortage in Europe. The current data collected in the database provides 105 programmes from 23 countries. The map is available on-line on the ENISA portal.

This unique database lists cybersecurity programmes in the EU, EFTA, and other European countries. The database was developed as a point of reference for all citizens looking to upskill their knowledge in the area of cybersecurity. It allows talented young people to make informed decisions about the variety of possibilities offered by higher education in cybersecurity and helps universities attract high-quality students motivated to keep Europe cyber-secure. The map makes it possible to search by country where the programme is held, by language used in the education of the programme, type of programme, e.g., master degree, postgraduate PhD course, bachelor degree, the type of delivery method, e.g., classroom, blended or on-line course. The selection of programmes is supported with information about the fee. The list of educational programmes in cybersecurity is not closed, as a protocol is available for further additions. Any higher-education institution can submit a recognized (by an EU Member State or EFTA country) programme by submitting the degree's information with the dedicated ENISA template. If the programme meets the basic quality-assurance parameters, the degree is accepted. Each degree becomes "out of date" after one year from the submission date as the submitter is responsible for updating the degree information each year. The requirements for the inclusion of a programme in the database are as follows: for a bachelor degree, at least 25% of the taught modules have to be cybersecurity topics; and for a master degree, at least 40% of the taught modules have to be cybersecurity topics. For a postgraduate specialization programme, at least 40% of the taught modules must be in cybersecurity topics and the programme must have a minimum of 60 ECTS. However, these requirements are just the basic information about the cybersecurity educational programmes in the EU and EFTA countries and will not, on their own, solve the skills shortage in Europe.

The major drawbacks regarding adequate education and training by high-level educational institutions found in the ENISA report point to the lack of strong interactions with industry. The identified barriers are mainly connected with the lack of technical support and funding availability. An important finding in the report is the poor understanding of the cybersecurity labor market and the fact that HEIs do not understand the requests of employers for manpower with the necessary skills. Similar findings can be read in the study of Catota [22]. A major factor that prevents good cybersecurity education is the lack of specialization of the professors and the lack of feedback from or cooperation with industry. In its study, ECSO [11] stressed that professionals need to understand all the disciplines that make up the area of cybersecurity, ranging from more technical topics to the subjects from social sciences. Most of these findings lead to the conclusion that there is a need for a sharper definition of the knowledge and skills that a student should possess and that activities like training and practice should take place after a student's graduation.

### 2.3 Standards, curriculum guidelines and accreditation

As studies have shown [23, 24] that a degree in cybersecurity can cover a wide spectrum of disciplines, depending on the area of emphasis of the educational programme. Many substantially different degree programmes are taking on the "cybersecurity" title or another similarly generic name. Due to the existing variety within the current programme and degree names, distinguishing a cybersecurity programme using some scheme of accreditation and certification appeared to be a very useful idea. Such a scheme could help in classifying the skills and the related competences. Different cybersecurity disciplines have different names that directly describe their areas of emphases, for example, network security, cyber criminology, or secure-software development. The latest studies from Dawson and Thomson (26) have discussed different views, like the impact of skills beyond the technical area of cybersecurity that are expected to have a major impact on the future workforce. Having this in mind, it is not surprising that some countries (Australia, USA, UK and France) have already established certification schemes for their national cybersecurity degrees that include items that are not directly technical. They award certification by attesting whether the degree meets the standards and criteria that a group of experts have decided are necessary to obtain a degree that focuses on cybersecurity. These certifications are overseen by the countries' main national cybersecurity institutions, i.e., the Agence Nationale de la Sécurité des Systèmes d'Information (ANSSI) in France, the Department of Homeland Security (DHS) and the National Security Agency (NSA) in the United States, and the National Cyber Security Centre (NCSC) in the United Kingdom. The exception being Australia, where the process is supervised by the Department of Education.

Although the accreditation schemes do not offer concrete solutions for the required content as an answer to the identified needs and problems related to the lack of a skilled work force in the labor market, they are still considered as a tool that certainly provides an adequate number of taught courses and activities that are specific to the cybersecurity area, even when a broader interdisciplinary focus in the programmes is maintained. Accreditation also enables, in great detail, visibility with regard to how the cybersecurity education is provided and the quality of the faculty engaged in the education. A common property of the presented accreditations is that they are awarded to degrees that provide an adequate number of taught courses and activities that are specific to cybersecurity.

## 3. Discussion

These findings indicate that cybersecurity encompasses a very broad range of specialty areas and work roles, and that no single educational programme can be expected to cover all of the specialized skills and sector-specific knowledge desired by each employer. However, it is also clear that there are certain knowledge sets and skills that are essential for any new employee in a critical technical work role, regardless of the field they are in or the specialty they adopt. This includes an understanding of computer architecture, data, cryptography, networking, secure-coding principles, and operating-system internals, as well as working proficiency with Linux-based systems, fluency in low-level programming languages, and familiarity with common exploitation methods and mitigation techniques However, even in that aspect opinions differ, Martin and Collier [25] claim that the mitigating current cyber issues mean that some countries and their education systems should adopt more interdisciplinary approaches. This will allow a better integration of people with different skill sets and a better comprehension of the cyber-security challenges. On the other hand, Dawson and Thompson [26], by considering the highly complex and heterogeneous cyber world, claim that the social aspects should have an important role in cybersecurity education and workforce development. In their paper they have identified six traits for the future cybersecurity professional: systematic thinking, collaboration, strong communication, continuous learning, a sense of civic duty and a mix of technical and social skills. On other hand, Malan et al. [27] and Cabaj et al. [28] argue that cybersecurity should be a very technical subject requiring years of study and training. Other experts claim that the specific and purpose-driven cybersecurity degrees at HEIs should better prepare the graduate for the labor market as one of the biggest concerns in cybersecurity education is students' lack of hands-on experience, resulting in a skills mismatch between what industry would like to see in a candidate and the skills that they actually possess [29]. The central theme of this concern is training versus education. Education tends to focus on the reasons, the theory and the mechanisms behind the material [4]. Industry prefers workers who are ready to work from day one. On the other hand, technology changes quickly and the students need to learn transferable skills that can be used throughout a lifelong career. Therefore, as a conclusion, many authors suggest that the cybersecurity-degree providers should balance the employability of the students with providing the foundations for future professionals capable of updating their skills in the current dynamic environment.

The Cybersec4EU study [23] found that the European education ecosystem with its new cybersecurity courses is growing, but it is very unevenly spread across Europe. This has contributed to different conceptualizations of the science of cybersecurity appearing and, as a consequence, there are currently a variety of educational offerings that introduce obstacles to the creation of a common cybersecurity educational framework. One of the problems identified was that there are still constraints on those students who wish to acquire an all-round skill set in cybersecurity, but they are pushed to specialize in either technical or societal cybersecurity issues, but not both [30]. Another challenge is the responsiveness of the content of the cybersecurity curricula to the evolution of the field as there is a lack of mechanisms for the rapid incorporation of material on new emerging threats or new skills.

In that context it is important to mention the work of four international organizations, i.e., the Association for Computing Machinery (ACM), IEEE Computer Society Association for Information Systems Special Interest Group on Information Security and Privacy (AIS SIGSEC), and the International Federation for Information Processing Technical, Committee on Information Security Education (IFIP WG 11.8), that have written a report about the "Curriculum Guidelines for Post-Secondary Degree Programs in Cybersecurity from 2017" [31]. Later, the leading author of this study Parriish with several other researchers published a paper that discusses the global perspectives on cybersecurity education for 2030, based on the research carried out within the ACM group, known as Innovation and

Technology in Computer Science Education – ITiCSE. Their study is based on the evaluation of all the educational institutions in the US from the CAE group. The ITiCSE group has provided reports on the subject of cybersecurity education for many years, starting with 2009. However, the main source of information used for developing educational prospects for 2030 was the NICE approach and the competency levels defined by the ITiCSE initiative [30]. Competences in cybersecurity in their study are understood as the ability to perform work activities at a stated competency level, which are denoted as roles like technician, entry-level practitioner, technical leader or senior software engineer. Competence itself is also recognized as the combination of knowledge, skill and abilities. The authors suggest that cybersecurity competence for the future, e.g., for 2030, can be constructed by developing two models of education [32]. The first is an information-technology programme with a cybersecurity track for students that are information-technology specialists with programme topics like governance, risk management, constraints and control. The second model is cybersecurity bachelor programmes with students that are cybersecurity specialists with a high level of expertise that should contain the same main topics as the first programme, but with a changed focus, e.g., risk management should address threat modeling, asset evaluation and vulnerability. Each of the topics should be taught at different levels within the selected model. This type of dichotomy, focusing on the needs of cybersecurity specialists, but also on IT specialists that need to know some cybersecurity, is becoming part of many opinions, like the one provided in the work of Moller and Crick [33] and Davenport et al. [26]. The recent evolution of cybersecurity education shows that it has begun to take shape as a true academic field, as a meta-science, as opposed to simply being a training domain for certain specialized jobs [19]. Other proposals appeared recently, e.g., that cybersecurity topics should be formally thought in schools as a part of school-level education.

## 4. Building the new educational ecosystem in EU: is this the way that we will close the skilled-workforce gap?

Interest in cybersecurity education and skills is long standing within the EU and it has been a policy concern since the publication by the European Commission of the first EU cybersecurity strategy in 2013 [34]. This document invites the Member States to increase their education and training efforts around the network and information security (NIS) topics and to plan for a "NIS driving license" as a voluntary certification programme to promote the enhanced skills and competence of ICT professionals and cybersecurity people. One of the actions was the setting up of competence centers, with the aim to develop the European Secure, Resilient and Trusted Ecosystem, including education. In 2019, the four competence centers, CONCORDIA, ECHO, SPARTA and CyberSec4Europe collected in the CCN network [35], were launched with tasks to establish and operate pilot projects with the goal to develop an innovation roadmap, including the development of a new educational ecosystem in cybersecurity. As a starting point, the views of the main stakeholders were collected in surveys carried out by the CCN network. The main message received was that the cybersecurity education and training in EU is still not sufficiently regarded as a factor that influences the success of the digital market's development. The main reason identified was the presence of only a few cybersecurity courses in computing curricula, poor alignment between educational offers at HEIs and the labor market's demands, little emphasis on multidisciplinary knowledge, and the prominence of theory-based education rather than hands-on training. All the collected comments revolve around the need to redefine the educational and training pathways in order to have a more unified standard for the knowledge and skills so that students should develop to meet these needs.

Regarding the required competences, a concerted effort to define the competences needed to be owned/developed by different European actors playing a role in the cybersecurity market or impacted by it, was pursued in a collaboration with ECSO and its members. The contributions from the CCN network in building the new educational ecosystem are related to different issues. Concordia (works on the development of the new cybersecurity education ecosystem with a number of courses collected from industry in a map as an answer to the needs for collaboration with industrial partners that are mainly representatives of the national and international corporate segment. A map showing the available courses was prepared, which is periodically updated with new courses. The industry fields covered are various, but the telecoms sector is the most addressed, although other industries are also covered, like the critical information infrastructure, IoT and cloud computing. The dominant language is English, but other European languages are also present. In addition, on the map, the industrial field is specified, as are the main target audiences, the type of courses (f2f, on-line or blended), entry requirements and the most important information provided is the type of certification given to the professionals that have successfully passed the course. Cybersec4Europe is working on the educational programmes at European HEIs. The ECHO pilot project (39) is looking to develop a cyber-skills framework (E-CSF) to address the needs and skills gap of the cybersecurity professionals based on a mapping of the cybersecurity multi-sector assessment framework developed in 2019. The E-CSF is composed of learning outcomes, a competence model and a generic curriculum, with mechanisms for improving the human capacity of cybersecurity across Europe. In the first year of the network, the CCN Education Cross-Pilots Group (covering all educational activities) produced the methodology for the creation of new courses for four types of professionals by specifying their role profiles (Concordia report). The ENISA map and Concordia industry map are interconnected and they are available on their respective websites. In addition, a general cybersecurity skills-certification scheme was designed to provide an examination mechanism for knowledge certification, skills and other competences for the defined profiles of cybersecurity professionals.

The outcomes from the four competence centers and the CCN Education Pilot promise a move towards a new EU ecosystem consisting of more structured curricula with a practical/training component, specific types of examinations and additional activities such as cybersecurity competitions and outreach activities as well as collaborations with the rest of the national cybersecurity educational systems. The cybersecurity knowledge topics and skills included are in line with the ACM study group and the NICE framework. However, missing topics, like organizational security (Security Operation and Personal Security) are recommended for inclusion in the curricula. The same applies to the issues dealing with anonymising data, as they are not currently sufficiently well addressed. Social Security (Customer service and technical support), Component Security (Procurement) and Connection Security (Physical interface and connectors) also need special attention due to the expansion of IoT-connected devices. Besides that, all programmes in cybersecurity education should acknowledge the importance of the human-centric factors, which include elements from sociology and psychology. Similar attention should be given to the areas of utmost importance, like privacy by design, which appeared to be present in less than 30% of the educational programmes.

On the other hand, despite the new HEI programmes in cybersecurity, companies still continuously face the problem of filling their cybersecurity-related positions. The total number of unfilled cybersecurity job openings in the 28 EU Member States remains stable from one year to the next, around 3500 a month. The fact that the total number remains almost the same suggests that education is adjusted to the company needs for professionals, as is being developed within the new ecosystem by the CCN network, and will help the situation to change. The current outcomes will certainly provide a positive impact on the current situation regarding the missing skilled work force in Europe; however, the transition will need some time for positive changes to happen.

## 5. Conclusion

The work presented in this chapter is a step towards a better understanding of the changing landscape of the cybersecurity education in the EU provided by surveys, actions and initiatives taken in both important fields: the high-level education and an industrial initiative. Both areas have shown that they are aware of the great demand for experts, professionals and other skilled people with competence and cybersecurity skills. The existing gap of skilled labor is not typical for Europe only; however, the identified shortage is demanding ways to be found for increasing the number of cybersecurity workforce applicants with actions and initiatives that will change the uneven distribution of qualified cybersecurity educational programmes in the EU and the training offers by industry.

The lack of cybersecurity-skilled people has its source in the nature of the new meta-science of cybersecurity, which is a rapidly changing discipline that has been evolving since the creation of the educational frameworks at both educational levels, including the training for experience offered by industry. The rapid development of the digital world and the needs for the protection of digital assets is another factor that contributes to the missing cybersecurity-skilled workforce all over the world. By taking this situation into account, the integration of the new topics within the existing frameworks supported by continuous training should become a continuous practice that will answer successfully the social and economic needs. Joint approaches will lead to an improvement of the current situation and the gap of missing skills to be closed. All these issues revolve around the idea of defining a sharper set of knowledge and skills that students should possess and the training activities they should undertake before they graduate with a degree in cybersecurity. When major stakeholders underline the poor alignment between the educational outcomes and the market demands and propose more multidisciplinary expertise to be acquired with a focus on the organizational and social challenges, they are actually asking the educators to include in the curricula a more hands-on approach to education and training. This is one of the major challenges in the reshaping of the European cybersecurity education landscape. One way to circumvent the existing situation is the relevant stakeholders – namely academia, governments and employers – to come together, discuss the foundational knowledge and skills to be developed and the activities that should be undertaken. Another task is a general European cybersecurity-degree accreditation and certification that should be promoted and applied in all EU Member States. Certification should be awarded to degrees that provide an adequate number of taught courses and activities specific to cybersecurity. Good examples and practices in the most developed countries in the EU are available, but their number is so small that an initiative for spreading a common accreditation scheme is necessary. Most of the national authorities support collaboration with foreign educational programmes that contribute to the educational quality, so cooperation and support in setting national certification schemes where the scheme is not present based on a common European framework will certainly be welcomed. It will facilitate the exchange of students and the mobility of the work force with standard levels of cybersecurity skills and knowledge.

## Author details

Borka Jerman Blažič
Institute Jožef Stefan, Ljubljana, Slovenia

*Address all correspondence to: borka@e5.ijs.si

## References

[1] EU, Resilience, Deterrence and Defence: Building strong cybersecurity for the EU, Brussels, (2017). https://eur-lex.europa.eu/legal-content/en/TXT/?uri=CELEX%3A52017JC0450

[2] British Airways, Customer data theft, (2019), https://www.bbc.com/news/business-48905907

[3] Caulkins, B. Marlowe, T. Reardon, A., (Cybersecurity skills to address Today's Threats, in Ahram T., Nicholson D., (eds) Advances in Human factors in Cybersecurity, AHFE 2018. Advances in Intelligent Systems and Computing, vol. 782. Springer, https://doi.org/10.1007/978-3-319-94782-2-2_18

[4] Ackerman, R., Too few cybersecurity professionals is a gigantic problem, (2019). https://techcrunch:com/2019/01/27/too-few-cybersecurity-professionals-is-a-gigantic-problem-for-2019/

[5] Carlton, M. Levy Y., M. Expert assessment of the top platform independent cybersecurity skills for non-IT professionals, (2015). Proceedings of IEEE Southeast conference on Privacy, Proceedings, Fort Lauderdale, FL, USA, https://ieeexplore.ieee.org/abstract/document/7132932

[6] ISC2 Cybersecurity workforce study, (2018). https://www.isc2.org/-/media/ISC2/Research/2018-ISC2-Cybersecurity-Workforce-Study.ashx?la=en&hash=4E09681D0FB51698D9BA6BF13EEABFA48BD17DB0

[7] Mirza, S., Brown, M., Computer weekly in April, (2020). https:computer.weekly.com

[8] Tripware, The Experts' Guide on Tackling the Cybersecurity Skills Gap (2020), https://www.tripwire.com/state-of-security/featured/expert-guide-tackling-cybersecurity-skills-gap/#:~:text=The%20skills%20gap%20is%20weighing,they%20did%20a%20year%20earlier

[9] Ventures Report (2018) - https://cybersecurityventures.com/cybersecurity-market-report-2018/

[10] ESG, Cybersecurity pending trends, (2018), https//www.esg-global.com/research/esg-brief-2018-cybersecurity-spending-trend,

[11] ECSO, Gaps in European Cyber Education and professional training, (2019). https://www.ecs-org.eu/documents/publications/5bf7e01bf3ed0.pdf

[12] Michael, P. Closing the information security skill gap, (2020) https://www.michaelpage.co.uk/our-expertise/technology/closing-information-security-skills-gap

[13] Hentea, M. Dhillon, H.S, Towards changes in information security education Journal of Information Technology, (2006) Number 1, 2006, pp 221-233

[14] UK Cabinet Office, The UK Cybersecurity strategy Protecting and Promoting the UK in the digital world, 2011, https://www.gov.uk/government/publications/cyber-security-strategy/

[15] ACM/IEEE-CS Joint Task Force on Computing Curricula. Computer Science Curricula (2013). https://dx.doi.org/10.1145/2534860

[16] NICE, National Initiative for Cybersecurity Education. Cybersecurity Workforce Framework. (2013)https://www.nist.gov/itl/applied-cybersecurity/nice/resources/nice-cybersecurity-workforce-framework

[17] ENISA, Cybersecurity eHEI data base, (2019), https://www.enisa.europa.eu/topics/cybersecurity-education/education-map

[18] Cybersec4Europe, Report on the HEI education in Cybersecurity, (2019) https://cybersec4europe.eu/

[19] ECHO, Cybersecurity Competence centre, https: https://echonetwork.eu/

[20] ENISA report of cyber skill development in EU, (2020) https://media.kaspersky.com/uk/Kaspersky-Cyberskills-Report_UK.pdf

[21] Concordia report on Cybersecurity education, Deliverable 3.4, Establishing a European Education Ecosystem for Cybersecurity, (2019) https://www.concordia-h2020.eu/

[22] Catota, M. Granger, M., Sicker, D.C., Cybersecurity education in a developing nation: the Ecuadorian environment, (2019) J. of Cybersecurity, 1-19, DOI:10-1093/cybsec/tyz001

[23] Davenport, J.H., Crick, T., Hayes, A. R. Hourizi, R., The Institute of Coding: Addressing the UK Digital Skills Crisis. (2018) In Proc. of 3rd Computing Education Practice Conference

[24] Galliano, J.S., Improved matching of cybersecurity professionals skills to job-related competence: an exploratory study, (2017) PhD University of Fairfax,,

[25] Martin A., Collier, J. Beyond Awareness: The Breadth and Depth of the Cyber Skills Demand, Center for technology and global affairs, (2019), Oxford University, https://www.ctga.ox.ac.uk/article/beyond-awareness-breadth-and-depth-cyber-skills-demand

[26] Dawson, J. Thomson, R., The Future Cybersecurity Workforce: Going Beyond Technical Skills for Successful Cyber Performance, (2018) Front. Psychol.,12. https://doi.org/10.3389/fpsyg.2018.00744

[27] Malan, J., Lale-Demoz, E., Rampton, J., Identifying the Role of Further and HigherEducation in Cyber Security Skills Development. Skills : Concepts, Measurement and Policy, Approaches, (2018) Journal of Economic Surveys 32 (4): 985

[28] Cabaj, I. Domingos, D., Kotulski, Z Respício, A., Cybersecurity education: Evolution of the discipline and analysis of master programs, Computers & Security, 2018 - ElsevierVol. 75, Pages 24-35

[29] Omolohunnu, R., Cybersecurity: A Nonexperimental Correlational Study of Organizational Employees' Security Perceptions and Vulnerabilities (2019). Information Technology Infrastructure, https://search.proquest.com/docview/2307785016?pq-origsite=gscholar&fromopenview=true

[30] Parr, C., Cybersecurity skills need boost in computer science degrees. (2014) https://www:timeshighereducation:com/news/cybersecurity-skills-need-boost-in-computer-science-degrees/2016933:article

[31] IFIP/ACM/IEEE/AIS/IFIP Joint Task Force Cybersecurity Education. Cybersecurity Curricula (2017), https://cybered.hosting.acm.org/wp/

[32] Parrish, A. Impagliazzo, J., Rajendra, K.R., Santos, H. Rizwan, M., Curriculum Guidelines for Post-Secondary Degree Programs in Cybersecurity, in A Report in the Computing Curricula Series, Joint Task Force on Cybersecurity Education, (2017)https://www.acm.org/binaries/content/assets/education/curricula-recommendations/csec2017.pdf

[33] Moller,F. Crick, T., A University-Based Model for Supporting Computer Science Curriculum Reform. (2018) Journal of Computers in Education, 5(4):415{434)

[34] European Commission, Policy, Cybersecurity Strategy of the European Union: An Open, Safe and Secure Cyberspace, (2013) https://ec.europa.eu/digital-single-market/en/cyber-security

[35] CCN - CONCORDIA, (2019) Cyber competence network– about, https://cybercompetencenetwork.eu/about

Chapter 4

# An Emerging Solution for Detection of Phishing Attacks

*Prasanta Kumar Sahoo*

## Abstract

In this era of computer age, as more and more people use internet to carry out their day to day work so as hackers performs various security attacks on web browsers and servers to steal user's vital data. Now Electronic mail (E-mail) is used by everyone including organizations, agency and becoming official communication for the society as a whole in day to day basis. Even though a lot of modern techniques, tools and prevention methods are being developed to secure the users vital information but still they are prone to security attacks by the fraudsters. Phishing is one such attack and its detection with high accuracy is one of the prominent research issues in the area of cyber security. Phisher fraudulently acquire confidential information like user-id, passwords, visa card and master card details through various social engineering methods. Mostly blacklist based methodology is used for detection of phishing attacks but this method has a limitation that it cannot be used for detection of white listed phishing. This chapter aims to use machine learning algorithms to classify between phishing E-mails and genuine E-mails and helps the user in detecting attacks. The architectural model proposed in this chapter is to identify phishing and use J48 decision tree classifier to classify the fake E-mail from real E-mail. The algorithm presented here goes through several stages to identify phishing attack and helps the user in a great way to protect their vital information.

**Keywords:** security attacks, phishing, fake E-mail, data mining

## 1. Introduction

It is one of the methods used by the phisher to steal user's most secret information in a fraudulent manner. It is a very serious security problem that the modern world is facing today in cyber space which leads to financial losses for individuals and the society at large. It is an unlawful act, the fraudsters use it to retrieve user's personal and secrete information by betraying them using various social engineering methods. It is becoming one of the major types of frauds where the phisher used to trick the user to reveal their own private information such as user id, password, pin and visa card details. Mostly phishing attack is done by E-mails. Very often a phishing messages may contain a uniform resource locator (URL) that redirect the user to visit an alternate web site. The redirected site is an extremely modified site and when the user clicks on that site, they are directed to enter their personal information which normally transferred to the phishing assailant [1, 2]. It is an offense in which a phisher sends the fake E-mails, that appears to be genuine and come from a trustworthy organization, instruct to enter their personal information such as online banking username, password, mobile number, residential address, details



IntechOpen

of the credit card and so forth [3–5]. There are many methodologies used by the phisher to trick the user to deceive them and to steal their personal credentials. Very often phisher used spoofed E-mails and forged websites to deceive the users. Web spoofing is one type of attack where phisher use artificial or forged sites to cheat users and to steal their personal information. The phishing E-mail seems to be a real one and even the website designed for the very purpose which directed the user to enter information looks real one. Mostly fake messages spread through E-mails, short message service (SMS), instant messengers, social networking sites, Voice over Internet Protocol (VoIP), and so forth, but E-mail is the most popular way and 65% of the phishing attack took place due to a click on the hyperlink attached to the E-mail [6]. Spear phishing is one of the methods used by the phisher to dupe organizations and individuals in Business E-mail Compromise (BEC). The very sophisticated spear phishing attacks [7–9] to target selected groups, individuals in an organization. Phishing is a type of attack that is very similar to fishing in a pond or river, but instead of trying to catch a fish, the phisher try to dupe user's most vital information [10, 11]. A user generally follows the authentication procedure by filing login id and passwords. The password should be strong password from security point of view to protect it from the attackers. Many anti-phishing tools were developed to provide stronger security which includes using image as input in the login process and hashing of passwords [12]. The web sites are specially designed by the phisher to looks to be legitimate one for which it is becoming very difficult for the user to detect fake website through their appearance.

### 1.1 Related work

Tan et al. [13] suggested an anti-phishing method to extract body tags and Meta from the URL. The uniform resource locator (URL) is broken down into tokens and after that the keywords are compared with yahoo search engine. The original domain name is compared against the given domain name and also with the country code of top level domain to check if there is a matching. The country code of top level domain is matched with that of web site and if found correct then it is considered as real web site otherwise fake website. Yan et al. [14] reviewed on Chinese phishing on Ecommerce sites. Sequential minimal optimization algorithm is used for the purpose and the features such as URL and the web features are used for detection of phishing. Genetic algorithm has been used to optimize the features. The data mining tool Waikato Environment for Knowledge Analysis (WEKA) is used to train the model that the system proposes. Li et al. [15] suggested using machine learning to detect phishing web pages. He has used document object model to optimize the features and emphases has given to web image that are extracted from the webpage. The features after optimization are passed into transductive support vector machine to differentiate between fake web site and real web site.

### 1.2 Existing work on phishing

Gemini is a well known tool used for the authentication process to protect the user against phishing. There were some anti-phishing techniques available today to prevent user from falling prey to the fake web sites by providing a strong secured authentication process. Some of the reputed sites display the security indicator for their sites to convey a message to the user that the site is not a fake website. The presence of URL indicator enables the users to identify the site as a real one [16, 17]. In some cases in the absence of such security indicators, the users avoid themselves from entering the passwords [13]. One of the examples of such is Sitekey [18] which is used by Bank of America for internet banking [19]. The user can choose an image as input into the login process and when the user trying to login, the system will validate the image. In case the input image is wrong then the user stopped form login and authentication failed. Dhamija et al. [20] in his paper titled "dynamic security skins" proposed to use personal identity for authentication by the remote server that the user can verify. So in this method the web site will be considered as fake web site if the identity of the web site cannot be proved. Parno et al. [21] presented an anti-phishing technique which uses hard ware devices such as smart phones and smart tokens to authenticate. Although a user unknowingly log into a phishing site, this process helps the user to protect the vital information from leaking out to phisher because of this trusted authentication procedure. Gemini does not require the support of other devices in comparison to other existing techniques. There are some anti-phishing techniques such as Antiphish [22] and Webwallet [23] already available to identify the actual intent of users browsing activity which helps the user from falling prey to phishing attacks. This research work takes user name as input to initiate anti-phishing technique which helps the user to protect their vital information whereas other techniques based more on passwords. Yue et al. [24] proposed a technique that is free from any kind of deceit to protect the user credentials being leaked out fraudsters by hiding the actual content from the fake sites. It makes the fraudsters very tough to retrieve user's secret info before the user identifies the site as fake. Some password management techniques such as PwdHash [19], Password Multiplier [15], and passpet [24] offer password hashing to provide better security strength for passwords. Because of rehashing of passwords and randomly changing the name of web sites a phisher could not make use of the stolen information. Birk et al. [12] suggested a different mechanism to track the identity of the attacker. He has proposed to use of fingerprint credentials to track the stolen information from fake sites.

## 2. Case studies in phishing

### 2.1 Case study: website phishing experiment

In this study a website was designed with an exact replica of website www.ahlionline.com, the original Jordan Ahli Bank website. The objective is to misleading the user's by targeted phishing E-mail attack to giving away their vital information. We intentionally put a lot of known phishing features during web site design to understand the user's awareness of these kinds of risk after getting authorization from the management. We used Internet Protocol (IP) address instead of domain name, http instead of https, poor design, spelling errors, absence of secure sockets layer (SSL), padlock icon and phony security certificate. We almost achieve our target to attack 120 employees through well planned phishing E-mail, informing them that their e-banking accounts are at high risk of being attacked and requested them to immediately log into their account through fake link attached to our E-mail to verify their balance in the account. We successfully deceive 52 from the group of 120 employees in our organization representing 44% of the sample, who followed the deceiving instructions and give away their actual credentials. The very surprising fact is 8 employees of the IT department and IT auditors are victims out of the 120 representing 7% of the sample. 44 employees from other departments out of 120-targeted victims representing 37% of the sample fell into the trap and give away their information without much hesitation. 28 employees are very cautious and given wrong information representing 23% of the sample and 40 employees choose not to respond at all after receiving the E-mail representing 33% of the sample. The experimental result shows that phishing is extremely dangerous to the whole society since almost half of the employees who responded were victimized. In particularly the very well educated and technically trained people from IT department and IT auditors are also among them. So increasing the awareness of all users who are using e-banking facility regarding this risk factor is highly recommended [25].

### 2.2 Case study: phone phishing experiment

A group of around 50 employees in an organization were contacted by their female colleagues to lure them into giving away their personal e-banking accounts details such as user id and passwords through friendly conversations with an aim to deceiving them. The results were very surprising as many of the employees fell for the trick. After having friendly conversations for quite for some time with them, the assigned team able to seduce them into giving away their e-banking details such as user id and passwords for false reasons. Some of these lame reasons which were used in the conversations are to check the account integrity, their privileges and accessibility and connectivity issues with the Web server for maintenance purpose. The assigned team managed to deceive 16 out of the 50 employees used for testing purpose into giving away their complete e-banking information such as user id and password, which is about 32% of the sample. Another eight employees (16% of the sample) agreed to give their user name only. The remaining 52% of the sample (26 employees) were very vigilant and decided not to reveal any information over the phone. The summary of the testing results reveals the high risk of the social engineering security factor. The results prove that there is a urgent need to increase the awareness of customers not to fall victims of this kind of threat which can have devastating results [26].

### 2.3 Case study: business email compromise (BEC)

The Nigeria-based Business E-mail Compromise (BEC) attack hit over 50 countries in 2017, targeting more than 500 businesses predominantly industrial organizations. The phishing scam directed the user to download a malicious file. When theses files were downloaded, malware would gain authorized access to their business data and networks [27].

### 2.4 Case study: shipping information

The internet security company Comodo found a new type of phishing scam specifically to target small businesses in July 2018. E-mails containing phishing spam was sent out to more than 3,000 small businesses firms, mentioning Shipping Information on the subject line. The E-mail was to inform about approaching delivery by United Parcel Service (UPS) and the user were asked to click on the delivery tracking link to get the delivery status. When the user clicked on the delivery tracking link it contained malware, potentially releasing a virus [27].

## 3. Proposed system architecture

Even though there are several methods exists today to detect phishing but still it has become a very difficult task to detect fake E-mails in the current scenario. Today there are a number of techniques exist for identification of phishing E-mails and some of them are white listing, heuristics, blacklisting and machine learning. A machine learning technique is proposed in this chapter to identify the phishing E-mails and protect the user from revealing their pin, user id and passwords. The objective of this chapter is to use J48 one of the machine learning algorithms to analyze incoming E-mails and helps in preventing the user from phishing attacks. This chapter presented an architectural model as shown in **Figure 1** below and uses the various sub-processes at different stages to classify between fake E-mail and genuine E-mails.

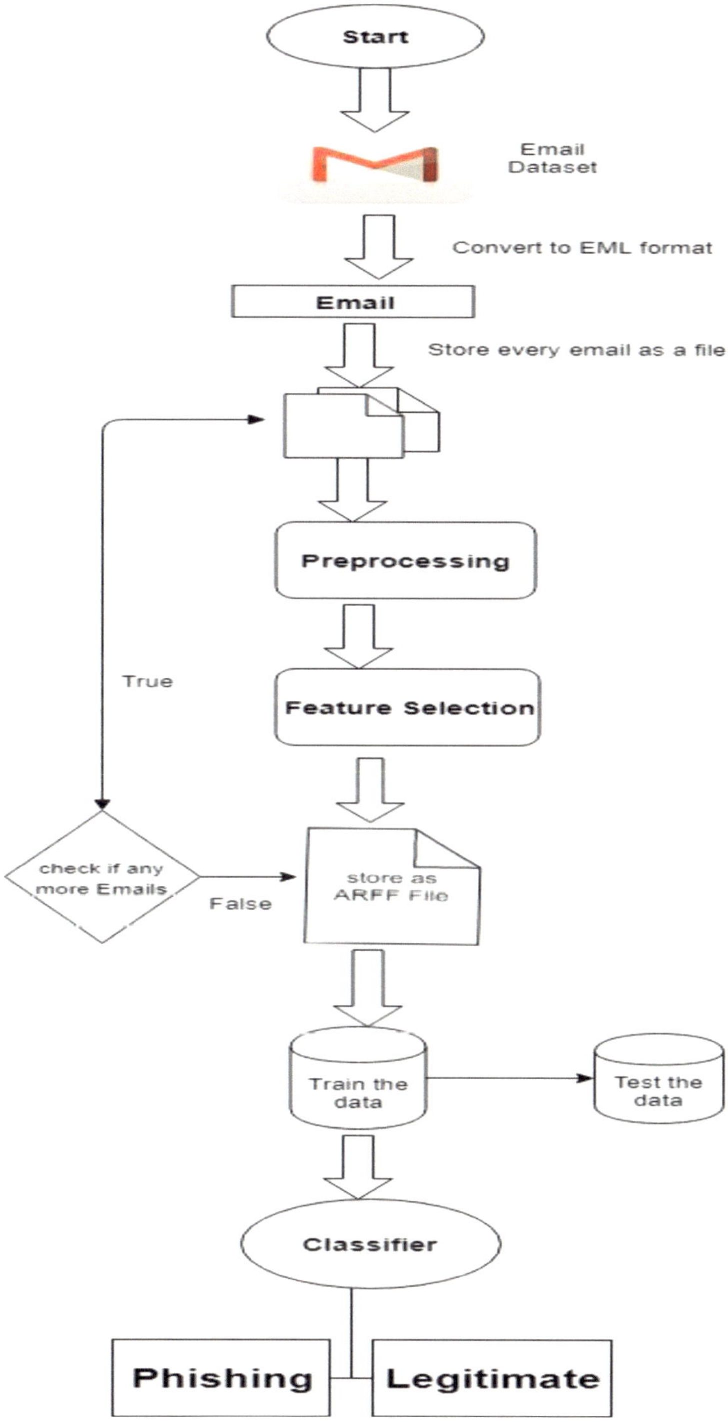


**Figure 1.**
*Shows the architectural model of the proposed work.*

### 3.1 The architectural model

The architectural model presented in the chapter as stated in **Figure 1** consists of seven sub-modules as Input Raw E-mails (data set), Covert to Electronic Mail Format (EML) format, Data Preprocessing, Feature Selection, Training Phase and using the model to classify test data. In the initial stage the system reads the raw E-mails data from Enron dataset. In the second stage convert them into EML (Electronic Mail Format) format and store them as a file. The third stage is data Pre-processing to removes unnecessary words through tokenization. The fourth stage is feature extraction. The features such as body, to, from, URL, carbon copy (Cc), blind carbon copy (Bcc) and the body of the E-Mails that is message are extracted from the input E-mails. In fifth stage the extracted data get converted into Attribute Relation File Format (ARFF). The sixth stage is training phase where model which is used for classification is trained using J-48 classification. The next stage is testing phase and the model is used to classify the E-mails to fake E-mail and real E-mails.

1. The very first step in E-mail classification is to select the suitable E-mail data-set which is a real sample of existing E-mails that includes both phishing and legitimate E-mails.

2. After E-mail data set is selected, splitting each and every E-mail and then converting them into Electronic Mail Format (EML). EML files are normally store each and every message as a single file and attachments may either be in the form of Multipurpose Internet Mail Extensions (MIME) content in the message or can be written off as a separate file.

3. Then data pre-processing is applied on to the above files to remove stop words and unwanted information. Then data reduction technique is applied to reduce the data size that needs to be examined. At the last step in the pre-processing phase lemmatization and stemming technique applied on token of words to convert them into their root forms.

4. After the data pre-processing step is over, then feature selection process starts with the cleaned data to extract different features form the E-mail data set. The features such as to, from, URL, carbon copy (Cc), blind carbon copy (Bcc) and the body of the E-Mails are extracted from the input data set. The process of feature extraction goes on unless the complete data is scanned properly and all the features are extracted. The most important features are E-mail header, Body, Java script and URL as given below.

    - E-mail Header: The header information is extracted from E-mail's data set. The header features are to, from, bcc, and cc fields. Some of the most popular phishing E-mail header includes keywords such as bank, debit, credit, Fwd:, Re:.

    - Body of E-mail: The body part of the E-mail is selected from the E-mails which contains the message part of the E-mail. Mostly phishing E-mail body include keyword such as dear, credit, click, log, identify, information, suspension and verify your account.

    - Java-script: It mainly contains a Java-script code in the email body. A phishing E- mail most of the time contain an On Click event, pop-up window code, or a code that links to an external website.

- URL: The uniform resource locator (URL) contains suspicious URLs. The phishing E-mail mostly contain "@" sign in the URL, port numbers in the URL, presence of an IP address in the URL.

- Network-based: The network-based feature mostly contains packet size and TCP/IP headers.

5. In order to apply classification algorithm to detect phishing E-mail the data needs to be converted into Attribute Relation File Format (ARFF). This chapter has suggested using J48 classifier for the E-mail dataset classification. Decision tree J48 algorithm is the extension of most popular ID3 (Iterative Dichotomise 3). This algorithm is most suitable for E-mail dataset classification where it can handle errors and missing values to some extent.

6. The model is trained in the training phase using the training data set and model is evaluated for its suitability.

7. After the model is thoroughly trained and evaluated properly, it is used to classify the test data set.

8. Finally the E-mail data set are classified into genuine, phishing E-mail and accuracy of the classifier is calculated from the confusion matrix.

### 3.2 Implementation and discussion on results

Enron data set is used to test the model being proposed by the chapter that includes both genuine E-mails and phishing E-mails. Initially the Data Pre-processing is performed on the data set to remove stop words, superfluous words and also the size of the data is reduced to get better result as shown below in **Figure 2**.

As stated above in **Figure 3**, the chapter is being implemented using J48 classifier for classification genuine E-mails and phishing E-mails with 98% accuracy. In order to measure the efficiency and performance of the proposed algorithm

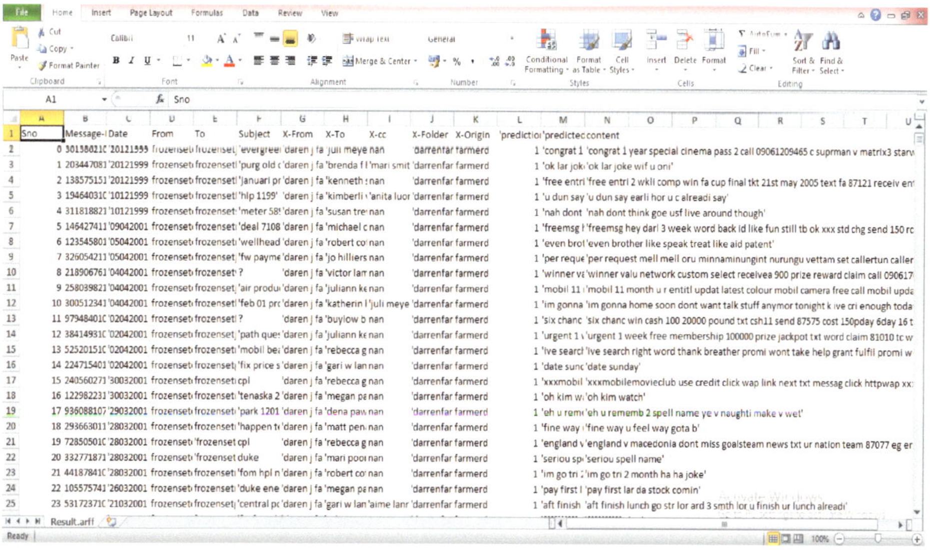

**Figure 2.**
*This shows feature selection process after data preprocessing.*

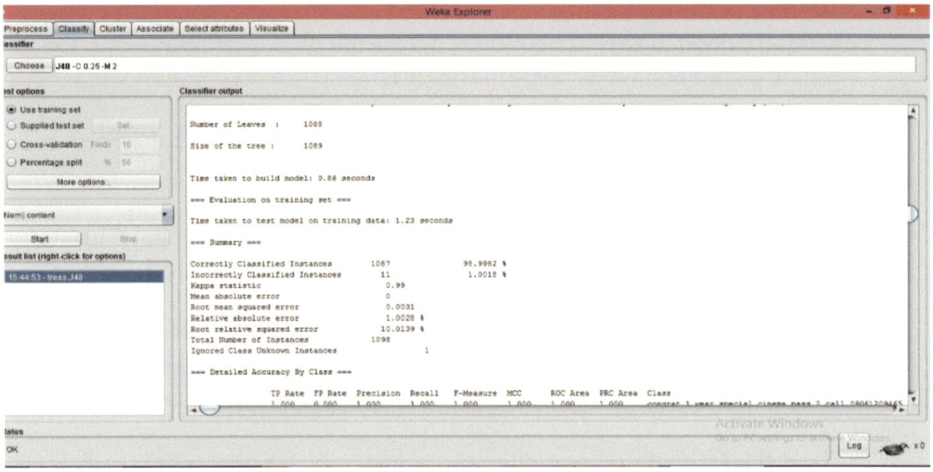


**Figure 3.**
*This figure show E-mails are classified using weka tool.*

in detecting phishing E-mails, False Positive (FP), True Positive (TP), True Negative (TN) and False Negative (FN) are computed and considered in the result. Then accuracy, Precision, Recall and F-1 score are computed using the formula given below.

1. **ACCURACY:** Accuracy is used to find the correct values; it is the sum of all true values divided by total values

(True Positive + True Negative)/(True Positive +True Negative +False Positive +False Negative)

$$\text{ACCURACY} = \frac{(TP + TN)}{(TP + TN + FP + FN)}$$

2. **PRECISION:** How often a model predicts a positive value is correct? It is all the true positives divided by the total number of predicted positive values.

(True Positive/True Positive + False Positive)

$$\text{PRECISION} = \frac{(TP)}{(TP + FP)}$$

3. **RECALL:** It used to calculate the models ability to predict positive values. How often does the model actually predict the correct positive values? It is true positives divided by the total number of actual positive values.

(True Positive/True Positive + False Negative)

$$\text{RECALL} = \frac{(TP)}{(TP + FN)}$$

4. **F-1 SCORE:** F1 measure is used when we need to take both Precision and recall.

$$F1 = \frac{2 \times PRECISION \times RECALL}{(PRECISION + RECALL)}$$

## 4. Conclusion

At this modern era as more and more people use internet for their day to day activities so as hackers on the network to steal their vital data through various security attacks. The objective of this chapter to presents a model using machine learning technique to detect phishing attacks and to prevent users from phishing. This chapter provides a very powerful architectural model in order to identify phishing E-mails. This chapter ends with a conclusion that phishing attacks is very dangerous to everyone in the society including organizations, person and hence must be detected accurately. Many researchers have contributed by giving their ideas to classify phishing E-mails from genuine E-mails but without much success. This chapter used J48 classification algorithm to classify between fake E-mails and genuine E-mails and it was observed that the model able to classify 98% accurately which is a far better result. Hence the model proposed in this chapter is very accurate and efficiently classify and could able to identify phishing E-mails. This chapter would provide a great help for ordinary man in protecting their important information by detecting phishing attacks.

## Conflict of interest

I the author of "An Emerging Solution for Detection of Phishing Attacks" states that this research works fully compile with ethical standards as per the Journal.

I have no direct or potential influence or impart bias on this research work.

I have no conflict conflicts of interests that are directly or indirectly related to this research work.

I have no funding from any funding agency or financial support from any organization.

## Acronyms and abbreviations

| | |
|---|---|
| E-mail | Electronic mail |
| URL | uniform resource locator |
| EML | Electronic Mail Format |
| SMS | short message service |
| VoIP | Voice over Internet Protocol |
| WEKA | Waikato Environment for Knowledge Analysis |
| IP | Internet Protocol |
| SSL | secure sockets layer |
| BEC | Business Email Compromise |
| UPS | United Parcel Service |
| Cc | Carbon copy |
| Bcc | blind carbon copy |
| ARFF | Attribute Relation File Format |
| MIME | Multipurpose Internet Mail Extensions |

## Author details

Prasanta Kumar Sahoo
Department of Computer Science and Engineering, Sreenidhi Institute of Science and Technology, Hyderabad, Telangana, India

*Address all correspondence to: prasantakumars@sreenidhi.edu.in

## References

[1] P. Liu and T. S. Moh, "Content Based Spam E-mail Filtering," 2016 International Conference on Collaboration Technologies and Systems (CTS), Orlando, FL, pp. 218-224.

[2] N. Agrawal and S. Singh, "Origin (dynamic blacklisting) based spammer detection and spam mail filtering approach," 2016 Third International Conference on Digital Information Processing, Data Mining, and Wireless Communications (DIPDMWC), Moscow, pp. 99-104.

[3] M. Khonji, Y. Iraqi, and A. Jones, "Phishing detection: a literature survey," 2013 IEEE Communications Surveys & Tutorials, vol. 15, no. 4, pp. 2091-2121.

[4] R. Islam and J. Abawajy, "A multi-tier phishing detection and filtering approach," Journal of Network and Computer Applications, 2013 vol. 36, no. 1, pp. 324-335.

[5] A. K. Jain and B. B. Gupta, "Comparative analysis of features based machine learning approaches for phishing detection," in Proceedings of the 10th INDIA-COM, New Delhi, India, 2016.

[6] Kaspersky Lab, "Spam in January 2012 love, politics and sport," 2013, http://www.kaspersky.com/about/news/spam/2012/Spam_in_January_2012_Love_Politics_and_Sport.

[7] B. Parmar, "Protecting against spear-phishing," Computer Fraud & Security, 2012 vol. 2012, no. 1, pp. 8-11.

[8] W. Jingguo, T. Herath, C. Rui, A. Vishwanath, and H. R. Rao, "Phishing susceptibility: an investigation into the processing of a targeted spear phishing e-mail," 2012 IEEE Transactions on Professional Communication, vol. 55, no. 4, pp. 345-362.

[9] T. N. Jagatic, N. A. Johnson, M. Jakobsson, and F. Menczer, "Social phishing," Communications of the 2007 ACM, vol. 50, no. 10, pp. 94-100.

[10] C. H. Hsu, P. Wang, and S. Pu, "Identify fixed-path phishing attack by STC," in Proceedings of the 8th Annual Collaboration, Electronic Messaging, Anti-Abuse and Spam Conference (CEAS '11), ACM, Perth, Australia, September 2011, pp. 172-175.

[11] N. A. G. Arachchilage and M. Cole, "Designing a mobile game for home computer users to protect against phishing attacks," https://arxiv.org/abs/1602.03929

[12] Rosiello, A., Kirda, E., Ferrandif F., et al. "A layoutsimilarity-based approach for detecting phishing pages", In the Proceedings of third International Conference on Security and Privacy in Communication Networks (Secure-Comm), 2007 IEEE, pp. 454-463.

[13] Choon Lin Tan, Kang Leng Chiew, San Nah Sze, "Phishing Webpage Detection Using Weighted URL Tokens for Identity Keywords Retrieval", in the proceedings of 9th International Conference on Robotic, Vision, Signal Processing and Power Applications, Springer Singapore 2017, pp. 133-139.

[14] Zhijun Yan, Su Liu, Tianmei Wang, Baowen Sun, Hansi Jiang, Hangzhou Yang, "A Genetic Algorithm Based Model for Chinese Phishing E-commerce Websites Detection in HCI in Business", Government, and Organizations: eCommerce and Innovation, Springer International Publishing, 2016.

[15] Yuancheng Li, Rui Xiao, Jingang Feng, Liujun Zhao, "A semi-supervised learning approach for detection of phishing webpages," 2013 Optik-International Journal for Light and

Electron Optics, vol. 124, Issue 23, December 2013.

[16] Wenyin, L., Huang, G., Xiaoyue, L., Min, Z., and Deng, X. "Detection of phishing web pages based on visual similarity", In the Special interest tracks and posters of the 14th international conference on World Wide Web (WWW), 2005 ACM, pp. 1060-1061.

[17] Whalent,T., and Inkpen N, K. M, "Gathering evidence: use of visual security cues in web browsers", In the Proceedings of 2005 Graphics Inter- face (GI), Canadian Human-Computer Communications Society, pp. 137-144.

[18] Rsa sitekey solution for enterprise. http://www.RsaSecurity.com, 2007. Bank of america, sign up for the sitekey service. http://www.bankofamerica.com/privacy/passmark/.

[19] Dhamija, R.,and Tygar, J, "The battle against phishing: Dynamic security skins", In the Proceedings of the Symposium on Usable Privacy and Security (SOUPS), ACM 2005, pp. 77-88.

[20] Parno, B., Kuo, C., and Perrig A., "Phoolproof phishing prevention", In the Proceedings of the 10th international conference on Financial Cryptography and Data Security, Springer-Verlag 2006, pp. 1-19.

[21] Kirda, E., and Kruegel, C, "Protecting users against phishing attacks with antiphish", In the Proceedings of the 29th Annual International Computer Software and Applications Conference (COMPSAC), IEEE 2005, pp. 517-524.

[22] Wu, M., Miller, R., and Little, G, "Web wallet: preventing phishing attacks by revealing user intentions", In the Proceedings of the 2nd Symposium on Usable Privacy and Security (SOUPS), 2006 ACM, pp. 102-113.

[23] Yee, K., and Sitaker, K., "Passpet: convenient password management and phishing protection", In the Proceedings of the 2nd Symposium on Usable Privacy and Security (SOUPS), 2006 ACM, pp. 32-43.

[24] Yue, C., and Wang, G H. Bogusbite, "A transparent protection against phishing attacks", ACM Transactions on Internet Technology (TOIT) 2010 Vol.10 n.2, pp.1-31.

[25] Aburrous, M., Hossain, M. A., Dahal, K., & Thabtah, F. (2010). Predicting Phishing Websites Using Classification Mining Techniques with Experimental Case Studies. 2010 Seventh International Conference on information technology: New Generations. doi : 10.1109/itng.2010.117.

[26] M. A. Hossain Dept. of Computing University of Brad fordBradford, Predicting Phishing Websites Using Classification Mining Techniques with Experimental" UK, 2010.

[27] https://smallbiztrends.com/2017/08/phishing-examples-small-business.html.

Chapter 5

# A Model for Auditing Smart Intrusion Detection Systems (IDSs) and Log Analyzers in Cyber Physical Systems (CPSs)

*Joshua Ojo Nehinbe*

## Abstract

Suitable models that auditors can adopt to concurrently audit smart Intrusion Detection Systems (IDSs) and log analyzers in Cyber Physical Systems (CPSs) that are also founded on sound empirical claims are scarce. Recently, post-intrusion studies on the resilience of the above mechanisms and prevalence of intrusions in the above domains have shown that certain intrusions that can reduce the performance of smart IDSs can equally overwhelm log analyzers such that both mechanisms can gradually dwindle and suddenly stop working. Studies have also shown that several components of Cyber Physical Systems have unusual vulnerabilities. These key issues often increase cyber threats on data security and privacy of resources that many users can receive over Internet of a Thing (IoT). Dreadful intrusions on physical and computational components of Cyber Physical Systems can cause systemic reduction in global economy, quality of digital services and continue usage of smart toolkits that should support risk assessments and identification of strategies of intruders. Unfortunately, pragmatic studies on how to reduce the above problems are grossly inadequate. This chapter uses alerts from Snort and C++ programming language to practically explore the above issues and further proposes a feasible model for operators and researchers to lessen the above problems. Evaluation with real and synthetic datasets demonstrates that the capabilities and resilience of smart Intrusion Detection Systems (IDSs) to safeguard Cyber Physical Systems (CPSs) can be improved given a framework to facilitate audit of smart IDSs and log analyzers in Cyberspaces and knowledge of the variability in the lengths and components of alerts warned by Smart Intrusion Detection Systems (IDSs).

**Keywords:** intrusion, Intrusion Detection Systems (IDSs), Network Intrusion Detection System, smart IDSs, IDS audit, IS auditor, Cyber Physical Systems (CPS)

## 1. Introduction

Pragmatic studies have recently shown that Cyber Physical Systems (CPSs) must be adequately protected with security tools to reduce the rising cases of Cyber Physical attacks and the destructive impacts of these attacks on global economy, international security, digital services and means of livelihood of many ethnic and social groups across the globe [1–3]. Further studies have shown that components of Cyber Physical Systems (CPSs) possess individual vulnerabilities that can endanger continuous usage of Cyber Physical Systems (CPSs) [4, 5]. The nature of the problems with different kinds of threats and cyber attacks on Cyber Physical Systems (CPSs) can correlate to severe disasters and complex confusion that may involve different stakeholders. The motives of some intruders may be complex to understand if they simultaneously attack the seamless integration of physical components and the computational elements of Cyber Physical Systems (CPSs) [6]. The impacts of some successful cyber attacks in this domain may corrupt or damage Cyber Physical data [2, 7]. Some intrusions can leak sensitive information to wider audience via social media with the aims to extort and discredit victims and service providers of Cyber Physical Systems (CPSs) [2].

The complexity and reoccurrence of threats and cyber attacks on the entire components of Cyber Physical Systems (CPSs) have made many organizations to develop the habit of deploying several categories of Intrusion Detection Systems (IDSs) within the peripherals and gateways of their connections to the entire Cyber Physical systems (CPSs) so that these devices can collect and analyze activities that signify evidence of intrusions against their corporate networks in real-time [8, 9]. Subsequently, analysts can quickly review the reports and respond to the attacks before the attacks achieve the objectives of intruders that launch them [10]. These issues have inevitably generated several challenges and concerns regarding the effectiveness of IDSs and analyzers of logs of IDSs in monitoring complex architectural systems peculiar to the above domains over the years. **Figure 1** illustrates Network Intrusion Detection System (NIDS) that is located in front of a firewall.

In other words, **Figure 1** demonstrates one of the two approaches organizations can adopt to position Network Intrusion Detection System (NIDS) in relation to firewall within the peripherals and gateways that connect them to the entire Cyber Physical Systems (CPSs) [7, 8]. Nevertheless, numerous studies often attest that Intrusion Detection Systems (IDSs) must always be upgraded to strongly help operators control the new dimensions and rising waves of intrusions against cyber physical resources across the globe. One of the pragmatic methods to achieve this security objective is to make IDSs smarter by connecting them to the Global Systems of Mobile (GSM) communication so that the toolkits can always send alerts to remote operators such that operators can promptly respond to cyber attacks at all time [11]. Thus, smart IDSs are IDSs that are configured such that operators can

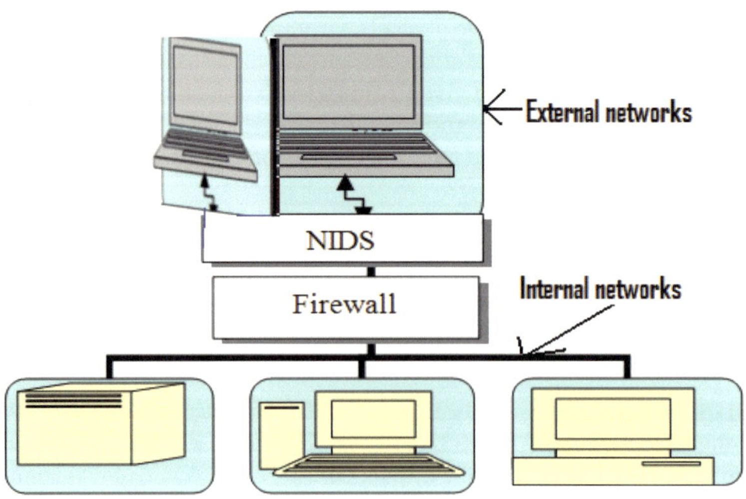


**Figure 1.**
*NIDSs in front of firewall.*

receive and respond to their alerts through Short Message Services (SMS) to the GSM or email addresses of the operators of IDSs in Cyber Physical Systems (CPSs). However, there are security and business requirements that underpin the framework upon which smart IDSs reside in private and corporate settings [2, 12]. The resilience and capacities of smart IDSs can be improved if operators can combine the information they gather from audit of log analyzers with the knowledge of the variability of lengths and components of alerts that smart Intrusion Detection Systems (IDSs) in the networks have generated. This can be used to ultimately design and improve the security policy on smart IDSs in the corporate elements of Cyber Physical Systems (CPSs) [3, 7, 13]. However, empirical studies on smart IDSs that specifically focus on audit of smart IDSs and log analyzers are inadequate over the years.

Basically, empirical studies on smart IDSs in the context of Cyber Physical Systems (CPSs) involve pragmatic examinations of specific experiments conducted with smart IDSs to concurrently correct security concerns and audit issues. These procedures can assist operators to improve the detection of intrusions against Cyber Physical Systems (CPSs) and cloud resources at large. The argument underpinning this chapter is that logs of smart IDSs should be concurrently audited during IDS audit. Otherwise, they may not be very useful for post-intrusion reviews. Similarly, lack of audit of logs of smart IDSs may render them ineffective for in-house training of newly recruited auditors and researchers exploring issues on identification, analysis, corroboration and mitigations of threats and security lapses in Cyber Physical Systems (CPSs) [5, 8].

Furthermore, smart IDSs are well-known for generating large quantities of alerts whenever they are configured to detect possible intrusions against Cyber Physical Systems (CPSs) [9, 11, 14]. It is inefficient to manually analyze massive alerts without incurring huge overheads and tradeoffs. Hence, data mining is often recommended as an underlying concept to automate tools that can reduce workload due to alerts from smart IDSs [14]. Another central issue here is that some companies use the reports obtained from the logs of smart IDSs to augment their networks security policies [8, 15, 16]. The necessity to audit smart IDSs alongside with log analyzers is not mandatory in the existing models for auditing Information Technology (IT). This generic audit framework seems to subsume IDS audit into security policy on computers and telecommunications [15, 17]. This weakness may eventually lead to lack of segregation of duties among internal auditors, IDS researchers and IDS operators. The human elements of the Cyber Physical Systems (CPSs) may place emphasize on Firewall and other forms of the Intrusion Prevention Systems (IPSs) over smart IDSs in the context of the organizational settings in the above settings. Moreover, it is plausible that some logs of regular IDSs that were archived might be relatively uninteresting details. One of the three central issues here is that the IDSs may be configured to send raw alerts to the mobile devices of the operators to analyze. This means that certain log analyzers that can analyze short messages must be installed in the Mobile phones of the operators of smart IDSs. Alternatively, remote log analyzers can send short text messages that indicate processed alerts of smart IDSs to the operators. Whichever the case, it is imperative to also audit programs that analyze logs of smart IDSs in Cyber Physical Systems (CPSs) to regularly establish the degree of information inherent in the archived logs at each time and to ascertain the patterns of packets intended to overload smart IDSs at certain period of time in the above settings [8].

Findings suggest that suitable realistic datasets that can be used to concurrently audit smart IDSs and logs analyzers are grossly inadequate for researchers due to security issues [17, 18]. Accordingly, the above domain of IDS audit in the security of networks and other components of Cyber Physical Systems (CPSs) continues to suffer a major setback over the years. Therefore, by using alerts from Snort and C++ programming language, this chapter presents a comprehensive review of the above research issues and further proposes a feasible model that professionals can adopt to lessen the problems. One of the significant contributions of this chapter is its ability to practically provide clear review and guidelines that experts and trainees can adopt to ensure perimeter defense of mobile and computer networks. The chapter uses four datasets to practically illustrate a new framework for concurrent auditing of smart IDSs and log analyzers within corporations in the entire Cyber Physical Systems (CPSs). Also, the chapter broadly justifies the importance of conducting audit of log analyzers in smart phones together with IDSs audit. The remainders of this chapter are organized in the following order. Section 2 will present background research work that relates to IDS auditing. Section 3 explains the scope of IDS audit in Cyber Physical Systems (CPSs). Section 4 discusses challenges confronting IDS auditors in auditing Cyber Physical Systems (CPSs). Section 5 provides the proposed methodology for auditing smart IDSs and log analyzers while section 6 concludes the chapter.

## 2. Background information on audit of smart IDSs and log analyzers in Cyber Physical Systems (CPSs)

Studies have shown that Cyber Physical Systems (CPSs) are mergers of collaborative networks of automatic systems that are strongly built on sound theoretical and scientific principles and seamless integration of many disciplines [1, 6, 12]. Some of the disciplines that contribute to progressive growth and modernize Cyber Physical Systems (CPSs) over the years include informatics, computer and, mobile systems, Wireless Sensor Networks (WSNs), cyberspace, system designs, software, process, robotic, automobile and mechanical engineering [1, 6, 12, 19]. The underlying benefit of incorporating integrated components to drive Cyber Physical Systems (CPSs) is easy connectivity of many devices and systems to Cyber Physical systems (CPSs) across the globe. This capability has resulted into wider applications of Cyber Physical Resources (CPRs) in the areas of medical services, agriculture, electric installations, space engineering and other notable facets of human life [6, 19].

Critical issues begin to surface with the inexhaustible growth currently recorded in this domain in recent years especially on the numbers of service users, service providers and revenue accrued from sales of products and services that relate to Cyber Physical Systems (CPSs) [4]. Empirically, experts have argued that security, computational efficiencies and degree of helpfulness of complex architectural framework that underlying seamless integrations of physical and computation components of Cyber Physical Systems (CPSs) are serious doubts whenever these components are evaluated on the basis of performance, quality of service, users' satisfactions and robustness to counter threats and challenges [5, 20, 21]. Yet, emphasis over the years has focused on the computational capabilities of Cyber Physical Systems (CPSs) but less attention has been paid to the link between the computational and physical elements of this domain [20]. These flaws have raised series of technical and research issues on how to forecast traffic flow, optimize Mobile Cyber-Physical applications and how to achieve high performances of social services and healthcare facilities like wearable devices that run on Internet of a Thing (IoT) [1]. The correlations between social settings and industrial applications of cloud-based services that interact with Cyber Physical Systems' designs; innovation and manufacturing of digital resources continue to generate new paradigms in manufacturing and design's settings [6, 22]. These necessitate the importance of measures to bridge the gap between the Cyber physical resources and social setting. Collaborative design of embedded systems and various algorithms that experts have designed to carry out co-modeling and co-simulation of novel innovations begin to emerge. However, majority of these algorithms often exhibit invisible flaws [19].

The above issues coupled with the alarming increase of intrusions against Cyber Physical Systems (CPSs) have resulted in the needs for organizations to adopt Intrusion Detection Systems (IDSs) [8, 10, 20]. These toolkits can then provide automated ways to monitor, analyze all incoming and outgoing network packets in their corporate networks, trigger and log alerts on suspicious packets they observe for security and decision purposes. Nevertheless, most of these mechanisms can only detect suspicious packets [9]. They have been criticized for lacking capabilities to make dependable decisions on suspicious activities of users that may signify security breach to Cyber Physical Systems (CPSs) [23]. Operators must carefully review alerts they generate to isolate false positives from realistic attacks. Alerts can be daunting and overwhelmingly difficult to manually analyze by operators. Series of log analyzers have been proposed over the years to compensate for these weaknesses [8, 9]. Studies have shown that significant numbers of log analyzers have limited capabilities required to categorize cyber attacks on the basis of all attributes of alerts [9]. A few numbers of researches has suggested that, the above devices should be upgraded so that they can intimate operators with alerts on real-time basis [11, 20]. The rationale is that operators should be able to remotely analyze intrusion logs and counter attacks on Cyber Physical Systems without the need to physically report to their offices.

These developments have led to the need to audit smart Intrusion Detection Systems (IDSs) to improve their efficacies. Audit of smart Intrusion Detection Systems (IDSs) or IDS audit involves comprehensive and thorough examination of the networking infrastructure and security controls upon which the management and operations of all smart Intrusion Detection Systems (IDSs) in an organization are established [18, 24, 25]. Ordinarily, one of the duties of IDS auditors is to thoroughly scrutinize IDSs, establish and report the efficacies of internal controls that the organization has implemented to safeguard each detector and resources related to these toolkits [26]. The evaluation and the reports of this kind of audit can go a long way to determine the level of compliance and operations of all intrusion detectors in the company with best global practices. Nonetheless, there are numerous challenges with research on audit of smart IDSs in corporate setting in the past years [18]. Studies advise that skilled intruders are common threats that are extremely disturbing corporate and private users of computer systems in Cyber Physical systems (CPSs) [2, 7, 10]. Unfortunately, researchers habitually ignore the audit of smart IDSs that should have established exploitable pathways, audit issues and novel paradigms on network security and perimeter defense since the inception of IDS technology. This neglect has countless impacts on digital resources that connect to cyber physical resources. This shortcoming is explicitly dangerous because it is generating warning signals service providers concerning data reliability and quality of service on local computing resources in many organizations. The impacts of some of these security concerns may appear negligible while significant numbers of them are grievous and hazardous to corporate existence considering the capabilities of demoralizing intrusions recently reported in some public media. Recently, the neglect of this aspect of IDS audit and lack of correlation of IDS audit with research findings have begun to subject sequence of findings from logs analyzers, integrity and compliance with professional standards and regulatory authorities to series of contentions [6, 21, 27].

Importantly, sudden changes in the classifications and dimensions of intrusions that often aim to attack computer and mobile services operating within the purview of Cyber Physical Systems (CPSs) are global concerns [7, 16]. Intruders have acquired more skills such that they can launch packets that have short and long datagram to achieve different motives in cyberspace. Studies of many trace files suggest instances whereby intruders have split some inbound and outbound packets into fragments. Some studies believe that attackers on Cyber Physical systems (CPSs) can suddenly varied the intensities of packets to smartly elude detections. Numerous audit and networking issues may begin to build up whenever new IDSs are installed in the perimeters of digital networks to complement existing IDSs that auditors have been previously audited. There are possibility that audit exercises may exclude auxiliary issues like log analysis on fragmented packets.

The location of IDSs relative to the firewall in an organization depends on their security policy. A growing numbers of opinions affirm that organizations can install Network Intrusion Detection System (NIDS) in the front or back of a firewall for different intentions [7, 16]. However, models that auditors can adopt to establish suitable approach to organizations are very scarce. Furthermore, current model of ICT audit restrict IDS auditors to the physical security, hardware and software components of smart IDSs [3, 24]. Auditors must use simulated attacks to investigate the initialization, configuration, interface, processing and performances of smart IDSs and to ascertain the tendency of the toolkits to dwindle after a prolonged usage. They must also evaluate the available disk spaces for both the toolkits and mobile devices that receive alerts from IDSs and log analyzers. They must assess the contingency plans in the organization to establish business continuity and preparedness of the toolkits to resume surveillance after intruders have attacked them or after downtime. Auditors must equally evaluate the internal and change controls designed to safeguard the smart IDSs from computer viruses and intruders. In addition, they will investigate the signatures, alert's mechanism, policies and possible rules that have been updated, their corresponding approvals and authorizers of the approvals to modify them [24, 25]. Nonetheless, the above procedures are flawed in the sense that both the experienced and inexperienced intruders may obfuscate and evade smart IDSs audited with the above model. Thus, intrusions on cyber components such as sensing, cyber communication mechanisms and physical resources like computer hardware, data center, employees and mobile devices that the detectors should have discerned and operators would have timely countered often achieve intruders' missions at long run.

One of the fundamental ways this chapter premises for operators and resident auditors to lessen the above problems is for both of them to periodically corroborate research with audit reports on smart IDSs in the perimeters of the organization. However, IDS audit is quite challenging nowadays because it is clearly different from the conventional IS audit process [18, 25]. Besides, IDSs audit requires the engagement of qualified IS auditors that also possess wide experience and knowledge in the above roles. Suitable IS auditors must also have practical experience on the installations of smart IDSs, logs' analyzers, reporting and countermeasures. Moreover, there are acute shortages of operators that also possess auditing skills. Besides, standard IDS audit templates and models that can serve as guiding principles to IDS auditors and operators in corporate environment in the context of Cyber Physical Systems (CPSs) are scarce [18, 24, 25]. Consequently, most IDS operators ignore the research aspect of their jobs that should be regarded as interim audit and concentrate on IDS operations.

Furthermore, approaches that most auditors frequently adopt to conduct IDS audit with generic Information System (IS) and audit process often exclude evaluation of the significance of log analyzers in the organization [27]. The dangers of the above methods are enormous especially if both reviews are inconclusive, unreliable and unsupported by empirical claims before major infringement occurs in the digital networks of the organization. Organizations can experience infringements in critical and less critical areas of their business operations. Intruders may attack resources or areas of corporate systems that attract little or no attention of IT managers, inspection and internal control's managers with the aims to have enough time to achieve their objectives and to equally evade detection. Consequently, feelers premise that smart IDSs should be strategically installed in the segments that will make it difficult for intruders to bypass them. Smart IDSs that are located at the hearts of huge inbound or outbound traffic should be thoroughly verified by IS auditors from time to time. Traffic that migrates across spanning mode can overwhelm smart IDSs that are technically weak to compromise.

Generally, research findings and related work in the domains of IDS audit and log analyzers are novel issues in network security and Cyber Physical Systems (CPSs) [18, 24, 26]. Conventionally, experts have justified the significance of IDS policy in the perimeter defense of networks of corporate organizations [8, 13, 27]. An empirical study that examined risk-based systems and process audit method has been carried out as a strategy to bridge the gap between auditors and architectural designs of IT resources [18]. The model was able to detect the weaknesses of the process in terms of risk of material deficiencies and thirteen control patterns. However, the research was basically a generalized audit process that has a better performance whenever the model is adopted to audit financial data. Moreover, a study on how to debug Network Intrusion Detection Systems (NIDSs) has been explored [16]. The proposed model uses detection rules to debug NIDSs and eradicate defective rules that are well-known for triggering repetitive alerts. The model can assist IDS operators to reduce workload. However, the major flaw of this model is that it has the tendency to be operationally proprietary. The model will require routinely extension and upgrade before it can broadly relevant to other categories of smart IDSs in the market.

## 3. The scope of audit of smart IDSs and log analyzers in Cyber Physical Systems (CPSs)

A systematic review of IDS audit is a methodical review or examination of the operational conditions of IDSs with the aims to ensure their protection and to guarantee efficient, effective and reliable IDS operations within the perimeters of computers; cyber physical and sensing resources and mobile networks in an organization [13, 25, 28]. The scope of Cyber Physical Systems (CPSs) varies from organization to organization. Algorithms are the underpinning mechanisms that control and regulate collaborative networks of theories, concepts and embedded disciplines that constitute Cyber Physical Systems (CPSs) in each organization [19]. Audit review should reflect components of computer and mobile systems to be audited. It should state cloud resources such as networks of computers, mobile systems, Wireless Sensor Networks (WSNs), front-end and back-end of the networks, software, hardware, human element, work flow and process engineering [6]. Audit of smart IDS can be performed in conjunction with or separated from the conventional audit exercises in an organization. The audit time table, management, misgivings and repeated outbreak of intrusions can influence the necessity to conduct IDS audit and its scope of coverage. For Cyber Physical Systems (CPSs), the scope of the audit should include the security of sensing processing, storage of large alerts, performance of hardware and software and reliability of the systems. It should also extend to validation of algorithms, automatic systems, theoretical and scientific principles and seamless integration of disciplines underlying the systems with best practices. Hence, this type of IDS audit is eventful [14, 18]. Examiners must carefully review and match the security policy of the organization with the implementations of smart IDS in the live and test environments to establish areas of compliance and noncompliance with best practice. Fundamentally, enterprise must have IDS policy. An IDS policy is a standard document stating a plan of actions an organization adopts regarding the administration and management of IDSs within their digital networks [8]. Besides, IDS policy should state IDS procedures, IDS rules and conditions that should be meant before rules can be activated, updated or deactivated [13]. The main challenge that IDS auditors often face is that most organizations do not have IDS policy [24]. Findings suggest that some companies do not isolate IDS policy from their security policies [8]. Hence, rather than separating both policies, some of them embedded a few sentences about IDSs in their security policies. Consequently, IDS audit and its ancillaries often lack exhaustive reviews over the years. Therefore, IDS auditor that wishes to conduct the above IDS audit must have well-established knowledge of IDS policy and major components of the smart IDSs within the networks.

In Snort for instance, the objectives of the audit must include critical review of IDS policy, physical security relating to the IDS (Snort in this case), the hardware component and software components of the toolkit. The audit must also include packet decoder, preprocessors, detection engine, logging and alerting system and output modules [8, 13]. Serious audit issues may arise whenever auditors lack strong knowledge of the above components and how they cooperatively work together to detect intrusions and to generate output in the required format.

## 4. Auditors' challenges in auditing smart IDSs in Cyber Physical Systems (CPSs)

Cyber Physical Systems (CPSs) lack the robustness to counter threats, challenges and cyber attacks due to weaknesses genetic to individual components that form these domains. Hence, there are critical challenges that face auditors and researchers of smart IDSs regarding IDS auditing and log analyzers in these domains. This section discusses and categorizes some of these issues into two groups; namely, the challenges with smart IDSs and challenges with log analyzers.

### 4.1 Research and audit issues on smart IDSs in Cyber Physical Systems

Different types of smart IDSs keep different categories of logs and alerts in different formats. The default settings of parameters that coordinate alerts of smart IDSs can enable the toolkits to trigger and log wordy and more explicit warnings than the setup that customize these parameters [25, 28]. **Figure 2** illustrates one

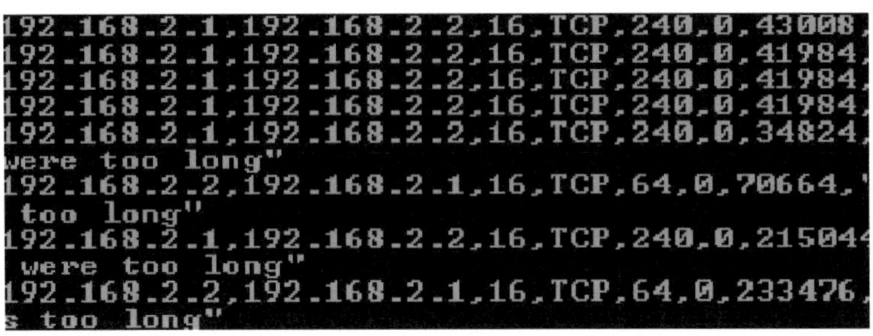


**Figure 2.**
*A sample of alerts from Defcon11 in comma delimited format.*

of the kinds of alerts that Snort can generate. The alerts are in comma delimited format because each attribute of an alert is separated by a comma. Operators of smart IDSs can implement the formats of alerts they want during implementation and before executing IDSs like Snort. The major issue is that the preferred formats of alerts cannot be reversed while the toolkits are working. This can create series of setbacks if operators if the formats they have implemented do not convey sufficient information operators will need to decide on the security matters of Cyber Physical Systems in the organization. **Figure 2** illustrates alerts that are expressed in comma delimited formats.

The alerts contain IP addresses to uniquely identify computers and their domain names on the Internet. The alerts are samples of comma delimited alerts extracted from Defcon-11 traces. Some of the attributes of the alerts were Transmission Control Protocol (TCP). However, further information is still required to ascertain attributes like the names, of the attacks to understand data transmission and exchange that occurred between sources and destinations of various attacks. **Figure 3** illustrates conventional kinds of alerts that the Snort would log whenever its default parameters on logs and alerts are implemented in Cyber Physical Systems (CPSs). This format is simple because each alert is explicit to human interpreters. For example, the signature generator (Sig_generator) of the first attack in **Figure 3**, the identification number (Sig_id) of the rule that triggered the alert and the number of times the rule has been reviewed or updated (Sig_rev) were 125, 1 and 1 respectively [25, 28]. The alerts are samples of default alerts extracted from Defcon-10 traces. The attack signified telnet's exploits. In other words, the Intrusion Detection System (Snort) detected telnet commands on the FTP command prompt or channel. The attack also indicated that someone used a computer with IP address 192.168.2.2 and port 21 to transfer file to a computer with IP address of 192.168.2.1 and port 1067 at 10:14 PM on 3$^{rd}$ of August. The problem with alerts that are formatted by comma delimiters is that auditors would require their documentations to properly understand them because they are not constantly explicit. **Figure 3** illustrates a sample of alerts of Snort in a default format.

It is imperative for the auditor to establish the directory where the alerts and systems files of the IDS are kept or recorded in the hardware before the beginning of the audit. By default, shows will Snort log alerts to */vary/log/snort/alerts*. However, the auditor begins to face further challenges if the directory is changed during implementation contrary to the conventional or documented standard. Additional challenges can occur due to the noncompliance of the organization to both the

```
[**] [125:1:1] (ftp_telnet) TELNET CMD on FTP Command Channel [**]
[Priority: 3]
08/03-22:14:26.756815 192.168.2.2:21 -> 192.168.2.1:1067
TCP TTL:64 TOS:0x10 ID:6518 IpLen:20 DgmLen:83 DF
***AP*** Seq: 0x17BA8D92  Ack: 0xFBCEEF87  Win: 0x7D78  TcpLen: 32
TCP Options (3) => NOP NOP TS: 116909 288736
[**] [125:1:1] (ftp_telnet) TELNET CMD on FTP Command Channel [**]
[Priority: 3]
08/03-22:14:26.757820 192.168.2.1:1067 -> 192.168.2.2:21
TCP TTL:240 TOS:0x10 ID:0 IpLen:20 DgmLen:66
***AP*** Seq: 0xFBCEEF87  Ack: 0x17BA8DB1  Win: 0x7D78  TcpLen: 20
[**] [125:1:1] (ftp_telnet) TELNET CMD on FTP Command Channel [**]
[Priority: 3]
08/03-22:14:26.762762 192.168.2.2:21 -> 192.168.2.1:1067
TCP TTL:64 TOS:0x10 ID:6519 IpLen:20 DgmLen:75 DF
***AP*** Seq: 0x17BA8DB1  Ack: 0xFBCEEFA1  Win: 0x7D78  TcpLen: 32
TCP Options (3) => NOP NOP TS: 116910 288736
[**] [125:1:1] (ftp_telnet) TELNET CMD on FTP Command Channel [**]
[
```

**Figure 3.**
*A sample of alerts of Snort in a default format.*

recommended disk space and accepted format for alerts in the IDS policy [8, 10]. The implication is that it will be difficult to compare the sufficiency of the information conveyed in the IDS logs and short text messages that are extracted from different segments of the perimeters of the same organization if they have heterogeneous formats. In essence, the above sample of the raw alerts explains the link between research on smart IDSs and IDS audit.

### 4.2 Issues with detection rules or policies of smart IDSs in Cyber Physical Systems

Practical experience shows that the formats of detection rules vary from Intrusion Detection System to another. The rules within the detection engine of smart IDSs are many and they are mostly protected by copyright. The rules usually instruct smart IDSs to discriminate by logging and raising alerts on specific packets that migrate from specific networks into local subnets. Some rules are also designed to instruct smart IDSs to indiscriminately log and raise alerts on all suspicious packets that migrate from any network into local subnets [9]. These rules can also instruct the toolkit to always trigger an alert whenever the device observes any TCP packet that contains "USER root" in its header [8]. Rules can be localized, designed or configure such that they will report suspicious packets heading towards a computer in the subnets of Cyber Physical Systems [10]. Several audit issues arise regarding to best strategies to audit rules or policies of IDSs. These toolkits have several inbuilt rules or policies. There may be some discrepancies between the rules or policies that have been implemented in the organization and the security policy driving the implementation of rules or policies of the smart IDSs in the system. Discrepancies can also occur if some IDSs in the networks are not configured to operate as smart toolkits. Professionalism is required in adapting framework for auditing smart IDSs to audit IDSs that are not configured as smart toolkits in other to adequately safeguard the entire components of cyber physical resources in the organization. One of the reasons behind these challenges is that the security policy of the organization might not fully reflect the totality of the rules or policies in the detection engines of all smart IDSs in the networks. The IS auditor needs to evaluate if the IDS policy actually states specific rules or policies that should be activated or deactivated during implementations of smart IDSs. It is also necessary for auditors to establish the level of compliance of the organization with best security practice on the detection rules or policies approved by the management of the organization [8, 24].

New rules or policies can be added to the smart IDSs in other to improve their efficacies. However, some rules or policies may generate redundant alerts. Hence, it is often difficult to immediately establish the criticality of new and old rules or policies without a critical exploration of log analyzers that process alerts that correspond to these rules or policies. Also, session printable policies or rules are difficult to recommend for deactivation because they enable the detector to log everything attackers have typed [8, 10]. It is possible that all sections of the IDS policy will not fully capture the sensitivity of detection rules or policies in organizations. The chapter encourages auditors to thoroughly audit available IDS policy to ensure the policy is providing suitable standard that covers all components of Cyber Physical resources adopted in the organization.

### 4.3 Issues with maintenance of smart IDSs in Cyber Physical Systems

Smart IDSs must undergo regular maintenance so that they can adequately monitor very high traffic rates migrating into or outside the organization [15, 16, 23]. The maintenance of smart IDSs is the process of performing system tuning and routine checks on all smart Intrusion Detection Systems in the organization; the directory of each configuration file, logs, text messages; available storage size, available disk space, disk space each toolkit has already utilized and the last time each toolkit was debugged to establish their readiness to promptly report intrusions that aim to exploit features of Cyber Physical Systems that provide opportunities for intruders to cause havoc without corrupting Cyber Physical data or leaking sensitive information from Cyber Physical Networks. Furthermore, constant maintenance of smart IDSs will enable their operators to correct new and past errors that were not recognized during the installations, configurations and testing phases of these devices. Usually, corrective maintenance is desirable because it will enable the operators of smart IDSs to perfect and improve the operations and performance of smart IDSs [15].

Intruders can compromise the mobile phones and email accounts of operators of smart IDSs [11, 21]. Therefore, the above maintenance will equally help operators of smart IDSs to fine-tune the toolkits so that they can effectively work in new environments and whenever the operators replace their mobile devices or renounce old email accounts. However, maintenance of smart IDSs requires extra efforts than the efforts required to configure and analyze their logs. Hence, most operators of smart IDSs often shy away from carrying out IDS porting, corrective and adaptive maintenance of these toolkits. From experience, IS auditor can perceive series of audit issues whenever the IDS policy does not recognize the significance of maintenance of smart IDSs in the enterprise networks.

### 4.4 Issues with configurations of smart IDSs in Cyber Physical Systems

There are hardware and software requirements for each smart IDS to exhibit performance that will always conform to best security practices. For NIDSs like Snort, the toolkit works on operating System like Linux, Windows 2003 Server Enterprise Edition and Microsoft Windows XP and hardware like Compaq 1600 Pentium III with dual Processor Server and Pentium IV workstation.

Using Snort as an example [7, 10], this premises that components such as Apache, Pretty Home Page (PHP), WinPcap and Analysis Console for Intrusion Databases (ACID) must be audited to ascertain their levels of compliance to best industrial practice [28]. The combination of Snort, Apache, database and ACID enable the NIDS to log alerts into a database. Two or more toolkits can be configured to centrally log alerts to unified database. Conversely, each toolkit may be setup to log its alerts to a different database. The above components also enable analysts to visualize and analyze alerts on web interface [8, 10]. Hence, the database (back-end) that may be MySQL must also be audited. IS auditors must always refer to the IDS policy for guidance. It is a good practice to complement the audit process by referring to the security policy of the organization to gain insightful evidence on degree of compliance and conformity of both documents.

The dangers are enormous whenever intruders compromise the back-end of the toolkit. Intruders can crash the entire toolkit, alter its cryptographic keys and render it bad and unintelligent [21]. Subsequently, they can illegally reconfigure the smart IDS to log no alerts or to suppress useful alerts [21]. New waves of stealthy attacks can shutdown IDSs; enable triggers and disable or re-start the back-end databases of the detectors. In the case of Snort, attackers can suddenly shutdown the Apache upon which the smart IDS runs. Hence, auditors must establish the level of control that safeguards all the components of smart IDSs in the firm. Usually, in Snort, Apache's server uses configuration file that is stored in the */etc/apache2/apche2.conf* [8, 24]. Therefore, auditors must also establish the last date the configuration's file was updated. Nonetheless, the above ideas are plausible whenever the auditors possess the needed skills to critically explore them.

## 4.5 Issues with IDS policy and security policy in Cyber Physical Systems

IDS policy is a document that is approved by top management in an organization [8]. This document reflects and states how all IDSs in the organization are implemented and managed. The document further reveals types of IDSs and their versions, configurations, license fees and expiry date and vendors. The document defines activities that managements of the organization have agreed to be regarded as normal and intrusive activities in their Cyber Physical Systems. It is expected to reflect the approved connectivity between log analyzers and logs of smart IDSs. It might be uneconomical to send overwhelming alerts directly to the operators of smart IDSs. Additionally, some smart IDSs can encrypt the email reports or alerts they intend to send to the operators or recipients. However, operators or recipients must install suitable tool in their mobile phones or computers to decrypt them. Thus, IDS policy should categorically state how the email addresses and mobile phones of operators of smart IDSs will receive concise and helpful alerts.

The security policy of an organization is the totality of security mechanisms that is approved by top management of the organization. This broad document usually states how the security's architecture of the organization should be deployed, monitored and managed annually. IDS policy is a segment of security policy. Auditors may find it difficult to challenge operators of smart IDSs in an organization whereby IDS policy is subsumed in security policy. In addition, the appropriateness of time that the organization must review their IDS policy will be difficult to criticize in this circumstance.

Most often, some intruders prefer to launch attacks that can probe or scan cyber networks to compensate for their inabilities to have access to the above policy's frameworks [7, 9, 10]. Information System auditors need to assess the security of the above policies in the organization to establish how they are kept, the custodian of both documents, access and procedures for granting approvals to the employees that have the rights to use and rights to know these documents.

## 4.6 Research and audit issues with log analyzers in Cyber Physical Systems

The quality of information that various log analyzers can derive from different formats of alerts that smart IDSs generate depend on many factors. Some analyzers of logs that originate from smart IDSs can process specific attributes such as Transmission Control Protocol (TCP), Internet Control Message Protocol (ICMP), Type of Service (TOS) and Internet Protocol (IP) length. Intruders that compromise the TCP and IP of computer networks will distort network conversations or communications and the exchange of data through application programs [10]. The attacks will also affect apps that send packets of data from one computer to another. Similarly, the values held in the flags of parameters or attributes of alerts also differ from one attribute to another. For instance, log analyzer that analysis the parameters of ICMP in Cyber Physical Systems intend to discover actions of intruders that have requested for certain details about the systems [29]. The intention of the intruder may be to establish computers or mobile devices that signify echo reply and destination unreachable. The attack may also reveal weaknesses in the configurations of router within Cyber Physical Systems (CPSs). The attack can publicize details of routers, timestamp, timestamp reply; redirect message headers, domain name request, domain name reply, mobile registration request, mobile registration reply, errors in the conversion of datagram; address mask request and address mask reply. Intrusions on trace route can provide trodden paths for Distributed Denial of Service (DDoS) attacks in Cyber Physical Systems (CPSs) [29].

In addition, TOS is designed to categorize and prioritize networks' data so that digital devices will process critical data packets before they will process data packets that of less significant. However, intruders have many ways they can check the reliability of the networks. Attacks on TOS intend to undermine the quality of services rendered by the host and routers in the networks. This category of attacks can indiscriminately affect the migrations of different kinds of inbound and outbound data within the networks of Cyber Physical Systems (CPSs) [2, 7]. Intruders can insert fake data into the networks given the knowledge of TOS in the networks. The impacts of this attack can be severe if it occurs at the peak of operations whereby it coincidentally hinders the priority and migrations of data of higher importance than data of less importance in the networks. Moreover, attack on TOS can increase the numbers of fragmented packets that lost in transit. It can also cause significant delay of packets to complete computer and mobile communications, reassembling of fragmented packets and routing of multimedia data.

Each of the above attributes of alerts conveys different meanings to different organizations [9]. The mode that every log analyzer adopts to write their results into the output files (folders) is very important. Programs that append new records with old records would require enough disk space than programs that always clear all the content of old records in the output files during execution. For these reasons, IDS auditors often face many challenges from company to company in conducting thorough investigations on outputs of log analyzers and establish the significance of the output files in accordance to best practice.

### 4.7 Issues with theoretical frameworks for designing log analyzers in Cyber Physical Systems

There are several theoretical frameworks that programmers can adopt to design log analyzers to analyze logs of smart IDSs within Cyber Physical networks. Studies show that Statistical techniques, subjective logic, Visualization, Artificial Intelligence (AI), Neural Networks (NNs), Ensemble techniques and data mining have been used to design log analyzers in recent years [23]. Some analyzers may adopt priority of alerts, similarity of values held in the attributes of alerts, human observations, attack scenarios, hierarchical graphs, attacks that overlap, subjective reasoning and evidence of the damage the attack has caused as underpinning philosophies to design log analyzers [23]. Auditors must be thorough in this regards because features of non-related attacks may overlap and this will lead to mismatch of intrusions [26, 27]. The maximum error of log analyzer will increase if it mismatches intrusions. In other words, reports from log analyzer that mismatches intrusions are misleading and ineffective to design strong counter measures against intrusions in progress.

In addition, it is necessary for auditors to establish how each analyzer select minimum similarity and expectation of similarity in other to establish how the toolkits merge related alerts together. Also, different algorithms and metrics can compute weighted average of related alerts in different ways. Hence, it is challenging for auditors to be vast in different algorithms for comparing overall similarity of the alerts and how various algorithms isolate patterns of alerts that are false positives from real positives.

### 4.8 Issues with metrics for designing log analyzers in Cyber Physical Systems

Programmers can design log analyzers that adopt multiple metrics and different data mining concepts to analyze logs of smart IDSs [14]. It is easy to compare outputs of closely related metrics together. IDS auditors must conduct routine research to ascertain strengths and weaknesses of statistical metrics that programmers have used to support intrusion detections in corporate organization that is under review. There are different ways to interpret and improve the quality of alerts from smart IDSs. Hence, the interface between log analyzer and logs of smart IDSs must be reviewed. These will enable auditors to establish suitable metrics for cross-correlation of alerts rather than interpreting uncorrelated attacks with heuristic methods. The instant that the design will update email addresses and mobile phones of operators of smart IDSs with new alerts should immediately IDS detects every suspicious event. Security issues begin to build up whenever there are networks failures such as poor Internet connection and poor mobile signals.

Auditors must review operational logbooks to determine whether operators of smart IDSs keep track of cases of networks failures such as poor Internet connections, inability to access emails and poor mobile signals in the organization. These will give insightful evidence into the effectiveness of Internet and mobile service providers that are supporting the organization. The findings in this case may also guide the auditor in recommending to the organization to sustain or review the Service Level Agreements (SLAs) they agreed with their service providers. The new threats to cyber physical resources how to mitigate intrusions that can co-occur together without sharing the same impacts on the targets. Outputs of log analyzers may indicate graphical illustrations of alerts [8]. Some operators of smart IDSs may prefer to adopt visualizations to interpret alerts in the form of histogram, pie charts, bar charts and simple correlation graphs [8]. **Figures 4** and **5** demonstrate graphical illustrations of alerts from Snort whenever the valued held in the TCP and TOS are used to analyze alerts from the same dataset. For these reasons, IDS audit must be able to establish audit issues concerning attributes and metrics the organization are adopting to differentiate sequences or patterns of alerts that have tendencies to possess different interpretations from alerts that have regular patterns even if these alerts are analyzed with different attributes. Some interpretations of alerts may not impact directly on business operations that human element of Cyber Physical Systems (CPSs) transacts on daily basis. In addition, it is plausible that some intrusions are seasonal threats to Cyber Physical Systems (CPSs). **Figure 4** illustrates log analysis of alerts on the basis of the values held in TCP of intrusive alerts.

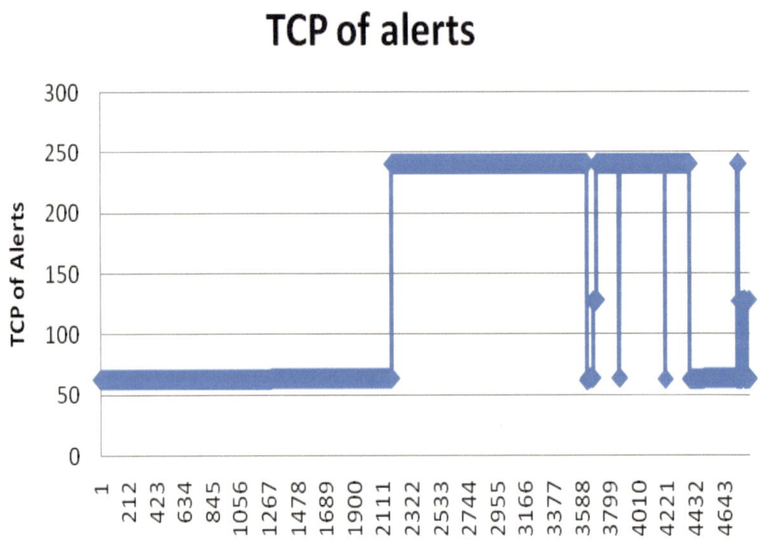


**Figure 4.**
*Log analysis of alerts by values held in TCP of alerts.*

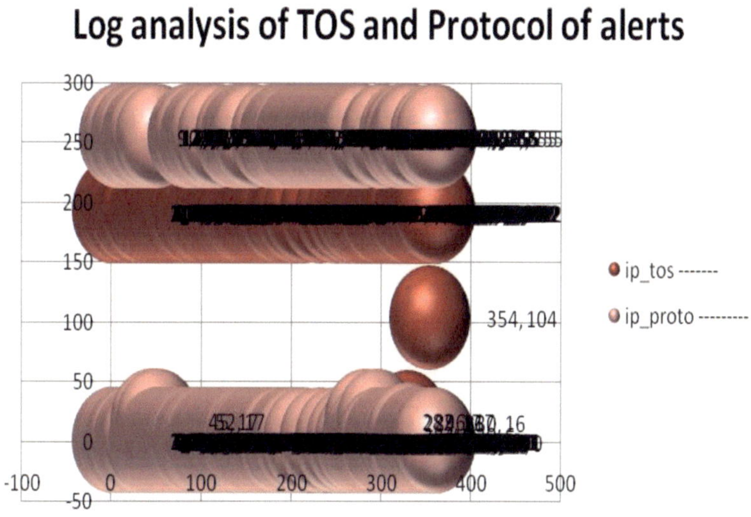


**Figure 5.**
*Log analysis of alerts by values held in TOS and Protocol of alerts.*

A seasonal rise in successful cases of cyber-attacks on corporate elements of Cyber Physical Systems (CPSs) can co-occur with a seasonal rise in unemployment and suspension of skilled workers. Therefore, IDS audit must establish the availability of inbuilt functionalities and capability of log analyzers in the organization to enable operators of smart IDSs to timely detect and mine frequent alerts from multiple sensors. Some IDS auditors can face challenges in recommending simple methods for graphical interpretations of IDS logs to organizations that do not include methods they prefer to illustrate intrusions against their Cyber Physical Systems in their IDS policy. **Figure 5** describes log analysis of alerts on the basis of the values held in the type of service (TOS) and Protocol of intrusive alerts.

## 5. Methodology for auditing smart IDSs and log analyzers in Cyber Physical Systems (CPSs)

Log analyzers are defined in this chapter as various programs that are designed to analyze logs of IDSs in a corporate setting [8]. Log analyzers have different objectives. The chapter proposes log analyzers that are interfaced with GSM to send short text messages after they have processed alerts of smart IDSs to operators. Log analyzers often have different objectives. For instance, log analyzers can be designed to debug NIDSs in the organization. There are log analyzers that determine the degree of predictability of attributes and information conveyed by attributes of alerts. Similarly, there are log analyzers that focus on correlation and aggregation of alerts. Sources of input data to each log analyzers in the same organization may also vary.

Some log analyzers may derive their input data from homogeneous logs of smart IDSs while significant numbers of them may receive input data from heterogeneous IDSs. By auditing them, operators and IDS auditors will be able to ascertain how the existing Log analyzers cluster alerts to arrive at the succinct texts they send to operators. For log analyzers that receive input data from several smart IDSs, it is necessary for the IS auditors to assess the locations of the contributing IDSs in relation to the log analyzers that aggregate or analyze their logs. Evaluators should ask questions like was the input modules of various log analyzers designed to override old alerts or append new alerts to previous ones and what programming language was used to design them? The time to upload new alerts to the input modules of the log analyzers should also be audited. **Figure 6** is a sample of execution of log analyzer of alerts that is implemented in this chapter.

The results from the above enquiry can determine log analyzers that should be recommended for upgrade and new development that should be incorporated to improve intrusion detection in the organization. **Figure 6** illustrates samples of execution of four categories of log analyzers that are designed to support the aruments raised in this chapter. These log analyzers are implemented with C++ language and they are based on the attributes of alerts from Snort IDS. The input to three of the analyzers were alerts that Snort triggered on the DATA01, DATA02 and DEFCON-10 dataset in IDS and offline modes. The input to forth analyzer was alerts that Snort triggered on DDoS datasets supplied by the DAPRA to assist research community. The IDS triggered 4,919 alerts and dropped 250 packets after analyzing the packet capture (PCAP) file of the dataset. Typical IDS research can explore many concepts with the above alerts.

The first log analyzer explores the rules that triggered the above alerts and a sample of its results is shown in **Table 3**. The second log analyzer explores the sources of the intrusions and all the addresses of computers they attacked and categorize them on the basis of date, time, sequence number, source IP address, source port number, destination IP address and port number of destination address. The third log analyzer explores the sources and destinations of the intrusions captured in the dataset. To ascertain the variability and quality of the alerts, the analyzer went further to compute Gini Index on the basis of sources and destnations of the attacks to further classify the alerts as shown in **Table 1**.

Given the probability of each cluster $[p(c_t)]$ and for each attribute (SIP or DIP), the Gini Index is expressed as [14]:

$$GIndex(SIP\,/\,DIP) = 1 - \sum_{t=1}^{n}(p(c_t))2 \qquad (1)$$

The fourth analyzer uses alerts from DATA01 and DATA02 to compute the lengths of alerts and the pattern within them.

## 5.1 A model for auditing smart IDSs and log analyzers in Cyber Physical Systems

The auditors of smart IDSs must have audit plan and feasible audit time table. The audit time table should categorically state the annual frequency proposes for conducting audit of smart IDSs and log analyzers in the organization [4, 24, 25, 27]. **Figure 7** describes a model for auditing Smart IDSs and Log analyzers in CPSs.

The audit plans can be an annual arrangement or a short-term plan that itemize the procedures the auditors will adopt to conduct IDS audit in the organization at the due dates. **Figure 7** illustrates the schematic diagram of a new framework for auditing smart Intrusion Detection Systems (IDSs) and log analyzers in this chapter. Accordingly, IDS auditors should preview the entire processes they will follow to carry out the audit of smart IDSs and log analyzers in advance. This is called the planning phase. This is the stage at which the auditors must delineate the objectives, scope, budget and resources they would require to comprehensively accomplish the audit [4, 5, 24]. The auditors will also need to establish the methods they will adopt to carryout fact-finding; the duration or time frame they will spend on each stage and the total time they will generally spend to conduct the review. The IDS audit team should categorically state the format of the IDS audit reports, potential challenges they envisage and the period they schedule to conduct exit meetings with the management of smart IDSs in Cyber Physical Systems (CPSs).

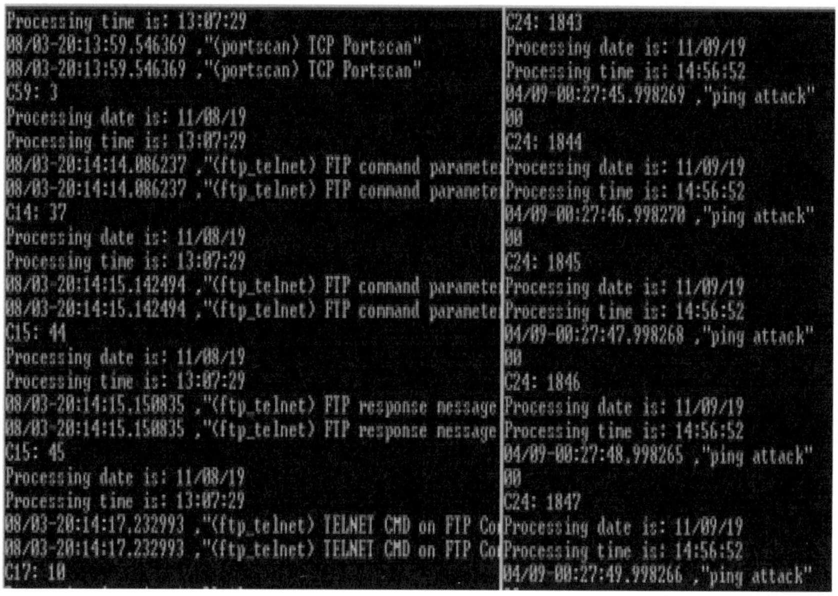


**Figure 6.**
*A sample of execution of log analyzer of alerts.*

| Dataset | Attribute | Number of cluster | Gini Index |
|---|---|---|---|
| DDOS-1-SIP | Source IP | 408 | 0.998 |
| DDOS-1-DIP | Destination IP | 1 | 0.000 |
| DDOS-2-SIP | Source IP | 265 | 0.996 |
| DDOS-2-DIP | Destination IP | 1 | 0.000 |

**Table 1.**
*Log analysis of online trace files.*

The second stage of this model is the preliminary examination of smart IDSs' controls and Log analyzers. In this stage, the IDS auditors ought to carry out initial assessment of the existing IDS resources, all related components of the IDS; operational procedures and the controls that were implemented in the enterprise to safeguard the smart IDSs and log analyzers. The auditors should interview or send questionnaires to main employees that are responsible for the management of different smart IDSs and all log analyzers in the organization [17, 18]. The review should cover all the IDSs in the organization together with infrastructure in the organization that relates to them, logical access and physical security of each smart IDS. The directory of each smart IDS, access to the root directory, procedure to log on to the root, permissions granted to read, write, execute and modify files and log analyzers; operating systems; hardware requirements including security, usage and available disk space; configuration files (signatures, profiles, etc) and respective logs kept by each smart IDS and log analyzer must be requested from the dedicated IDS operators. The review of the log analyzers and other programs that interface with the logs of the smart IDS should also be carried out at this stage using simulated attacks.

Furthermore, at the third stage of this model, the IDS auditors begin to critically examine Service Level Agreement (SLA) on the smart IDSs and verify the SLA for

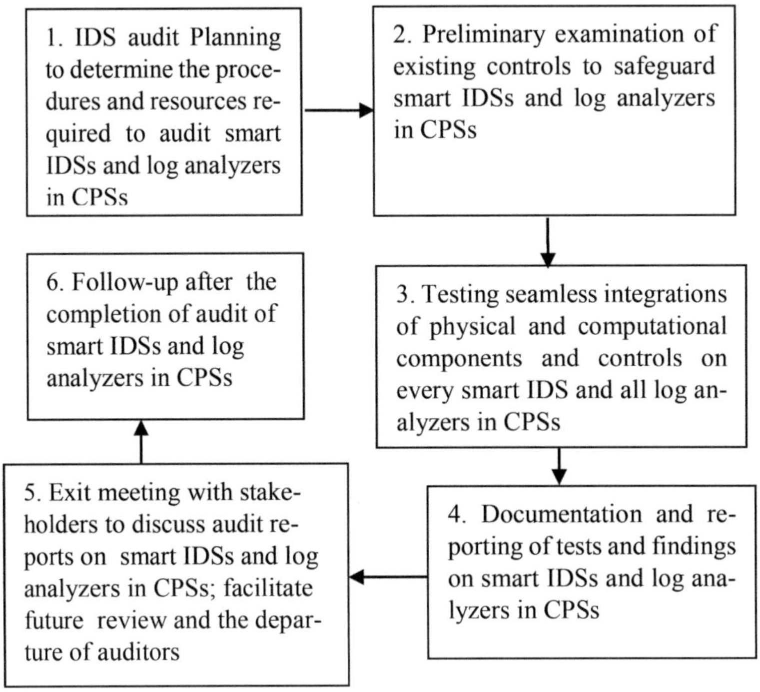


**Figure 7.**
*A model for auditing smart IDSs and log analyzers in CPSs.*

proprietary log analyzers [18]. They will scrutinize process flow, incident reporting procedures; relevant features of physical and organizational structures; training and users manuals in the organization that is using Cyber Physical System to support their business operations. They must test and validate the level of security and controls that have been implemented to counter likely threats and attacks on smart IDSs and related infrastructure in the networks [7, 13, 25]. Auditors must examine the seamless of the entire components of the engineered systems and quantify the level of protection smart IDSs in the organization can render to them. They must review controls and configurations of operating systems, security of smart IDSs and database access controls. The review at this stage should include various strategies the organization has implemented to hardening the host computer(s) and the networks so that auditors can establish the levels of compliance of operations of smart IDSs in the company with best practices [5, 21, 25].

In the fourth stage, proper documentation and reporting are critical elements that auditors must carryout to achieve comprehensive auditing of smart IDSs and log analyzers [4, 18, 25]. Hence, it is imperative for the IDS auditors to document key findings they observe at each stage of the audit. This chapter proposes that the IDS auditors should appoint dedicated scribers among the audit team to document tests and respective findings as the audit progresses. IDS audit reports should include executive summary, suitable headings, controls investigated during the audit and corresponding findings the team of auditors have observed in the organization [17, 24]. They must include remarks, recommendations and practical suggestions on how IDS operators and designers of existing log analyzer can fix audit issues they have identified in the review. Thus, this chapter proposes that documentation and reporting of findings should be incorporated into stage 4 of a comprehensive audit of smart IDSs and Log analyzers in Cyber Physical System.

Exit meeting is the fifth stage for a comprehensive audit of smart IDS and log analyzers in the context of Cyber Physical Systems. The auditors and audit team from the organization that is under review must gather together in interactive conferencing to discuss the audit reports before the audit team will exit the organization [17, 25]. The meetings are avenues for both teams to agree on the date and how various audit issues raised on the smart IDSs, log analyzers; computational and cyber physical infrastructure in the organization will be fixed. The meetings should state the date the representatives of audit team will revisit the unit of the organization to check that issues raised in the IDS audit reports have been fixed.

Finally, follow-up is the sixth and last stage of the above framework. The representatives of the IDS audit team must revisit the organization to examine documents like visitor's diary and access log to the above resources. They need to also report on the status of all the issues that have been raised in the audit reports they recently submitted to the organization [25]. To conclude the audit, the reports of this team should categorically state audit issues on smart IDSs and log analyzers that have been fixed, pending issues and reasons behind the delay on audit issues that end-users have not fixed. We suggest that auditors must advise the organization to develop a suitable IDS policy whenever they have none.

### 5.2 Results and discussions

The attacks illustrated with the DDOS-1 and DDOS-2 datasets in **Table 1** did not vary on the basis of their respective destinations' IP addresses when compared with the sources' IP addresses of the attacks. The results sugest that the entire alerts that originate from the dataset are mostly repeated information that belongs to one group of destination's IP address. Hence, the Gini Index was 0.000.

**Figure 8** illustrates log analysis of lengths of alerts in DATA01 dataset.

Therefore, IDS auditors must as well audit codes and Log analyzers to establish the input data, their functions and capabilities in other to establish the strenghts and limitations of each analyzer. Such systematic review will enable the auditor to establish Log analyzers that analysts should optimize either by splitting them or by merging two or more codes together. **Table 2** illustrates cumulative length of attributes that Snort has used to report 4919 and 75,390 alerts on DATA01 and DATA02 respectively. **Table 3** interprets the attacks from the above evaluation and the rules that detected them. Thus, auditors can adopt information in **Tables 2** and **3** to conduct risk assessments and identify strategies of some intruders in Cyber Physical Systems (CPSs).

**Figure 9** is a description of log analysis of lengths of alerts in DATA02 dataset.

Essentially, **Figures 8** and **9** illustrate the patterns that lengths of alerts from both datasets can generate. Thus, the chance that intruders can overload smart IDSs over time depends on the quantity of alerts the detectors can trigger on daily basis. The results further suggest that automated strategy for forecasting length of alerts smart IDSs generate is critical to auditors in conducting audit of smart IDSs in the context of Cyber Physical Systems (CPSs). This can assist operators to forecast patterns of attacks, workload and how human aspects of security and privacy can link to Cyber Physical Systems (CPSs).

### 5.3 Suggestions for improving security in Cyber Physical Systems

The above models have practical implementations in protecting computational, human, mechanical and physical components that are fundamental to Cyber Physical Systems (CPSs). IDS policy must state the configurations and various types

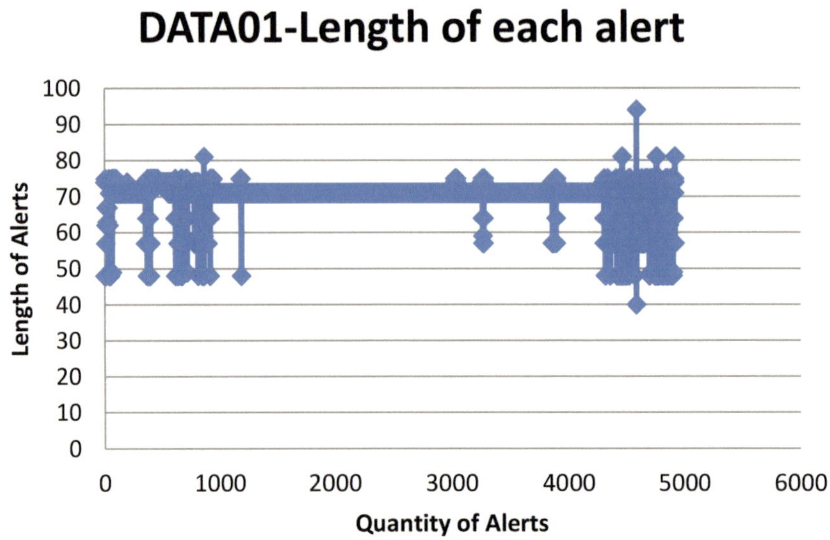


**Figure 8.**
*Log analysis of lengths of alerts (DATA01).*

| Dataset | Total alerts | Total attributes |
|---|---|---|
| DATA01 | 4919 | 345375 |
| DATA02 | 75390 | 2893183 |

**Table 2.**
*Log analysis of components of alerts.*

of smart IDSs in the above settings. This document should state the vendors of Network Intrusion Detection Systems (NIDs) and Host-based Intrusion Detection Systems (HIDSs) installed to safeguard all entities in Cyber Physical Systems (CPSs). Auditors must verify whether the policy approves software-based IDSSs or hardware-based IDSs, or combinations of both detectors. Among other things, auditors should further investigate this document to ascertain if it contains information regarding license fees, number of users, expiration date for the payment of license fees and bank accounts of the vendors of smart IDSs procured in these settings.

IDS policy must reflect operators of smart IDSs responsible for the administration and monitoring of various smart IDSs and Log analyzers in the organization. Recently, intruders keenly probe source codes to establish their limitations. Therefore, it is imperative for IDS auditors to carefully scrutinize IDS policy. The document must categorically state allowable length of time to train supervised learning algorithms as well as the acceptable level that log analyzers must reduce workload due to IDS alerts in other to undermine the generality of intrusions IDSs have warned. What is the acceptable way to classify similar alerts and similar intrusions? Should similar intrusions be classified on the basis of temporal relationships, intrusive objectives, capabilities to support subsequent intrusions or values held in the attributes of alerts? The audit must be able to match IDS policy with the above questions for the document to be useful for mitigating problems of alert correlations that have raised serious concerns among security experts in recent time. IDS policy document should not reflect ambiguity in any aspect. The document should be simple and explicit. It should also include the incident and reporting team; processes of escalating cases of intrusions and response strategy approved by the

| Sig_generator | Sig_id | Sig_rev | Description of alert/attack | Summary of attack |
|---|---|---|---|---|
| 119 | 2 | 1 | Double decoding attack | The attack was an http exploit. The intuder inllegally inspected HyperText Transfer Protocol (http) to gather information about application protocol for distributing hypermedia data in the networks |
| 119 | 18 | 1 | Webroot directory traversal | The attack was an http exploit. The intuder possibly accessed data, codes, files, etc via root directory of the web server in the networks |
| 122 | 1 | 0 | TCP portscan | The intuder inllegally scanned a computer port with intention to gather information about open ports, close ports and services running in the computer |
| 125 | 2 | 1 | Invalid FTP command | The intuder used invalid FTP command to possibly transfer files in the networks |
| 125 | 3 | 1 | FTP command parameters were too long | The attack was buffer overflow exploits with FTP client. The intruder used telnet's client to possibly transfer files that exceeded maximum length in the networks |
| 125 | 4 | 1 | FTP command parameters were malformed | The intruder used badly formed FTP command to possibly transfer files on FTP client |

**Table 3.**
*Log analysis of rules that generate alerts.*

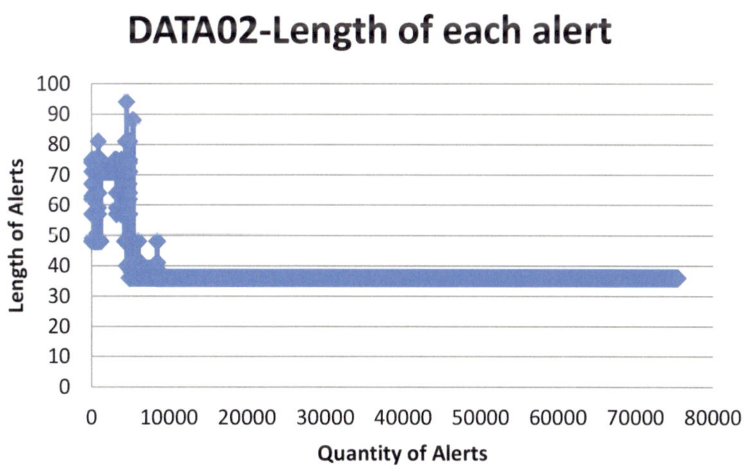


**Figure 9.**
*Log analysis of lengths of alerts (DATA02).*

management. In all, it is equally suggested that IDS policy should include methods for handling public awareness and lessons learnt in the case of devastated attacks that require the organization to intimate the general public.

An organization may deploy smart IDSs that run on different operating systems. The performance of smart IDSs becomes necessary whenever they run on different operating systems. For instance, experience shows that Bro usually operates in Linux/Unix, FreeBSD and Solaris' environment while Snort can run with Windows and Unix/Linux operating systems. There are different ways to hardening different operating systems. Therefore, auditors must familiar with different ways to hardening common operating systems in the industry. Some smart IDSs require installations of client software on computers in the networks of Cyber Physical Systems (CPSs). Hence, auditors must also ensure they audit client software on computers in the networks that interface with smart IDSs. Uninteresting activities and activities that are important attacks can vary from organization to organization. Hence, auditors must be professional at all time. They should professionally handle recommendations aiming to limit the number of false positives especially while suggesting extra policy scripts that should be included with existing rules for detecting cyber-attacks.

Some toolkits can express their signatures as regular expressions or as fixed strings. Audit of smart IDSs in Cyber Physical Systems (CPSs) should establish how signatures are designed in each detector. This information is needed in recommending suitable training and professional development to operators of smart IDSs whenever audit reports suggest that operators lack sufficient knowledge to carry out their daily jobs' specifications. Auditors of smart IDSs and log analyzers should evaluate the effectiveness of training facilities that are available for conducting in-house training in the organization. In-house training can be recommended to operators in case the required facilitators are available in the organization. It is ethical for auditors to recommend training outside the organization to operators of smart IDSs whenever there are insufficient facilities to conduct in-house training in the organization [25, 27]. Operational training should include topics such as network or traffic content, false positives. false negatives, policy scripting or writing rules or signature, signature-matching, uninteresting activities, interesting activities, cyber threats and attacks, security, user privileges, front-end and back-end of smart IDSs; installation, configuration, maintenance and execution of smart IDSs and log analyzers to empower operators of smart IDSs in Cyber Physical Systems (CPSs). Auditors should ascertain operators if smart IDSs that aware or unaware of the official websites of various smart IDSs in the organization during audit of smart IDSs and log analyzers. The audit should establish operators of smart IDSs that subscribe or unsubscribe to news update in the official websites of IDSs in the organization. The reason is that official websites of IDSs often contain helpful documentations and new tips about bugs and attacks and strategies to fix them. There should be no bandwidth limitations in the networks for most smart IDSs to be effective. Organizations should strictly adhere to the hardware requirements such as hard disk and processor of host computers; software requirement such as operating systems (Linux, Windows and Solaris) and the required versions of auxiliary tools such as libpcap, Perl and tcpdump that service providers recommend for smart IDSs to ensure high performance. Audit reports should state the location of smart IDSs in the organization; other options for location the toolkits and their respective benefits to enlighten the organization. For instance, smart IDSs can be installed behind an external firewall in the networks. This will enable the firewall to reduce numbers of suspicious packets that smart IDSs in CPSs will analyze. Some organizations may install smart IDSs before the external firewall. This method will enable smart IDSs to detect potential attacks migrating into the networks. The trade-offs is that smart IDSs will produce high number of alerts for log analyzers and operators to analyze. Smart IDSs can also be installed inside internal firewall if the human element in Cyber Physical Systems (CPSs) aims to detect internal hosts that are vulnerable to computer worms and computer virus.

DOI: http://dx.doi.org/10.5772/intechopen.94569

Audit reports should specify agencies that require external reports of incidents from the organization that is being audited. Statistics on incident information can suggest prevalence of security breaches of Cyber Physical systems (CPSs) nationwide. Auditors can evaluate compliance of the organization to the various requirements of regulatory bodies by reviewing information about the frequency regulators required for submitting mandatory reports to the government and National Agency for Incident Analysis (NAIA). The formats of the reports may be summary of critical incidents or all cases of security violations on monthly, quarterly, biannual or annual basis. Interview with someone who inspects and forwards the reports to the required external recipients will appropriately establish details of how and when the reports are due for submission. The reports to agencies should be informative in case they require the reports in specific formats. Operators should express the date and time the incident begin and end. The number of each type of incident could be included in the report period for statistical purpose.

Smart IDSs and log analyzers merely detect suspicious events. They cannot make authoritative decisions if a suspicious event is an attack or not attack. These mechanisms also lack the intelligence to decide whether an attack is successful attack or a failed or unsuccessful attack. Therefore, operators and recipients of alerts from smart IDSs and log analyzers must constantly investigate the reports they receive from the above mechanisms. Furthermore, IDS audit reports and reports on log analyzers should be simultaneously made available to the IDS operators in the organizations to address all audit issues pinpointed in the reports.

Above all, the above audit model is an integral part of the information security of an organization. Host machines, hardware-based IDSs and repository for storing reports on smart IDSs should be regularly protected from intruders like burglars. For software-based IDSs, the logical security of databases of the IDSs; web servers and various infrastructural components on the networks such as router, firewall and location of the smart IDSs in relation to the firewall should be thoroughly reviewed to ascertain their levels of compliance with best security standards. Segregation of duties among network engineers, Database Administrators (DBAs), internal control and operators of smart IDSs in Cyber Physical Systems (CPSs) is highly recommended. It is disastrous if the logs are deleted while the toolkit is running. Auditors should recommend enforcement of strong access controls to restrict illegal logging in to the configurations and logs of smart IDSs as panacea to information leakages and attacks on smart IDS through the back-end of applications in Cyber Physical Systems (CPSs) [12].

The root causes of intrusions are dynamic security and privacy issues in Cyber Physical Systems (CPSs). Broad audit should be able to reveal how log analyzers adopt classification rules to segment logs of smart IDSs in Cyber Physical Systems (CPSs) and classify alerts into normal and abnormal events. Without sound understanding of data mining procedures, IDS auditors might face difficult challenges to audit association and episode rules necessary to expose hidden relationship among alerts that are not obviously related. Research has discovered that sequence of the intrusions on cyber physical resources in an organization can occur within different timestamp. Practically, it is difficult to find the mean of categorical datasets that have no numerical attributes. Instances whereby the designers of log analyzers have adopted weighted values to transform alerts in the logs of smart IDSs must be clearly reviewed during audit. The reports will enable end users to establish limitations of algorithms that adopt concepts like k-nearest-neighbor (KNN) classifiers and how to improve on the underpinning concepts for transposing alerts into human readable form in the organization. Auditors should establish types of Security Information and Event Management (SIEM) and other threat solutions in Cyber Physical Systems (CPSs).

The above results submit that auditors must audit log analyzers irrespective of whether they are locally designed or they are proprietary models in the organization. The reports should reveal expert rules that are used to process events' logs and their characteristics. Auditors should strongly recommend proper documentations for log analyzers and other threat solutions in Cyber Physical Systems (CPSs). Essentially, the above audit model should establish the existence or absence of audit team in the organization. Reports obtained from the audit should be submitted to the unit in charge of monitoring smart IDSs in the organization. Thereafter, auditors should notify them and management with written reports stating past audit issues that have been suitably addressed [16, 26]. Otherwise, a terminal date to ensure that all pending audit issues must be addressed and potential impacts of noncompliance must be issued to the above stakeholders as well.

## 6. Conclusion

This chapter shows that pragmatic studies on audit of smart IDSs in the context of Cyber Physical Systems (CPSs) are erroneously taken lightly over the years. This gap has generated negative impacts in the security of computational components, cyber and physical resources of Cyber Physical Systems (CPSs) over the years. Manufacturers of smart IDSs can design rules or policies that are deactivated by default because they are not immediately needed to protect Cyber Physical Systems (CPSs). Such rules or policies can be completely useless if smart IDSs are not periodically audited. Operators can waste huge resources to redesign inactive rules or policies due to lack of information about possible threats and cyber attacks in Cyber Physical Systems (CPSs) and ignorance of the existence of similar rules or policies in the detection engines of smart IDSs. Consequently, the chapter demonstrates that log analyzers can serve diverse objectives in a corporate setting. It has also been stated that series of intrusions can elude smart IDSs whenever the periodic audit of smart IDSs in Cyber Physical Systems (CPSs) is not based on empirical findings. The idea is that smart IDSs and all log analyzers in a corporate setting must be specially audited and their readiness for packets processing must be routinely verified to ascertain their compliance with best security practices.

There are several concerns that may arise if the computers hosting smart IDSs are weakly protected or if they are not protected at all. The toolkit can be compromised by intruders, thereby under-reporting or over-reporting security breaches in Cyber Physical Systems in the organization. Intrusions that overpower hosts of smart IDSs can suddenly shutdown the toolkits without the awareness of operators. The smart IDSs can begin to generate series of false alerts. These devices can suddenly stop to trigger alerts if intruders cleverly re-configure them without the awareness of dedicated employees. Experienced intruders may modify rules or policies of smart IDSs and compromise the passwords for logging to the root directories of smart IDSs in Cyber Physical Systems (CPSs). They may delete logs, modify alerts and other related components of these toolkits. Some intruders may disable smart IDSs in Cyber Physical Systems (CPSs) before they will attacks the networks. The integrity of the log analyzers that analyze logs of compromised smart IDSs in these circumstances will also be subjective. Therefore, smart IDSs and log analyzers in Cyber Physical Systems (CPSs) must be periodically audited to establish lapses or hidden faults in the validity and the strength of the protection that the internal controls offered to the detectors and to help the company to settle on the cost of ownership of their smart IDSs.

This chapter has proposed an audit model that should contain significant and explicit information necessary to guide human elements in Cyber Physical Systems

(CPSs). The chapter also substantiates the importance of smart log analyzers in the security of Cyber Physical Systems (CPSs). These groups of log analyzers are configured to remotely send brief statements that present the main points about alerts/attacks and in the form of short text messages to the operators of smart IDSs in Cyber Physical Systems (CPSs). The message may include "source IP, destination IP, short descriptions and time of occurrence of the attacks". The above model has also suggested that audit reports should contain executive summary on audit of smart IDSs and log analyzers in Cyber Physical Systems (CPSs); objectives or purpose and scope of the audit. The reports must also include all proprietary and locally developed log analyzers that relate to smart IDSs in the review. The reports will be informative if they convey information about the available resources, challenges and date of the audit. Columns that outline the serial number (S/N); control tests that auditors have carried out, findings, risk assessment of each problem, suggestions that can mitigate the problems; human elements in Cyber Physical Systems (CPSs) that should fix the problems and remarks or explicit comments (that will state whether the problem has been fixed or is still a pending issue) should be incorporated in the audit reports. Useful explanations regarding the entire phases of the audit, signatories to the reports and annotations should be included in the reports to clarify and substantiate the validity of the reports to stakeholders in Cyber Physical Systems (CPSs).

Furthermore, auditors must periodically verify that logs of smart IDSs and log analyzers in Cyber Physical Systems (CPSs) are regularly archived and operators strictly adhere to the modality for maintaining them. This chapter has further provided a new pathway on how to investigate the sufficiency of IDSs intelligence and log analyzers and the degree at which they conform to IDS policy and best security practices in a real-life environment and in the context of Cyber Physical Systems (CPSs). Since empirical studies have shown that IDS policy is a well-established fact in IDS manuals, similarly, future studies should provide best standards and frameworks for concurrent auditing of smart IDSs and log analyzers in Cyber Physical Systems (CPSs) using non-statistical metrics. Finally, strong cooperation between organizations, GSM operators and research community can help to lessen issues and challenges in Cyber Physical Systems (CPSs) that have been identified in this chapter.

## Author details

Joshua Ojo Nehinbe
ICT Security Consultant, Nigeria, West Africa

*Address all correspondence to: nehinbe@yahoo.com

## References


[1] A. W. Colombo, T. Bangemann, S. Karnouskos, J. Delsing, P. Stluka, R. Harrison, F. Jammes, and J. Lastra: Towards the Next Generation of Industrial Cyber-Physical Systems in: Industrial Cloud-Based Cyber-Physical Systems: The IMC-AESOP Approach. Pp. 1-22; Springer Link, ISBN 9783319056234 (2014)

[2] J. Epstein: Security Lessons Learned from Société Générale. IEEE Security & Privacy, Vol. 6, Issue 3 (2008)

[3] W.H. Baker, A. Hutton, C.D.Hylender, C. Novak, C. Porter, B. Sartin, P.Tippett: Data Breach Investigations Report, Verizon Business (2009)

[4] L. George: Cyber-Physical Attacks: A growing invisible threat. Oxford, UK; Elsevier Science. ISBN 9780128012901 (2015)

[5] Gubb P, Takang A. Software Maintenance. New Jersy, USA: World scientific Publishing; 2003

[6] IANA: Internet Control Message Protocol (ICMP) Parameters https://www.iana.org/assignments/icmp-parameters/icmp-parameters.xhtml

[7] D. Adams and A. Maier: Confidentiality Review & Audit of GoldBug-Encrypting E-Mail-Client & Secure Instant Messenger (2016)

[8] J.O. Nehinbe: Automated Technique for Debugging Intrusion Detection Systems, 1st International Conference on Intelligent Systems, Modelling and Simulations (ISMS2010), proceedings of IEEE Computer Society's Conference Publishing Services (CPS), London (2010)

[9] J.O. Nehinbe: Methods for reducing workload during investigations of Intrusion Logs; PhD Thesis, University of Essex, Colchester, London (2011)

[10] J .Fitzgerald, P.G. Larsen, M. Verhoef (Eds.): Collaborative Design for Embedded Systems: Co-modelling and Co-simulation. Springer Verlag, ISBN 9783642541186 (2014)

[11] K. Julish, C. Suter, T.Woitalla and O. Zimmermann: Compliance by Design – Bridging the Chasm between Auditors and IT Architects. *Computers & Security*, Elsevier. Vol 30, Issue 6-7 (2011)

[12] D. Wu; D.W. Rosen; L. Wang and D. Schaefer: Cloud-based design and manufacturing: A new paradigm in digital manufacturing and design innovation; Computer-Aided Design, Vol 59, pp 1-14 (2014)

[13] P.R. Bitterli, J. Brun, T. Bucher, B. Christ, B. Hamberger, M. Huissoud, D. Küng, A. Toggwhyler and Wyniger: Guide to the Audit of IT Applications. ISACA (2009)

[14] R.E.: Cascarino, Auditor's Guide to Information Systems Auditing. John Wiley & Sons publication (2007)

[15] R. Ciprian-Radu; H. Olimpiu; T. Ioana-Alexandra and O. Gheorghe: Smart Monitoring of Potato Crop: A Cyber-Physical System Architecture Model in the Field of Precision Agriculture; Agriculture and Agricultural Science Procedia, vol. 6, pp. 73 – 79 (2015)

[16] R.U. Rehman: Intrusion Detection Systems with Snort: Advanced IDS Techniques Using Snort, Apache, MySQL, PHP, and ACID, Library of Congress, New York (2003)

[17] Snort Users Manual 2.9.11:The Snort Project; Cisco and/or its affiliates (2017)

[18] S. Senft and F. Gallegos: Information Technology Control and Audit; Auerbach Publications (2009)

[19] T.S. Kumar and P. Radivojac: Introduction to Data Mining:- Lecture Notes (2017)

[20] ISACA: Information Systems Auditing: Tools and Techniques Creating Audit Programs (2016)

[21] The Global Information Assurance Certification (2003), Snort Intrusion Detection System Audit: An Auditor's pers-pective; GSNA practical version 2.1 (2007)

[22] D.E, Robert: IT Auditing: An Adaptive Process. Mission Viejo: Pleier Corporation (2005)

[23] The National Science Foundation-US: Cyber-Physical Systems (CPS) (2020)

[24] T. Phatak; P. Isal, O. Kadale; A. Nalage and S. Bhongle: Smart Intrusion Detection System, International research journal on engineering and technology, Vol. 4, Issue 04 (2017)

[25] R. Alder, A.R. Baker, E.F. Carter, J. Esler, J.C. Foster, M. Jonkman, C. Keefer, R. Marty and E.S. Seagren: Snort: IDS and IPS Toolkit, Syngress publishing, Burlington, Canada (2007)

[26] R. K. Rainer, C.G. Cegielski, I. Splettstoesser-Hogeterp, C. Sanchez-Rodriguez: Introduction to Information Systems: Supporting and Transforming Business, 3rd Canadian Edition, ISBN: 9781118476994 (2013)

[27] W.H.Murray: Data security management: Principles and Applications of Key Management; Auerbach publication (1999)

[28] W. Buchanan: *The Handbook of Data and Networks Security* (1st Edition), Springer-Verlag New York, Inc. Secaucus, NJ, USA (2007)

[29] W. Stallings: Network Security Essentials: Applications and Standards, 4th edition, Prentice Hall (2011).

Chapter 6

# Digital Culture: Control and Domination of Technical Images in the Era of Psychocapitalism

*Rodolfo Augusto Melo Ward de Oliveira*

## Abstract

This Chapter aims to conduct a theoretical study in order to understand the transmutation of modern culture into digital culture, which is intrinsically linked to technological, political, economic, artistic and cultural advances. Our goal is to unite components of the visual culture and the culture of convergence to explain how new realities and new forms of control and domination are created through images and used on a large scale by the neoliberalist system in the network society, inaugurating the new phase of capitalism, i.e., psychocapitalism. Until recently, mobile phone devices were used solely for calls (oral language), being then followed by the era of text messaging (written language). Today, everyone has cameras (image language) and Internet connectivity. The Internet is part of people's daily lives, and the trend is for us to increasingly connect to devices connected thereto and to connect electronic devices of daily use to the Internet. This ensures connectivity as a common space in the social construction and identity of the social being in such a way that there is no longer a distinction between "online," "offline," "real," and "virtual." The disciplines of arts, sociology, philosophy, anthropology and social communication are used as a basis.

**Keywords:** psychocapitalism, digital culture, image, contemporary philosophy, control, domination

## 1. Introduction

In order to understand the new challenges in cybersecurity, it is necessary to understand the functioning of the contemporary social body, digital culture, and the rise of technical images and their use for the construction of new realities. This encompasses new forms of control and domination used on a large scale, in the network society, by the neoliberalist system, inaugurating the new phase of capitalism, i.e., psychocapitalism.

This Chapter, produced based on a philosophical approach, aims to collaborate with the discussions on technical images in the contemporary times using photography as an object of studies to facilitate this analysis. We address the main issues surrounding the production of images in the field of documentary and artistic photography, delimiting their borders, transgressions, and points of convergence. This should contribute to the understanding of contemporary society, cyberspace, cybersecurity, and how psychocapitalism has used images as a form of control and domination.



IntechOpen

Anthropologist Bittencourt [1] argues that the use of photographic imagery as a representation of the real by anthropology – notorious as an academic discipline for scientifically studying the human being – has become a powerful instrument for generating and maintaining a regime of truth. For political, power and control interests, photography has been used to maintain and, in some cases, create the regime of truth that stigmatized criminals, the mentally ill, the poor, indigenous people, quilombolas, Arabs, blacks, Asians, and all segments considered subordinate.

For a long time, anthropology used photography for the purposes of surveillance and stigmatization "of the wild and the exotic as Other." According to Bittencourt [1], this means of surveillance created a specific regime of truth and built stereotypes that positioned the "Other in relation to a notion of Us as producers" of images. They created exotic images of people and places, hitherto unknown to society, i.e., they created, in addition to images, the people and places themselves. In anthropology, photographic documentation was widely used as a means to justify an idea related to race and anthropometric systems in the second half of the 19th century [1]. Photography proved to be a powerful tool for creating realities, regimes of truth, and power.

The general purpose of this Chapter is to analyze, through a theoretical study, how the technical and photographic images contributed to the rupture of the modern concepts of truth, cooperating in the creation of new regimes of truth and new less standardized power structures, which have provided greater freedom to contemporary photographic production. Concomitantly, this Chapter will also shed light on how power systems have been transmuting and shaping this "image civilization" in which we live, while offering illusory images of freedom in a cyclical system of repetition of human actions[1] that feeds itself back and feeds on data.

We will define an instrument, apparatus and machine and enter a brief history of the evolution and convergence of these objects based on Flusserian thinking. The conceptualization of these terms aims to facilitate the understanding of current discussions about the interaction between man and machine, cybersecurity, and the current conception of man and machine co-authorship that surround the debate about the post-human and photography in post-modernity. The reflections written here should be expanded and applied to other fields of knowledge. We will start with the definitions and origin, which are so important and often overlooked by the desire to talk about the now, which in my view, in a way, would result in a shallow Chapter.

## 2. Instrument, machine and apparatus

Flusser [3] states that instruments are tools used by man to modify the world or to make human life easier. According to him, these tools would comprise empirical extensions of the body's organs, generally simulating the functioning of the organ that they extend. The difference lies in how they are more powerful and efficient, as they reach farther distances and deeper in nature and thus fulfill their role as an instrument. This instrument, after being discovered and mastered, is incorporated into human experience and culture. In each society, the instruments were removed from nature to fulfill a specific human need in that location. Human beings, then, transferred this knowledge of the use of instruments to their successors, learning

[1] Man, excluding his intellectual integration and mobilization of consciousness, has an animal machine that is identical to that of other mammals, subjecting himself to the "digestion movement," eating at fixed times, "following the crowd and, like sheep, the pace of the pace collective" ([2] p. 85).

about the usefulness of instruments used by other peoples and creating, adapting and converging their instruments into new instruments that would make their life easier. The instruments contributed to the evolution of the human being and evolved alongside them.

Let us then take a leap in time to the period of modernity. After the Industrial Revolution, instruments passed through the sieve of science, were considered technical instruments, and received technological and scientific investments, becoming more powerful in their functions and programming, being then called machines. Based on this transformation, their relationship with man was inverted. Man has ceased to be the constant and has become the variable in this relationship. The instruments that used to work for men now witness part of humanity working for the powerful machines, which have also come to dominate the production lines and become essential for economic development.

This change caused by the rise of machines in the post-Industrial Revolution period promotes and accelerates countless social, political and economic changes, as one of the main causes of what Flusser [3] called "alienated work." This process was responsible for dividing society into "capitalists" and "proletariats," comprising, respectively, the owners of the machines and those who work for the owners of the machines as salaried employees.

The alienated work problematized by Flusser [3] is linked to the displacement of manufacturing and production information from artisans to machines. He emphasizes the historical and social importance of this enormous transformation that took place at the time, as customs, traditions, social relations and economics were rapidly changing over a short period of time. According to Flusser, the allocation of traditional craftsmanship knowledge from the hands of the artisan also removed their power over the value of their product, as the value of the product or consumer good was linked to artisanal making, i.e., to knowing how to make. The artisan materialized the information during the making and attributed value to it. Flusser referred to it as the information about "pieces of the world." Following the Industrial Revolution, the tool began to preserve the information on production of products, transferring the value of goods and products to the tool and, subsequently, to the owners of the tools, the capitalists.

### 2.1 Technical objects and technical images

In order to understand the current discussions about digital culture – the cyberspace –we must approach Simondon's thinking. We do not intend to exhaust the complexity of thinking about the evolution of technical objects, but rather elucidate issues that are related to the interaction between man and apparatus, which Flusserian thought did not have the opportunity to resolve. It is necessary to rescue the thought of this author, specifically the concept of human interaction with technology.

Simondon [4] builds on the thought of his teacher, Canguilhem, and bases his reflection on three fundamental problems that, according to Lopes ([5] p. 308–309), comprise "(1) the meaning of the technical object as to be technical, genetically conceived, (2) which also implies thinking about its evolution, and (3) the question of its absolute origin within the vital invention "of technical objects, instruments, machines, and devices. When analyzing the "technical object" as a technical "being," the author appropriates and is based initially on the "genetic method," which implies thinking about the evolution of technical objects and their origin.

According to Simondon [4], the technical object was naturally invented without being correlated with economic, social and cultural factors. He associates the evolution of technical objects with human evolution, as a joint and natural evolution. He attributes objects to their own genesis, separate from the genesis of the human being. In this process of attributing its own genesis to the technical object, the author gives it autonomy so that they become a technical "being," which evolves and develops through convergence and adaptation. As Simondon argues ([4] p. 20), "the technical being evolves through convergence and adaptation to itself; it is internally unified according to a principle of internal resonance."

Based on the fusion between the thoughts of Flusser, Canguilhem and Simondon, we understand that the camera may have evolved by adapting both the visual and technological needs of contemporary society, converging with other more current and powerful technological devices, such as the smartphone. In Flusser, machines were powerful because of their size; in contemporary times, we notice a certain inversion in which mobile devices have become smaller and more powerful. Large machines still have their space, although they are expensive and have little mobility, which puts them in the background in today's society, with the possibility of being classified, in some cases in photography, as handcrafted devices.

One of the main thoughts in Simondon's theory [4] consists of arguing that the idea of opposition between culture and technique is false, just as the opposition between man and machine. This "ignorance" in relation to the nature of machines and technical knowledge would be one of the causes of the recurrent malaise in contemporary society and which would in some way result in technophilia and technophobia – while some wish to follow the technological flow and prevent their obsolescence, others, conservatives, would not assimilate technological innovations.

Technophiles are generally people who interconnected the different spheres of their lives in new technologies, creating a certain dependence on these technologies, because, as Flusser [3] says, man transferred his interests from the objective world to the symbolic world of information. This type of phobia is very common in today's connectivity society. Technophilia would then comprise the fear of failure due to some technological breakdown or failure.

In turn, technophobia is the reverse. It is the fear of technology. This is also a very common phobia nowadays. Many people have lost their jobs, being replaced by machines. We have an interesting example, within the world of photography, relating to technophobia: the transition from the analog photographic device to the digital device. Here, we can also speak of the fear of hackers and data theft by large companies that monetize this information.

Following this brief introduction, and the limitation that the work involving this Chapter imposes on us, we will address the definitions of image and technical image. According to Flusser [3], images are codes that replace events with scenes with the purpose of representing, comprising maps or instruments to guide the human being in the world, mediating the relationship between man and the world, gaining more and more power over time and replacing even informative texts. This, however, is a mistake, in the author's view, as images and texts should complement and not replace one another. In his studies, Flusser already pointed to the emergence of the culture of convergence.

With the advent of technical images, images leave the field of imagination and enter the field of alienation, and man begins to use them as screens for reality and to create images to represent his own life and to live according to the production of images. This promotes the inversion of the function of images, creating a form of idolatry in relation to images and neglecting the reason why images are produced – to serve as an instrument and to guide man in the world. "Man, instead of using images in function of the world, begins to live in terms of images. He no longer deciphers the scenes of the image as meanings of the world, but rather the world itself is experienced as a set of scenes" ([3] p. 9).

The transmutation of the imagination into a hallucination is marked by man's inability to reconstruct the abstracted dimensions of the image and thus decipher them. By losing this potential, the image ceases to be a mediator between man and the world, losing its magical aura, to become its own credible reality. This type of image, called a technical image, apparently does not need to be deciphered, as it is confused with the very representation of the world, leading the observer to trust the image as much as they trust their eyes. We can see this in the use of social media, as will be explained later in this text.

Flusser questions the replacement of texts with images because the technical images themselves have text in their essence, being produced by photographic devices that have, in essence, the union of research and studies in the form of technical texts that were applied in the construction of this device, which in turn create the technical images. This dynamic in the construction of the technical image grants it credibility and the potential to replace traditional images, which, in Flusser's view, contributes to idolatry regarding the image. It would be up to photography to reunify thought, freeing us from text-centered culture and the domain of the conceptual, guiding us to (re)think through images. This is another point that will be discussed below, but, first, let us get into the study of space–time called contemporaneity.

### 2.2 The clipping of the contemporary space-time

The post-Industrial Revolution world has advanced rapidly, with new technologies changing the entire global geopolitical system and beginning to command the economy through control over the production of goods and products. With the rapid advance of science and technology, new technologies have become more accessible and exponentially incorporated by society in order to facilitate the activities of daily life, being used both at work and in the mediation of personal relationships. We realize that scientific and technological advances have created better living conditions for the population that has access or the purchasing power to do so.

We have presented the main characteristics of the changes from the historical period known as modernity to postmodernity. We have shown both positive and negative characteristics and alert to the use of technology by the current hegemonic power system, financial capitalism, which acts with precision and works with specific data for each individual, using technology as a form of control, inaugurating a new phase of capitalism, i.e. psychocapitalism.

The social transformations of the last decades are not constituted solely by economic and technological changes, but also by profound social transformations that are still boiling, requiring an analysis of dense circumstances, to name the main ones, which is not the object of study of this Chapter. Nevertheless, it is relevant for a better understanding of how photographic images are consumed or shared on social networks to understand how and where these networks are structured in contemporary times. It is also necessary to show how the construction of social identity has changed and is changing due to the rupture from the concepts of truth and modern meta-narratives.

In this Chapter, the main characteristics of cyberspace are presented, without the aim of exhausting the subject. We wish solely to provide the reader with clear guidance as to the issues raised in this research and how photographic production and creation are following, being influenced and influencing decisively the imagery construction of the globalized collective identity in the current era.

Today, we are moving towards ensuring that everyone is connected to the Internet, producing and sharing data. Until recently, mobile phone devices were used only for calls (oral language), being then followed by the era of text messaging (written language). Today, everyone has cameras (image language) and Internet connectivity. The Internet is part of people's daily lives, and the trend is for us to increasingly connect to devices connected thereto and to connect electronic devices of daily use to the Internet. This ensures connectivity as a common space in the social construction and identity of the social being in such a way that there is no longer a distinction between "online," "offline," "real," and "virtual" [6]. "The Internet is no longer merely an instrument, becoming part of the political action of a wide network of social stakeholders" [7].

A number of theorists see connectivity as the characteristic of our time, placing it above a simple connection between people and things and linking it to the very time in which we live – the era of connectivity – wherein participation becomes self-motivating, as contents are received and shared exponentially on the network, with many of these images. We are moving towards a "civilization of the image."

Today's photographic devices already have Wi-Fi functions for quick connectivity and diffusion of photographs, and most photojournalists, particularly those from major media outlets, work with this type of equipment to disseminate images quickly in the cyberspace. Smartphones have also been frequently used to produce photographic images. The network society is massively using the mobile phone camera as an alternative for producing images due to portability and direct connection to the Internet.

The main advantages of the smartphone are its size, which facilitates transportation and provides agility; connectivity to the Internet, which allows the rapid dissemination of images on the network; and ease conducting research on the spot, besides being more discreet than a professional camera. The cost–benefit ratio is also of fundamental importance. Being present in the cyberspace is crucial for the contemporary artist, having also become, for the modern individual.

The cyberspace is gaining more and more prominence as a stage for political debate and has attracted different social spheres, such as companies and public officials, to social media platforms. It is necessary to understand the context and the global conjuncture of why, who and where the discussions take place. as they guide the collective agenda, influencing and converging with the collective social imaginary. The following will be a summary of the thinking of scholars who study the subject of postmodernity or supermodernity[2] and how social movements are developing in this new field.

## 3. Psychocapitalism

The contemporary photographic image has been used on social media platforms as a means of self-promotion for the individual who acts as an image idolater. The image in the consumer and spectacle society takes on a primary role in personal

[2] "From the 1950s, the term began to be used in American literary theory to classify the main schools of the 20th century. Initially, the term was used in a pejorative sense, i.e., to designate an uninspired moment compared to previous productions in the area of Humanities. By the mid-1960s, however, the word began to gain an affirmative connotation. In 1969, American literary critic Leslie Fiedler (Cross the Border) described his time as a death struggle between modern and postmodern literature. The postmodern slogan would be: "Cross the border" between supposedly elitist art and the more popular art" [8].

relationships, particularly in the cyberspace. People begin to create images to represent their own lives and to live according to the production of images, thereby promoting the inversion of the function of images, which some theorists refer to as image society or "image civilization."

The current hegemonic regime of power, aware of the underpinnings of today's society, has used the power of images to create regimes of truth and regimes of power to watch and control society. It is not something new for photography, which has been used since its inception to create real regimes that have stigmatized peoples and cultures. Next, we will deepen the understanding of how power groups have used scientific and academic knowledge – such as the concepts of civilization of connectivity and civilization of the image – to control and subdue entire societies. In future research, we will address the issue of photography as a meeting place between art, science, and technology, proposing possible relations with psychocapitalism.

Photography has always been linked to the construction of realities through images. Throughout history, these images have been used for different purposes and interests. Both photography and the photographer were linked to the role of observer of society and undertook to record it for the purposes of domination or for liberation.

Based on the understanding of the concepts of market[3], signal[4], spectacle society[5], the era of connectivity, and civilization of the image – which are the result of social research produced in the last decades – we can approach the current discussion on contemporary society[6], also referred to as the transparency society. The concept of a transparency society encompasses all the concepts presented, unifies them in a single definition, and proposes a systematic analysis of the way of life in today's society, simplifying this dense subject for academic studies.

We understand that, as from the 1970s, in Germany, the consequences of the gradual integration of the political state with civil society could be observed. Industrial, commercial and banking capitalism were joined in the form of financial capital, giving rise to organized capitalism, i.e., an organized group with political and economic strength capable of influencing the internal politics of the state.

"The 1970s and 1980s saw major changes in different dimensions of social life. We can observe the disorganization of the accumulation pattern implemented with greater force in the post-war period, with changes in the productive structures, production relations, consumption patterns, forms of sociability, and the various spatialities of the world economy. At the same time, and in an articulated manner, welfare states were gradually dismantled. Social and political stakeholders of crucial importance for the understanding of the political and economic scenario of the central countries until the 1970s, such as unions and the major American banks, lost

[3] This conception of a consumerist society speaks to the thought of Baudrillard [9] who proposed to explain contemporary personal behavior through consumer society and the objectification of things, of life itself, plotting a reality in which the object has more value than its functionality, i.e., consuming a particular object is more important than its usefulness.

[4] The characteristic feature of this time is that no human being, without exception, is able to determine their life in a sense that is to a certain extent transparent, as used to be the case in the evaluation of market relations. In principle, all are objects, even the most powerful [10].

[5] [...] people do as much as possible and use the best resources available to them to increase the market value of the products they are selling. And the products that they are encouraged to market, promote and sell are themselves ([11] p. 13).

[6] We are mainly talking about large urban conglomerates.

strength, while other sectors such as the finance industry gained prominence. The national states themselves had their power significantly changed, redrawing the map of power in the world. Simultaneously, the 1970s and 1980s represent a milestone in the social sciences. With the explanatory exhaustion of macro-theoretical models, represented mainly by functionalism and Marxism, facing a changing world, we are witnessing a great theoretical effervescence and the consolidation of the search for new paths for social theory. The most general feature of this search for paths is convergence" ([12] p. 1).

Currently, according to economist Ladislau Dowbor (2017), we live in the era of unproductive capitalism, which consists of a process of financialization of the planet. For the author, banks and financial institutions have come to dominate the productive system by extracting from it, through interest and tariffs, volumes of incomparably greater resources of contribution than production, generating a society of "unproductive rentiers." In his book The Age of Unproductive Capital, Dowbor ([13] p. 17) criticizes the current financial system:

"We wish to outline how three dynamics are articulated that structurally unbalance development and quality of life in the world. In simple terms, we are destroying the planet for the benefit of a minority, while the resources necessary for sustainable and balanced development are sterilized by the global financial system."

For the sociologist Alfredo Pena Vega ([14] p. 16), we are experiencing another moment in which the situation of the world reveals to us that the model of hegemonic civilization, based on economic growth, has become exhausted. Society does not have the skills to deal with the environmental crisis. Our ancestors bequeathed to present generations a great environmental burden, believing that we, with our technology and evolution, could end hunger, social separation, and the finitude of natural resources.

We do not intend to delve into socioeconomic or geopolitical factors. What we wish to bring address is how these factors act to govern our daily lives, creating social inequalities and destroying the planet, which tend to worsen over time. Today's society is sick because the system that controls and governs our lives is unhealthy and Machiavellian. The chronic disease of financial capitalism is psychological illnesses, which are transmitted through invisible frequency bands, the host being often one's mobile device.

### 3.1 The power of the image in the society of tiredness and transparency

South Korean Eastern philosopher Byung-Chul Han, based in Germany and author, among other works, of The Burnout Society [15] and The Transparency Society [15], argues, when studying the historicity of society, that humanity developed a characteristic social disease in each time. For instance, in the last century, pathologies were bacteriological or viral, while the pathology of contemporary society is neuronal, or psychic. For the author, the neoliberal system deployed a new phase of capitalism – emotion capitalism – marking the transition from biopolitics to psychopolitics, from disciplinary society to a society of control by income, in which man is obliged to surrender, becoming the very inspector of his performance and the accuser of his failure.

We currently live in a society formed by multitasking people who carry in their minds the constant demand of the neoliberal system to produce and be the best in everything they do. They must be the best in all areas of life, with no possibility of failure. It may appear controversial – although therein lies the strategy – that such a system is based on the excess of positivity, incentive and reward, as an update of the punishment system proposed by Foucault[7]. As an example, to clarify our discussion, we can analyze the images posted and shared on social media, such as Instagram or Facebook. Pictures of supposedly successful people, living spectacular, healthy lives, only possible through much effort and sacrifice, which led them to great rewards provided by the capitalist system and only possible in that system: financial success. It is very clear the purpose of these images is to motivate, encourage, and seduce. They talk to us and tell us that it such images are the images of success, happiness, self-realization, while everything that they are not, or which is not contained in them, means failure. The power of these images over us is intense, as they approach human desires that we do not wish to show or admit, such as envy, greed and desire. They are malicious images that corrupt us at the same time as they motivate us. They interact with us and tell us that we can do what we want, that is, become entrepreneurs, become our own bosses, bring our jobs home, or be financially successful to buy and consume. Thus, we can be happier to acquire products and consumer goods and produce more images that will be shared worldwide, creating a system that feeds itself back, satisfying the wishes of power of the images and the system. The images want the body of those who see them, the observer, and those who look at them desire what they show or are seduced by the mystery they hide.

Also known as the labor society and the performance society, the contemporary social body imprisons people by promising a false illusion of freedom in which the master himself has become a slave to work and without time for recreation. In this coercive society, each one carries their field of work. The individual explores themselves and believes that this is a form of personal fulfillment. This exploratory self-collection generates self-criticism and leads the individual to develop psychological diseases that, alongside other factors of postmodern life, induce hyperactivity, work fatigue, attention disorders, and burnout syndrome, in addition to causing depression and other psychological illnesses.

Another major point pointed out by Han [15] is related to surveillance in today's society, which, unlike that analyzed by Foucault in the 1970s, is made by the social individuals themselves. It would be a kind of digital panopticon in which people undress, i.e., they put valuable personal information on social media, the majority of which comprising the imagery. Images have increased their power to create and

[7] The new technologies of power are only possible due to the advent of the "subject" category, and the physical bodies of people comprise the first space in which a new form of power has been exercised. Disciplinary power is a technology of individualized power, "man-body," which trains the subject, tames them, automates habits and transforms them into an obedient and useful instrument for the society of economic production. One of the main tools of disciplinary power is the idea of a panopticon, which induces the subject's mind, leading them to think that they are being watched even without being observed. This tool replaces the physical violence of the time of slavery with psychological violence. Biopower is an extension of the application of the individual's disciplinary power to society, "species-man." It is a technology of collective and massive power that is established on the "fundamental biological fact that the human being constitutes a human species," a society, and the primary thoughts are that of "let live," preserving life and society, and "let die," which eliminates everything that is useless for economic production and which may come to threaten life and society. These new forms of power that emerged in Europe in the 18th century are the evolution of sovereign power, of monarchs, who had the right to "let live" or "let die." From this rupture, we can understand what the author says about "micro power," which is an analysis of the power that is not central, but rather in the peripheries, and which today is so current if we consider the current decolonial movements that cross the entire social fabric, in all social structures, at the global level. "Power is everywhere; not because it encompasses everything, but because it comes from everywhere" ([16] p. 89).

sustain regimes of truth and power. The prosumer, in the illusion of being authentic within a given social circle, creates their fictional images loaded with neoliberalist power and narrative, fostering and validating the hegemonic imagery system. All of this is stored in Big Data, which generates, through artificial intelligence, highly accurate statistical data, processing huge amounts of personalized information about certain human groups with common interests that elucidate many characteristics regarding these segmented groups.

The idolatry of image purported by Flusser [3] makes a lot of sense today. Life in sameness, in monotony, demands dreams and adventures. Han [15] says that the images are not just "reproductions, but also models where we take refuge to be better, more beautiful and more alive". The neoliberal system identified this, and apparently, the communication team in that system read Flusser, studied the history of photography and visual culture, and learned about the power of images. The knowledge produced in the academy has been applied by groups of power for the surveillance and domination of society.

Social networks have several uses, although they place people inside social bubbles of artificial realities. When analyzing this system fed by fictional images, Han [15] argues that these groups create a type of violence of excess positivity that forces us to be happy all the time, leading to an exhaustion of happiness. Another important observation about this happiness is that it is an artificial happiness, created as a way of controlling and maintaining this system.

Individuals have an artificial notion of freedom, as they have the impression of control over their lives and actions. They are situated within a system programmed to alienate people and bring them into subgroups of common interests. Because they have the freedom to choose among some possibilities of their subgroup of interests, these individuals are led to believe that they are free. From the moment they believe they are free, they enter the game of psychocapitalism, which uses psychological images to exert dominance.

The virtual social circle, which concentrates the social dynamics of postmodern life, consists of a controlled environment in which users are able to block people with whom they do not wish to have any contact. It would be like a life linked to the algorithm of the place of comfort, wherein individuals only relate to people similar in terms of ideas and behaviors. We agree with the author on the harms of this type of escape from problems and not facing one's challenges. It is detrimental to the maturation of the individual, who does not learn to deal with life's frustrations and is deprived of finding solutions to complex problems, always opting for the easiest route. Such route is already pre-established, i.e., a utopian and perfect life that collaborates with the homogenization of people's behavior. As individuals do not acquire emotional maturity and social skills, they also do not know how to identify stealers and energy vampires.

On social media platforms, people create images of themselves with the aim of selling themselves as authentic, as each one wishes to be different while following the same fashion trends and rules. In the past, people were aware that they were dominated; today, they no longer have this awareness, as they have been delegated the power of self-supervision and self-punishment, which is mistaken for freedom. We have moved from a disciplinary society to a society of control for income, in which man is required to surrender, and if he fails to surrender, he is makes demands from himself. The person has the illusion of freedom and that he is his own boss, thereby being able to explore himself. Those who fail in neoliberal society make themselves feel responsible and ashamed, instead of questioning the system. They direct the aggression on themselves and do not become critics of the system or the economic model, but rather persons who are depressed for taking on the full weight of failure.

Han [15] proposes the rupture between Foucault's biopolitical theory, based on the domain of the individual by the body, and the new phase of capitalism, i.e., emotion capitalism, which is the raw material of this new model. The current power system controls the individual's psyche, in the same way as the control model used by Christianity, which controls the followers by their own mind, encouraging martyrdom and self-pity, imprisoning their mind at the same time as it preaches false freedom. In this era of society, only the capital, which explores, governs and feeds on images, data, information and emotions, is free to circulate the world and transform the psychic force into a work force (**Figure 1**).

As an example of this new technological data market, we can mention advertisements, which appear to us right after accessing an online sales website. The product usually appears in the advertising area of Facebook, or Instagram, or even in the Web browser. It is not necessary for the user to visit a website, however; if they try on a shoe at a physical store, the GPS on their mobile device will inform their location and propose shoes for the user's profile. There are also advertisements that are suggested on social media platforms due to the capture of sound information by smartphones.

New communication and information technologies have been assimilated by the market, creating a digital economy that circulates capital through the sale of data; examples include the data sales scandal on Facebook (2018), the presidential elections in the United States and Brazil, which involved massive use of artificial intelligence. Power groups linked to financial capital use the new possibilities of ICTs to influence political elections, democracies, and people's ways of living, mainly because they use and apply the complexity of academic knowledge for domination purposes.

Han [15] views a possible way out of the civilizational crisis that we are experiencing in art and contemplation. Art is a possible way out to find other narratives to live the Self, to better understand the world and its functioning, and to acquire self-knowledge. The author states that, in order to live better, moments of idleness are necessary, with deep reflections on our lives – moments when we do not exploit ourselves.

**Figure 1.**
*Control devices (2021).*

We understand that social, political, cultural and economic issues are directly linked to photographic production today and are not able to divide these matters, as contemporary photography could only exist due to technological, scientific and artistic evolution. Because it is a hybrid language, it continues to evolve and is used in artistic production in an intelligent search for criticisms of this system, it being understood that the system dominated the minds of a large portion of the population, which mocks the resistance, which, in this case, would be beneficial to themselves.

## 4. Conclusions

We understand that photography has accompanied the cultural, political and socioeconomic changes experienced by society in the past three centuries. These transformations, by integrating the sociopolitical system as the creator of images of power, contribute to the cultural construction of a homogenized society. In contrast, we propose a reflection on reality and society through artistic photography, as a solution for creating alternative realities based on the thinking of the tripod of author and co-author, individual and society, and observer and image.

Through this brief bibliographic survey on the cyberspace and social relations in contemporary times, we have sought to explain the current context and conjuncture of documentary and artistic photographic creation and how these images have been used as a means to homogenize behaviors and transform them into data. Such data is then monetized and sold by large technology companies to multinational conglomerates and political-electoral campaigns, directly influencing democracy. We also demonstrate that there is an Image System that induces people to offer their data of their own initiative, and that Image System feeds itself back. Our goal was not to exhaust the subject, but rather to provoke the reader into facts that are inherent in our society. We seek to show, through authors from different areas, that there is a dense social transformation that directly influences social reorganization through the power that images and their representation exercise on humanity. We also seek to demonstrate that the status of the image is being changed and that, consequently, the status of the observer is also changing. The images are no longer linked to the truth, but rather to a fictitious representation. All of this has a direct bearing on issues related to cybersecurity and cyber warfare since, through the image system, people give their data of their own initiative, sometimes causing damage to themselves.

In coming studies, we will deepen the discussion on the production of contemporary images – the photography produced by mobile phones – explaining and exemplifying how they have played an active role in science and in the construction of regimes of truth and power. Photography has converged, in terms of media and culture, maintaining itself as the main image-producing device in both modernity and postmodernity.

## Author details

Rodolfo Augusto Melo Ward de Oliveira
Brasília University, Brasília, DF, Brazil

*Address all correspondence to: rodolfoward@unb.br

## References

[1] BITTENCOURT, Luciana. Anuário Antropológico/92. Rio de Janeiro: Tempo Brasileiro, 1994. p. 225-241.

[2] LEROI-GOURHAN, André. O Gesto e a Palavra –II –Memória e Ritmos. Lisboa: Edições 70, 2002.

[3] FLUSSER, Vilém. O mundo codificado: por uma filosofia do design e da comunicação. São Paulo: Cosac Naify, 2013. O universo das imagens técnicas: elogio da superficialidade. São Paulo: Annablume, 2008. Ficções filosóficas. São Paulo: Edusp, 1998. Bodenlos: uma autobiografia filosófica. São Paulo: Annablume, 2007a. O mundo codificado. Org. Rafael Cardoso. São Paulo: Cosac Naif, 2007b. Língua e realidade. São Paulo: Annablume, 2004. Ser judeu. São Paulo: Annablume, 2014. Filosofia da caixa preta: ensaios para uma futura filosofia da fotografia. Rio de Janeiro: Relume Dumará, 2002. O instrumento do fotógrafo ou o fotógrafo do instrumento. Íris, agosto de 1982.

[4] SIMONDON, Gilbert. Du mode d'existence des objets techniques. Paris: Aubier, 1989.

[5] LOPES, Wendell Evangelista Soares. Gilbert Simondon e uma filosofia biológica da técnica. Cientiæ Zudia, São Paulo, v. 13, n. 2, p. 307-334, 2015.

[6] HINE, C. Ethnography for the internet: Embedded, Embodied and Everyday. London: Bloomsbury, 2015.

[7] TEIXEIRA, Ana Cláudia; ZANINI, Débora; MENESES, Larissa. O fazer político nas mídias sociais: aproximações teóricas sobre ação coletiva em rede. 41o Encontro Anual da Anpocs GT2 – Ciberpolítica, ciberativismo e cibercultura. 2017.

[8] FEITOSA, Charles. Pensamento pós-moderno. In: TEIXEIRA, Francisco Carlos (Org.). Enciclopédia de guerras e revoluções do século XX. Rio de Janeiro: Campus, 2004. p. 702-703.

[9] BAUDRILLARD, J. Simulacres et simulations. Paris: Galilée, 1981.

[10] ADORNO, Theodor W.; HORKHEIMER, Max. Minima Moralia. São Paulo: Ática, 1992.

[11] BAUMAN, Zigmunt. Vida para consumo: a transformação das pessoas em mercadoria. Rio de Janeiro: Zahar, 2008. Modernidade líquida. Rio de Janeiro: Zahar, 2001. Tempos líquidos. Tradução de Carlos Alberto Medeiros. Rio de Janeiro: Zahar, 2007.

[12] MARQUES, Eduardo Cesar. Notas críticas à literatura sobre estado, políticas estatais e atores políticos. São Paulo: Editora da USP, 1996.

[13] DOWBOR, Ladislau. A era do capital improdutivo. São Paulo: Outras Palavras & Autonomia Literária, 2017. 316 p. Além do capitalismo: uma nova arquitetura social. São Paulo, novembro 2018. 86 p.

[14] PENA VEGA, Alfredo. Wawekrurê: distintos olhares./Rodolfo Ward, organização, fotografias. Brasília: Senado Federal, Conselho Editorial, 2019. 156 p.: il., fotos. Edições do Senado Federal, v. 213.

[15] HAN, Byung-Chul. A sociedade da transparência. Lisboa: Relógio D'Água Editores, 2014. Sociedade do cansaço. Tradução de Enio Giachini. Petrópolis: Vozes, 2015. No enxame: Perspectivas do digital. Tradução Lucas Machado. Petrópolis: Vozes, 2018.

[16] FOUCAULT, Michel. Historia da sexualidade: a vontade de saber. Paz & Terra; 9ª edição, 2014.

Chapter 7

# The Impact of Denial-of-Service Attack for Bitcoin Miners, Lisk Forgers, and a Mitigation Strategy for Lisk Forgers

*Davi Alves*


## Abstract

Bandwidth depletion Denial-of-Service (DoS) attack can impact the propagation of a mined block in the Bitcoin blockchain network. On Bitcoin Proof-of-Work (PoW) consensus several machines try to resolve an expensive cryptographic puzzle faster than anyone else and succeed to mine a valid block. Despite a DoS attack impedes one machine to propagate its mined block allowing it to become valid for most peers, there will be several other peers to resolve the puzzle in time, hence the blockchain will continue to grow. However, from the perspective of the owner of the attacked machine, this can be critical because it will not receive a mining reward. This chapter covers such an attack in the Lisk blockchain that utilizes the Delegated Proof of Stake (DPoS) consensus mechanism. A mitigation strategy was created based on two tools that I have created allowing a delegate account to be configured in more than one node, allowing to forge a block even when one of its nodes is under DoS attack. Also, the transaction flood DoS attack is explored, and a mitigation strategy was created for a specific sidechain in the Lisk ecosystem. The mitigation strategy identifies spam transactions and rejects them to be included on the Lisk nodes transaction pool, hence they will not be propagated into the blockchain. Towards the end, I evaluated scenarios and mitigation strategies created for each attack demonstrating solutions for several scenarios.


**Keywords:** Lisk, DoS, PoW, DPoS, bandwidth depletion attack, transaction flood attack, mitigation strategy, dynamic programming

## 1. Introduction

The necessity of a solution to allow transactions between peers without a third-party authority was the main reason for the Bitcoin [1] blockchain creation. The Bitcoin whitepaper demonstrates this necessity as follows: "Commerce on the Internet has come to rely almost exclusively on financial institutions serving as trusted third parties to process electronic payments. While the system works well enough for most transactions, it still suffers from the inherent weaknesses of the trust based model. Completely non-reversible transactions are not really possible, since financial institutions cannot avoid mediating disputes. The cost of mediation increases transaction costs, limiting the minimum practical transaction size and cutting off the possibility for small casual transactions, and there is a broader cost in the loss of ability to make non-reversible payments for nonreversible services. With the possibility of reversal, the need for trust spreads. Merchants must be wary of their customers, hassling them for more information than they would otherwise need. A certain percentage of fraud is accepted as unavoidable. These costs and payment uncertainties can be avoided in person by using physical currency, but no mechanism exists to make payments over a communications channel without a trusted party. What is needed is an electronic payment system based on cryptographic proof instead of trust, allowing any two willing parties to transact directly with each other without the need for a trusted third party. Transactions that are computationally impractical to reverse would protect sellers from fraud, and routine escrow mechanisms could easily be implemented to protect buyers [1]".

Blockchain technology promises to redefine trust in distributed systems by serving as a tamper-proof and transparent public ledger that is easily verifiable and difficult to corrupt [2]. Hence, it is utilized a consensus protocol that allows participants, for example, all copies of the blockchain, to agree on a unique version of the true state of the network without a third authority [3]. Despite blockchain are publicly verifiable and tamper-proof, each node on a public blockchain is a computational node that is exposed on the Internet by default, therefore, exposed to denial-of-service attacks or distributed denial of service attacks (DoS/DDoS), it will be used DoS for DoS or DDoS attacks from here. On Delegated Proof of Stake (DPoS) consensus, a consensus composed by a numeric quantity of nodes configured with delegate accounts, unique accounts responsible to forge blocks and change the state of the network, each node configured with a delegate account has a determined slot of time to forge a block in the network [4].

This chapter exposes two types of DoS attacks that can have a great impact on the Lisk Blockchain network. One attack is called a bandwidth depletion attack that sends several UDP packets at high speed against a computational node. Hence, at the moment a delegate account configured on a single node is successfully attacked by a DoS during its time slot for forging a block, then it cannot forge a block during that specific amount of time exclusively allocated to it. The second type of attack is called transaction flood attack and the main purpose is to send spam transactions that are valid in format, but they have small value and fee costs. The goal of such an attack is to fulfill a queue that resides on each node of the Lisk blockchain called transaction pool. When the transaction pool of a node is full then the node cannot accept any other transaction from anyone in the blockchain, this way all new transactions created and sent to any node are rejected.

A solution for the bandwidth depletion problem was already discussed in [4] and this chapter brings an update on the solution. However, the necessity of a solution for the transaction flood attack is discussed also in [5] and the results demonstrate the resilience of the mitigation strategy that was implemented against such attacks. It was shown two different types of a flood attack, one more expensive, it sends a transaction with proper relay fee and mining fee that would make them first selected for a block not allowing other transactions to be selected first, and another one attack cheaper and powerful in Bitcoin ecosystem. The latter was based in send several transactions with a proper relay fee but a small mining fee, this way such transactions were not selected for a block and always went to mem pool, a queue in Bitcoin.

The necessity for a solution to mitigate transaction flood attacks in the sidechain context and bandwidth depletion attack were the main reason for writing strategies to such problems.

This chapter is organized as follow: Section 2 abords related works, Section 3 presents Lisk version 2.3.8 and brings the first look at Lisk version 5, Section 4 details the impact of DoS attacks in Lisk blockchain, Section 5 demonstrates the strategies to mitigate bandwidth depletion and transaction flood DoS attacks, Section 6 demonstrates results, and Section 7 concludes the chapter.

## 2. Related works

In the context of Blockchain and transaction flood mem pool attacks, there are some papers, and it was identified [5] as relevant for this chapter. It analyzes two specific ways to perform flood attacks in the Bitcoin network. One is based on sending several transactions with appropriate relay fees and relevant mining fee to allow spam transactions to be included in a block not allowing real transactions from real users be included in a block, hence the transaction from real users go to mem pool. In this form of attack, the mem pool starts to grow as a valid transaction is not been chosen by miners since the spam transaction has more relevant fees to be included in a block. However, this is an expensive attack, and a transaction fee already difficult in this scenario. The second mem pool attack [5] states that spam transactions are created by Sybil accounts with a relay fee above the minimum relay fee required for a transaction, however, the transactions mining fee is below the minimum fee to be included directly in a block, this way transactions go to mem pool and stay there. Also, mem pool size grows, and for a real user to create a transaction and have it included in a block it is needed to include a relevant price for the transaction fee. After the same procedures, it was discovered that it increases Bitcoin transaction fee price by time and keeps other transactions away from been included in a block. Finally, [5] proposes a solution for such a scenario that can detect transactions spams and reject properly such transactions.

Vasek et al. [6] presents an empirical study of DoS attacks on the Bitcoin ecosystem, it was identified that most of the attacks occur on currency exchanges, then mining pools. Also, it was analyzed how was constructed the dataset of DoS registers and currency exchanges that already suffered attacks and took countermeasures of anti-DoS protection. Among the conclusion was presented that big mining pools are bigger targets for DoS attacks than smaller mining pools especially because of the mining race on Bitcoin. A mining pool can launch a DoS attack against other mining pools if it realizes that the concurrent mining pool can have mined a block and tries to spread it into the network.

## 3. Lisk Blockchain

The Lisk Blockchain utilizes DPoS as its consensus mechanism to forge blocks and updates the state of the network [2]. DPoS is a consensus that elects the top 101 active delegate accounts based on the higher-weight voted delegates. Only delegate accounts can vote for delegate accounts. The voting mechanism in Lisk 2.x can be represented by the formula below and in **Table 1**:

$$\sum_{i=1}^{n} Xi$$

Lisk nodes communicate between them using a P2P network based on transaction propagation and block propagation. Each node on Lisk utilizes Javascript Object Notation (JSON) objects with blocks and transactions compressed to

| Labels | Definition |
|---|---|
| X | Amount of LSK voter holds |
| i | voter |
| n | Amount of voters |

**Table 1.**
*Vote mechanism formula in Lisk version 2.X.*

communicate [4]. The P2P networks enable scalability on the network, avoid a single point of failure, and prevent a small group of participants controls the network [3]. Also, a consensus mechanism allows establishing a new state in the network. On every 10 seconds, a block is forged on the network including a maximum of 25 transactions in it and only delegate accounts can forge a block in Lisk.

The 5 components of a blockchain that are important to achieve a consensus protocol are: Block proposal that generates blocks and attaches essential generation proofs, Information propagation that disseminates blocks and transactions across the network, Block validation that checks blocks for generation proofs and the transactions within, Block finalization that reaches consensus on certain blocks, and Incentive mechanisms that encourage honest participants and drive the system to move forward [7].

### 3.1 Delegate accounts

Delegate accounts are the unique accounts that can forge a block in the Lisk network. To forge a block each delegate account among the 101 top active delegate accounts has a specific time slot of 10 seconds [2]. There is no competition between delegate accounts during a time slot, each time slot belongs to a single delegate account and only that specific delegate account can forge a block at that moment.

### 3.2 Transaction pool

Transaction pool is a queue that resides in a Lisk blockchain node [2]. By default, this queue has a capacity of 1000 transactions plus 1000 multi-signature transactions. Any transaction created and broadcasted to a Lisk node is stored in its transaction pool. When the moment to forge a block arrives for a delegate account, it gets transactions from its transaction pool and includes them in a block. In Lisk version 2.x the transaction pool queue sorts transaction by their timestamp.

### 3.3 Lisk sidechain SDK 2.3.8

"Lisk sidechain is an exclusive blockchain that accepts custom transactions developed with the Lisk transaction library. Despite that a sidechain accepts only transactions supported by the Lisk blockchain network and custom transactions registered in the sidechain, this is a remarkably interesting characteristic especially because the sidechain does not allow transactions from different sidechains. Furthermore, the transaction space on a sidechain block is reserved only for the custom transactions supported by itself and the transactions supported by the Lisk blockchain. Each node in the sidechain network executes and accepts the same type of transaction. However, until the version used in this paper, 2.3.8, there is no communication yet between Lisk blockchain and the Restaurant sidechain [8]".

### 3.4 A first look in Lisk SDK 5.x

Lisk introduces, on version 3.0, Lisk-BFT, a customizable fault-tolerant framework of consensus algorithms from the famous Paxos protocol [9] to improve efficiency and resistance against Byzantine faults [4]. The Lisk-BFT protocol is a forkful protocol where there is no requirement for a block proposer to achieve consensus before adding more blocks to the block tree, for more information see [10]. Many improvements were added in Lisk SDK 5.x, like an increase of block size to allow a capacity of 128 transactions instead of the only 25 transactions of version 2.x. Also, the increase of the size of the transaction pool, the inclusion of dynamic fees on transfer transactions, and much more can be verified in [11].

## 4. Impact of DoS in Lisk Blockchain

This section starts by bringing two types of DoS attacks that can directly impact the performance of Lisk Blockchain. These DoS attacks are bandwidth depletion and transaction flood attacks in the transaction pool.

### 4.1 Denial-of-service bandwidth depletion attack

Bandwidth depletion attacks can have a great impact on blockchain application owners in the Lisk environment and on delegate accounts. This affirmation is important especially because of DPoS consensus mechanisms in Lisk. In DPoS, delegates are the unique accounts that could forge a block in Lisk, hence if a node configured with an active delegate account is attacked during its time slot and prevents the forge of a new block then the blockchain will lose at least 10 seconds. A delegate time slot is attached to one specific delegate, and only it can forge a block. Another problem caused by a DoS attack against a delegate account is the transactions accumulated in the transaction pool, in this period, no block with transactions can be created during the time slot of the attacked delegate. Any new transactions created by users will arrive in the transaction pool increasing its occupancy rate.

**Figure 1** demonstrates a use case of a Lisk application that allows users to request food online, and each food request represents a single transaction in the blockchain. **Figure 2** demonstrates a bandwidth depletion attack.

**Table 2** shows a scenario of transaction requests in the Lisk application and how much it can be affected by a DoS attack during its most important period of usage.

**Figure 1.**
*Users requesting food online on a Lisk application. Each food request generates a transaction to be submitted into the blockchain.*

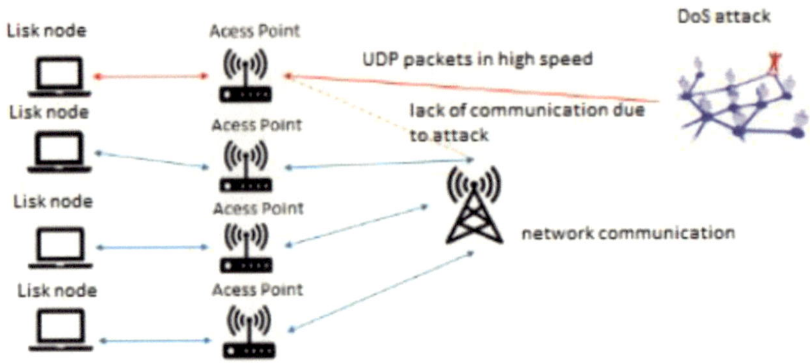


**Figure 2.**
*Bandwidth depletion DoS attack against a delegate account configured on a Lisk node [4].*

| Labels | Restaurant 1 | Restaurant 2 |
|---|---|---|
| Number of tx | 50 | 90 |
| maximum Request time without dos | 20 seconds | 40 seconds |
| Dos duration against 1 delegate account | 15 minutes | 15 minutes |
| total waiting time of a user | 30 seconds | 50 seconds |

**Table 2.**
*DoS attack on a single delegate account affects waiting time. Since a delegate account forges only a single block in a round of 16 minutes, the waiting time during a DoS increases at least by 10 seconds. The most impacted in this scenario is the attacked delegate account that cannot receive a reward as it did not forge a block.*

### 4.2 Transaction flood attack

Transaction flood attack consists of sending an immense quantity of transactions that necessarily do not are related to the business itself. For example, using the same use case of Restaurants and food requests, a transaction flood attack would consist of sending several transactions of small value that are not food requests, they are just transactions with small amount value, but in large volume to surpass the capacity of a block and increase the number of transactions into transaction pool until it gets full. After achieving the capacity of the transaction pool, no other transaction created by any user will be accepted in the transaction pool, they will just be refused and discarded not getting a chance to be included in a block. **Figure 3** demonstrates a scenario that the transaction pool is full, and valid transactions created by a user online on the restaurant website are discarded.

**Table 3** shows a scenario of transaction requests in the Lisk application and how much it can be affected by a transaction flood DoS attack during its most important period of usage.

The next section will investigate mitigation strategies for bandwidth depletion DoS attacks and flood transaction attacks.

## 5. Strategies to mitigate DoS attacks on Lisk Blockchain

In this Section, it will be presented the mitigation strategies for transaction flood attacks and bandwidth depletion attacks.

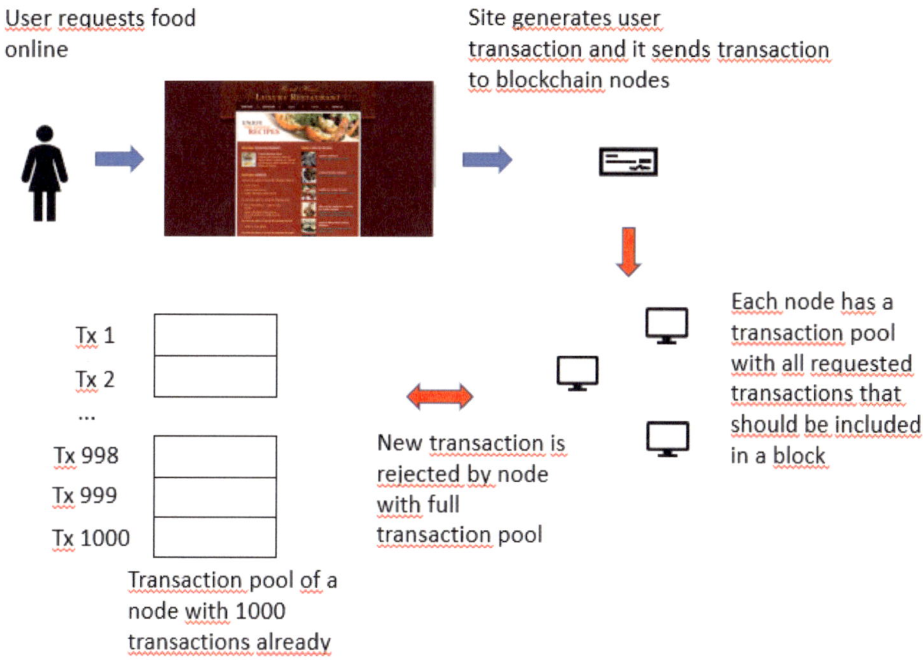


**Figure 3.**
*The transaction pool capacity of 1000 transactions is already full. Any new transaction that arrives on a node is rejected until the transaction pool has some space after including transactions on new blocks.*

| Labels | Restaurant 1 | Restaurant 2 |
|---|---|---|
| Number of tx | 50 | 90 |
| maximum Request time without dos | 20 seconds | 40 seconds |
| Transaction flood Dos duration with full capacity loaded | 15 minutes | 15 minutes |
| total waiting time of a user | 15 minutes +20 seconds | 15 minutes +40 seconds |

**Table 3.**
*Transaction flood DoS attack on blockchain. When the transaction pool capacity is full no other transaction can be included in it. Sporadically, a valid transaction from a user can be added into the transaction pool by chance because of the normal flow of block creations by forgers and the inclusion of transactions from the transaction pool into a block. The most impacted in this DoS scenario are users, applications, exchanges that cannot include transactions because any transaction is rejected.*

## 5.1 Transaction flood DoS mitigation solution

The proposed solution for transaction flood DoS attack is based on the use of dynamic programming to verify if a transaction was already sent before and to verify if a transaction has specific characteristics of a valid transaction in the context of the restaurant business. It was used a use case of a restaurant sidechain to explain the flood transaction mitigation strategy.

### *5.1.1 Restaurant use case mitigation solution*

In a restaurant sidechain [8], it is possible to request food online using a specific type of transaction, the food transaction type. This specific type of transaction has a unique identifier for any transaction and a specific transaction type code. Despite that a sidechain can accept regular transfer transaction types, from a restaurant business perspective, only the food transaction type should be accepted to buy food in the sidechain. Hence, any spam transaction that is not a food transaction should be rejected. Also, if spam transactions are specified as food transaction type, the food type is verified based on another transaction type called menu transaction (MT). The MT type lists all foods accepted by a restaurant with detailed information as price, name, description of all foods. The transaction id is verified to not allow the same transaction id to be used several times into the same block in the blockchain. Finally, spam transactions are also validated in amount and fees. Sender balance is verified before a transaction is spread to other nodes in the blockchain, this reduces the verification impact in case of spam attacks. Any transaction that does not fit in the specified criteria is considered a spam transaction and therefore rejected by the solution. Despite this solution was utilized in a sidechain, it can be adapted to be used directly in a blockchain.

#### *5.1.2 Dynamic programming approach in the solution*

To allow the success of the proposed solution it was specified a threshold number of transactions to be verified for transaction flood attack. This is important because the transaction pool of any node has the size of 1000 transactions capacity by default. To allow a response in time is important to specify a threshold, this way the problem becomes an NP-Complete problem to solve. If no threshold is specified, then as much spam transaction arrives harder the problem becomes to solve, and a solution to mitigate such a scenario becomes more expensive to verify.

### 5.2 Bandwidth depletion DoS mitigation solution

The proposed solution of bandwidth depletion DoS attack mitigates it on an active delegate account configured on monitored nodes of Lisk blockchain as published in [4]. The solution uses tools to monitor the synchronization level of correct blocks in blockchain between connected nodes and allows a delegate account to forge a block and spread it into blockchain nodes even when a specific monitored node is under bandwidth depletion attack. This specific synchronization level is called Broadhash Consensus and is an aggregate rolling hash of the last 5 blocks on de node data storage. When a specific tool called Forge Verifier (FV) detects that a monitored node is under attack, it verifies between all monitored nodes which one has the best synchronization level of blocks in the blockchain, and then it selects the best node for forging at that moment setting the forging status of the best-synchronized node to true and all the other monitored nodes forging status to false. Hence, when a forging slot of a configured delegate account arrives then it can forge a block even when another monitored node is under bandwidth depletion attack. Furthermore, the solution allows the continuity of block generation by the configured delegate account without wasting the slot time allocated to it on each forging round.

#### *5.2.1 Architectures elements*

For the mitigation strategy proposed in [4], there are 3 main architectural elements. The blockchain node API allows to perform HTTP requests to know the synchronization level of a monitored node and therefore allows the FV tool to specify the forging node at that moment. The FV tool continuously monitors nodes configured in a file, called monitor.json, based on synchronization level, then it sends a request to a tool called Forger Lisk (FL). The new possibility in the FV tool

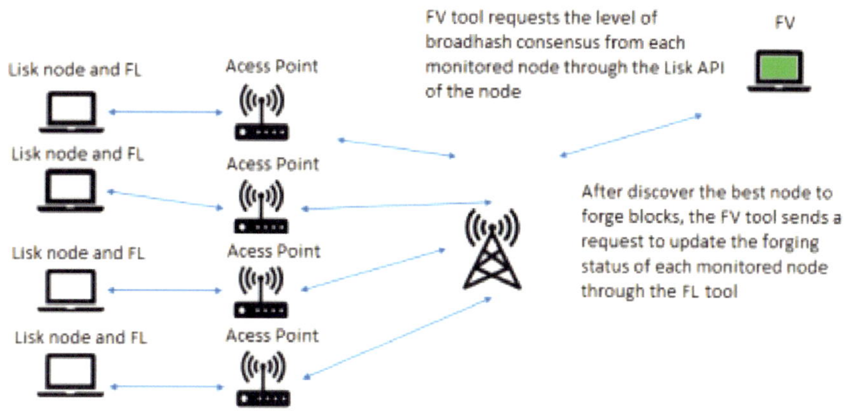


**Figure 4.**
*Architecture elements of bandwidth depletion mitigation solution [4].*

is to configure, in the monitor.json file, the maximum waiting time that FV should wait to retrieve the synchronization level from the monitored nodes specified there. For example, if FV is monitoring 3 nodes, and the maximum waiting time is specified to 10 seconds, then FV requests each node for its synchronization level, which goes from 0 to 100, and all monitored nodes should respond in 10 seconds otherwise they will be considered not accessible nodes by FV. After wait 10 seconds for an answer, FV will choose a node from the nodes that responded to the synchronization level request to be a forger in that round. After FV performs this step, it sends a request for an update to the FL tool, the goat is to update the forging status of monitored nodes through nodes API where the FL tool resides. FL tool exists because it is only possible to change status on any Lisk node through local requests. Hence, FV can reside on any computer that has access to the internet, however, FL needs to reside in the same computational node of a monitored Lisk node (**Figure 4**).

## 6. Performance evaluation

The contribution of this chapter was performed evaluating both DoS scenarios and mitigation solutions in a sidechain network for the transaction flood DoS attack and in the Testnet network for the bandwidth depletion attack. The tools utilized, links, and GitHub source code can be found in Appendices Section.

### 6.1 Transaction flood sidechain performance evaluation

The sidechain results were performed using Lisk SDK 2.3.8 version, 101 delegate accounts, a backend representing one restaurant connected to sidechain nodes, a web application connected to the restaurant backend, a script to generate spam transactions and send them to the restaurant backend. In this solution, the restaurant backend provides the mitigation strategy on its API method (**Table 4**).

#### *6.1.1 Testing environment*

The Lisk SDK 2.3.8 was utilized to create the restaurant sidechain and it was executed in all blockchain nodes. The backend was developed in nodeJS and connected with sidechain nodes. Web application representing restaurant website was developed using React technology.

| Scenarios | DoS flood transactions different from food transaction | DoS flood transactions as food transaction but with different food offered by the restaurant | DOS flood with same transaction ID | Dos flood transactions wallet without enough balance |
|---|---|---|---|---|
| with proposed solution | Mitigated | Mitigated | Mitigated | Mitigated |
| without solution | Denial-of-service | Denial-of-service | Broadcasted to sidechain nodes that refuse spam transaction (overhead) | Broadcasted to sidechain nodes |

**Table 4.**
*In **Table 4** above, it is possible to understand use case test scenarios performed with DoS attack and mitigation solution.*

### *6.1.2 Evaluation and use cases*

A transaction flood attack was performed using a valid balance transfer transaction that was sent every 100 ms against the restaurant backend. During the attack, it was accessed the Lisk restaurant website and performed a valid food request online successfully. The video was recorded and included in Appendices Section.

## 6.2 Bandwidth depletion Testnet performance evaluation

The Testnet results were provided already by [4] and are commented on here. Testnet delegate accounts can be found at Lisk Testnet explorer. The Lisk version utilized was 2.3.x, also it was utilized a new relic tool to record monitored nodes API requests and it was calculated response time for API nodes.

### *6.2.1 Testing environment*

"The Lisk Core version 2.1.3-RC.0 was used on all monitored nodes during the tests on Testnet network and it implements Lisk protocol. It was used Visual Studio Code to implement the tools FL and FV and they were executed on NodeJS version 10+. The chosen network for the tests was Testnet. It was assumed as a premise that bandwidth depletion DoS attacks using UDP protocol against one of the monitored nodes by the FV tool. There are some tools and sites that can perform such types of attacks. Also, videos were recorded, calculated average of requests per minute, and response time was monitored with Newrelic. Furthermore, it was captured Pcap files allowing network data to be analyzed with the Wireshark tool or reproduced with Tcpreplay for better comprehension of the tools developed, the solution strategy, and their behavior on Lisk [4]".

### *6.2.2 Performance analysis*

In the following scenario, it was tested bandwidth depletion attack against one of 4 monitored nodes. Even with the attack against a delegate account configured in one of all 4 monitored nodes, it was possible to forge blocks with a single forger node while the other ones were updated to be non-forgers. Also, a video demonstration of a similar attack was performed and recorded, it is available in Appendices Section. **Table 5** shows the result [4]:

| Definition | node 1 | node 2 | node 3 | node 4 |
|---|---|---|---|---|
| number of requests per minute on node api | 1–2 | 1–2 | 1–2 | 1–2 |
| response time on node API | Good | Good | Good | Insufficient |
| dos number of requests | 0 | 0 | 0 | +5000000 |

**Table 5.**
*Test results of DoS bandwidth depletion against node 4 [4].*

## 7. Conclusions

This paper presented a strategy to mitigate transaction flood denial-of-service attacks reducing overhead in the blockchain, and allowing the spread of valid transactions between nodes. Also, it was presented a strategy to mitigate bandwidth depletion denial of service attack on Lisk allowing, in most situations, the continuity of blocks been forged by a delegate account reducing the probability of creating forks and loss of forging block time slots. As a result of the analysis, it was observed that a restaurant online solution continued to provide service even during the spam transaction attack. Also, it was observed that during the bandwidth depletion denial-of-service attack monitored nodes attended the requests from FV while attacked nodes struggle to respond in time. For future works, I expect to adapt proposed solutions to the new Lisk SDK version 5 with Lisk-BFT consensus.

## Acknowledgements

Our thanks to Sidechain Solutions for an idea of DoS flood attacks that helped me to create DoS flood scenarios.

## Conflict of interest

The authors declare no conflict of interest.

## Notes/thanks/other declarations

I would like to thank Manu from the Lisk team for reviewing Lisk information: "It's possible to configure transaction pool to increase the pool size to accept more transactions, this doesn't solve the DoS attack, but allows a restaurant-like application to process valid transactions in sidechain if required."

### Appendices and nomenclature

Lisk SDK. https://github.com/LiskHQ/lisk-sdk
Visual studio code. https://code.visualstudio.com/updates/v1_50
Nodejs. https://nodejs.org/en/
ReactJs. https://reactjs.org/
New Relic https://newrelic.com/
Bandwidth depletion videos: https://github.com/davilinfo/ACM_conference/tree/master/videos/testnet

Source code mitigation solution of DoS flood attack Lisk restaurant Backend.: https://github.com/davilinfo/intechopen_2020

Lisk Restaurant http://liskrestaurant.com:5000/

Bandwidth depletion and flood transaction videos: https://github.com/davilinfo/intechopen_2020/videos

## Author details

Davi Alves
UFBA, Salvador, Brazil

*Address all correspondence to: davi.alves@ufba.br

## References

[1] Nakamoto, S. 2008. Bitcoin: A peer-to-peer electronic cash system. Available from: http://bitcoin.org/bitcoin.pdf. [Accessed: 2020-12-20]

[2] Kordek, M., and Beddows, O. 2016. White paper: Lisk. Technical report. Available from: https://whitepaperdatabase.com/lisk-lsk-whitepaper/. [Accessed: 2020-12-29]

[3] Pahl, C.; EL Ioini, N. and Helmer, S. A Decision Framework for Blockchain Platforms for IoT and Edge Computing. In Proceedings of the 3rd International Conference on Internet of Things, Big Data and Security - Volume 1: IoTBDS, 105-113, 2018; Funchal, Madeira, Portugal; DOI: https://doi.org/10.5220/0006688601050113

[4] Davi Alves. A Strategy for Mitigating Denial of Service Attacks on Nodes with Delegate Account of Lisk Blockchain. In Proceedings of The 2nd International Conference on Blockchain Technology (ICBCT'20); 2020; Association for Computing Machinery, New York, NY, USA, 7-12. DOI: https://doi.org/10.1145/3390566.3391684

[5] Saad, Muhammad & Kim, Joongheon & Nyang, Daehun & Mohaisen, David. Contra-*: Mechanisms for Countering Spam Attacks on Blockchain Memory Pools. Available from: https://arxiv.org/abs/2005.04842

[6] Vasek, M., Thornton, M., and Moore, T. 2014. Empirical Analysis of Denial-of-Service Attacks in the Bitcoin Ecosystem. In Proceedings of the International Conference on Financial Cryptography and Data Security (Christ Church, Barbados, March 07, 2014). FC'2014, 55-71. DOI: https://doi.org/10.1007/978-3-662-44774-1_5

[7] Xiao, Y., Zhang, N., Low, W., and How, Y. T. 2019. A survey of distributed consensus protocols for blockchain networks. ArXiv, https://arxiv.org/abs/1904.04098v3.

[8] Davi Alves. Proof-of-Concept (POC) of Restaurants food requests in the Lisk Blockchain/Sidechain. ISAIC Conference (2020); Journal of Physics Conference Series, ISSN: 1742-6596, 2021. DOI: https://doi.org/10.1088/1742-6596/1828/1/012110

[9] Lamport, L. 2001. Paxos made simple. ACM SIGACT News 32(4), 51-58. [Online]. Available from: http://lamport.azurewebsites.net/pubs/paxos-simple.pdf. [Accessed: 31/12/2020]

[10] Hackfeld, J., Lightcurve 2019. A lightweight BFT consensus protocol for blockchains. ArXiv, https://arxiv.org/abs/1903.11434.

[11] Lisk 2020. Launch of Betanet v5. Available from: https://lisk.io/blog/development/launch-betanet-v5. [Accessed: 2020-12-30]

Chapter 8

# On Telecommunications Thorn Path to the IP World: From Cybersecurity to Artificial Intelligence

*Manfred Sneps-Sneppe*

## Abstract

The chapter is devoted to the discussion of the telecommunications development strategy. Communication specialists all around the world are facing the problem: how to shift from circuit switching to packet switching. The same problem is the main challenge for the US Department of Defense. We discuss the Defense Information System Network move from circuits to packets, namely, "Joint Vision 2010" doctrine - the implementation of signaling protocol #7 and Advanced Intelligent Network, and "Joint Vision 2020" - the network transformation by the transition to Assured Services Session Initiation Protocol and Multifunctional SoftSwiches. We describe some packet switching shortcomings during the implementation of Joint Vision 2020, namely, the failed GSM-O contract and Joint regional security stacks failures. The Defense Department's newly released cloud strategy positions the general-purpose Joint Enterprise Defense Infrastructure (JEDI) cloud initiative as the foundation. The strategy emphasizes a cloud hierarchy at DoD, but JEDI cloud strategy leaves a series of unanswered questions relating to the interoperability of clouds. The JEDI cloud strategy has based on Artificial Intelligence Initiative. We conclude that the long-term channel - packet coexistence seems inevitable, especially in the face of growing cyber threats.

**Keywords:** circuit switching, packet switching, joint vision 2010, advanced intelligent network, joint vision 2020, SS7, IP, AS-SIP, softswitch, defense information systems network, defense red switched network, artificial intelligence

## 1. Introduction

The chapter is devoted to the discussion of the telecommunications development strategy. Communication specialists all around the world are facing the problem: how to shift from circuit switching to packet switching. The same problem is the main challenge for the U.S. Department of Defense.

*"The DoD today still has analog, fixed, premises-based, time-division multiplexing (TDM) and even asynchronous transfer mode (ATM) infrastructure,"*- is the AT&T view [1]. Really, the DoD has one aging network based on circuit switching point-to-point circuits. This "old" technology requires an expensive support of hardware and additional upgrades with difficulties carried on in the IP era.

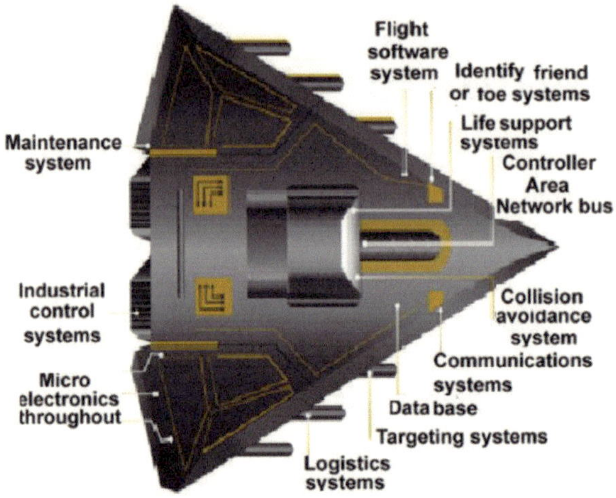


**Figure 1.**
*Software and information technology systems in aircraft (shown for classification reasons) [2].*

Cyber threats are another hard obstacle in a move to IP world. In October of 2018, the Government Accounting Office (GAO) has reported [2], the United States weapons systems developed between 2012 and 2017 have severe, even "mission critical" cyber vulnerabilities. DoD weapon systems nowadays are more and more software dependent (**Figure 1**). We observe the weapons, from ships to aircrafts; use more software than even before. For example, the aircraft F-35 Lighting II software contains eight million lines of code [3].

The rest of paper is as follows. Sections 2 and 3 are about DoD's strategies "Joint Vision 2010" and "Joint Vision 2020," respectively. In Sections 4 and 5, we consider the target DISN infrastructure and Joint regional security stacks. In Section 6, the up-to-date JEDI Cloud Strategy and Artificial Intelligence Initiative have given in short. In the concluding Section 7, we point out rather unsuccessful US Army Regulator fights for IP technology. It is exampled by Defense Red Switch Network using 40 years old ISDN technology.

## 2. Joint vision 2010

The Defense Information Systems Network (DISN) is a global network. It provides the transfer of various types of information (speech, data, video, multimedia). Its purpose is to provide the effective and secure control of troops, communications, reconnaissance, and electronic warfare.

The new DoD Doctrine [4] had issued by General J. Shalikashvili in 1995. This is the keystone document for Command, Control, Communications, and Computer (C4) systems up to now. At that time, "Joint Vision 2010" doctrine met a strong criticism from the US GAO side [5]. The GAO pointed out that the military services are operating as many as 87 independent networks. DISA initiated a similar data call after GAO survey and identified much more - 153 networks throughout Defense.

General J. Shalikashvili had met the technological uncertainty and the controversial requirements. Under these conditions, DISA (Defense Information Systems Agency) has made a very important decision - to use the "open architecture" and commercial-off-the-shelf (COTS) products only for military communication networks. The decision was – to use widely tested developments of Bell Labs, namely, the telephone signaling protocol SS7 and the Advanced Intelligent Network (AIN). These products were rather 'old' at that time: SS7 protocols had developed at Bell Labs since 1975 and defined as ITU standards in 1981.

The details regarding the transition to SS7 and AIN we found in a paper [6] from Lockheed Martin Missiles & Space – the well-known Defense contractor.

SS7 is an architecture for performing out-of-band signaling. In supports the call establishment, routing, and information exchange functions as well as enables network performance. In own order, the Advanced Intelligent Network was originally designed as a critical tool to offer sophisticated services such as "800" calls and directory assistance. The functional structure of the SS7 makes it possible to create the AIN by putting together functional parts: Service Control Point, Service Switching Point, the Service Creation Environment, Service Management System, Intelligent Peripheral, Adjunct, and the Network Access Point. **Figure 2** describes the AIN components that operate in the worldwide military telecommunication network, as well

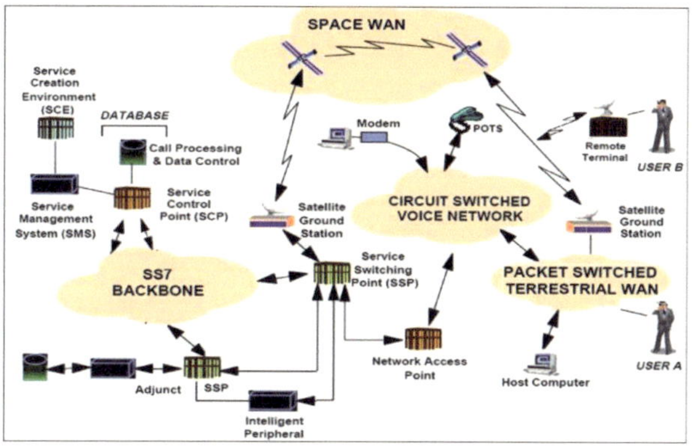


**Figure 2.**
*Advanced intelligent network military service architecture [6].*

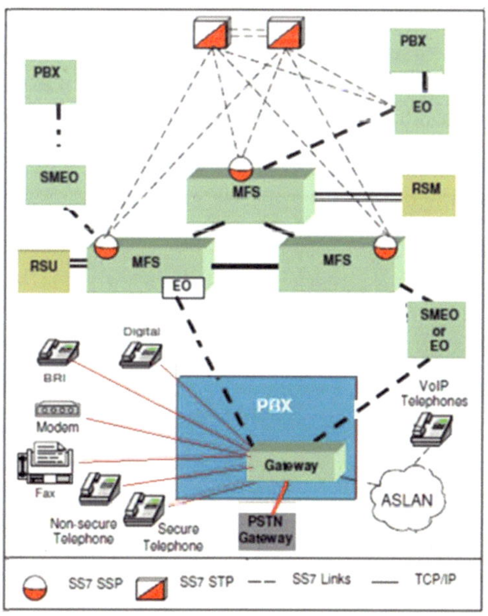


**Figure 3.**
*The simplified DISN view: The current state [7].*

as how they are deployed in SS7 backbone, the space Wide Area Network (WAN), circuit switched voice network and the packet switched terrestrial WAN.

To illustrate the current DISN architecture (**Figure 3**) we refer to the certification of Avaya PBX by DISA Joint Interoperability Test Command in 2012 [7]. The SS7 network is some kind of the nervous system of DISN up to the resent time. It connects the channel mode MFS (MultiFunctional Switches) and many others network components. That is, within the DISN network, the connections have established by means of SS7 signaling. All new terminal equipment what appears is largely IP type, nevertheless SS7 network retains its central place.

## 3. Joint vision 2020: all-over-IP

Just a few years later as "Joint Vision 2010" had introduced, namely, in 2007 the next Pentagon strategy "Joint Vision 2020" appeared. Pentagon published a fundamental program [8]. There we find the most important point: DISN have been built on basis of IP protocol (**Figure 4**). IP protocol should be the only means of communication between the network's transport layer and all available applications. The following 10 years have shown it is an extremely hard challenge.

To implement Joint Vision 2020, the most important step is the replacing of channel switching electronic Multifunctional switches (MFS) by packet switching routers. The transition to IP protocol has based on the use of Multifunctional SoftSwiches (MFSS) and new signaling protocol AS-SIP (Assured Services Session Initiation Protocol). MFSS operates as a media gateway (MG) between TDM circuits switching and IP packet switching components. During the transition phase, MFSS operates under the control of the media gateway controller (MGC). Communications control protocol H.248 has used between MG and MGC. As shown in **Figure 5**, MFSS should be pure packet switch besides DRSN 'island' using ISDN protocol.

A few words about SIP signaling. The SIP protocol widely used now for internet telephony is not able to provide secrecy during transmission (under cyber warfare conditions) and to provide priority calls. Therefore, the Department of Defense ordered to develop one new secure AS-SIP protocol [10]. The AS-SIP protocol turned out to be extremely difficult. AS-SIP uses the services of almost 200 different RFC standards while ordinary SIP uses only 11 RFC standards.

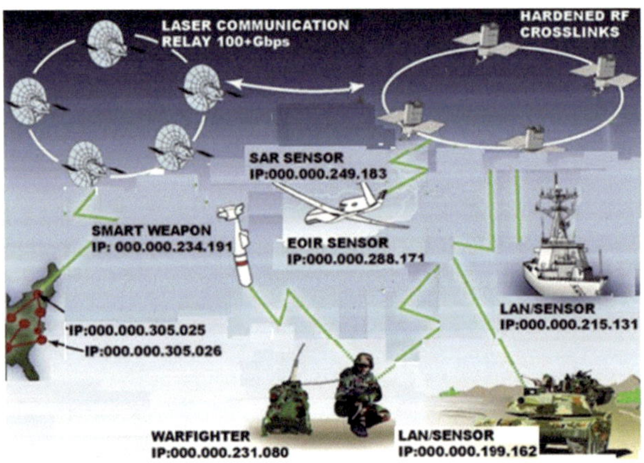


**Figure 4.**
*Joint vision 2020: Each warfare object has own IP address.*

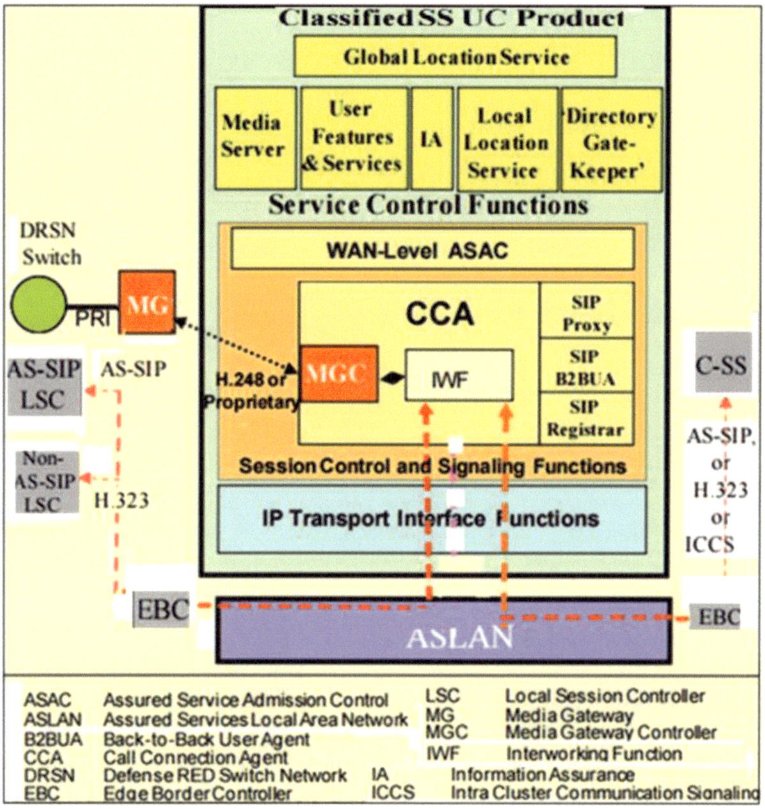


**Figure 5.**
*Reference model for multifunction SoftSwitch [9].*

The aim of "Joint Vision 2020" concept is to implement unified services based on Unified Capabilities concept. Army Unified Capabilities (UC) have defined as the integration of voice, video, and/or data services. These services have delivered across secure and highly available network infrastructure [11].

The following are the basic Voice Features and Capabilities:

- Call Forwarding (selective, on busy line, etc.)
- Multi-Level Precedence and Preemption (MLPP)
- Precedence Call Waiting (Busy with higher precedence call, busy with Equal precedence call, etc.)
- Call Transfer (at different precedence levels)
- Call Hold and Three-Way Calling and many others.

The Unified Capabilities services are covering a plenty of communication capabilities: from point-to-point to multipoint, voice-only to rich-media, multiple devices to a single device, wired to wireless, non-real time to real time, etc. A collection of services include email and calendaring, instant messaging and chat, unified messaging, video conferencing, voice conferencing, web conferencing (**Figure 6**).

**Figure 6.**
*Rich information services surrounding a soldier: not too much?*

## 4. The target DISN infrastructure

The target DISN infrastructure contains two level switching nodes: Tier0 and Tier1 (**Figure** 7). Top level Tier0 nodes interconnect as geographic cluster and a cluster typically contains at least three Tier0 SoftSwitches. The distance between the clustered SoftSwitches must planned so that the return transmission time does not exceed 40 ms. As propagation delay equals 6 μs/km thus the distance between Tier0 should not exceed 6600 km. The classified signaling environment uses a mix of protocols including the vendor-based H.323 and the AS-SIP signaling. The use of H.323 has allowed only during the transition period to all IP protocol based DISN CVVoIP (Classified VoIP and Video). Classified VVoIP interfaces to the TDM Defense RED Switch Network (DRSN) via a proprietary ISDN PRI as a temporary exception.

In October 2010, the US Army Cyber Command had set up. USCYBERCOM is now a part of the Strategic Command along with strategic nuclear forces, missile defense and space forces [13]. One of Cyber Command key tasks is to build Joint Information Environment (JIE) and to implement Single Security Architecture (SSA).

It is worth noting the US Cyber Command activities significantly slow down the transition to IP world. Cyber Command shall receive UC network situational awareness from all network agents including DoD Network Operations Security Centers (NOSCs), and the DISA Network Operation Center (NOC) infrastructure (**Figure** 8). Thus, DISA and the other DoD Components shall be responsible for end-to-end UC network management providing the strong cybersecurity requirements. The solution of cyber defense tasks radically changes the all DISN network modernization plans.

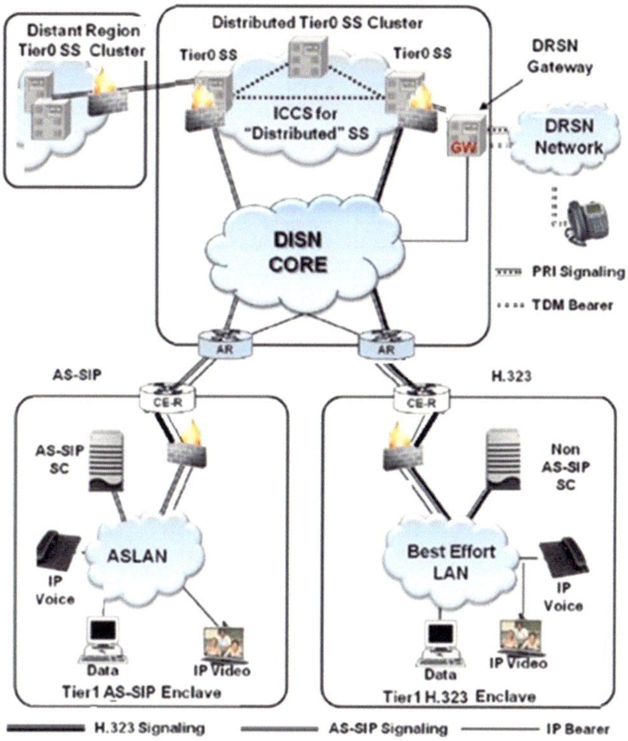


**Figure 7.**
*DISN classified VoIP and video signaling design [12].*

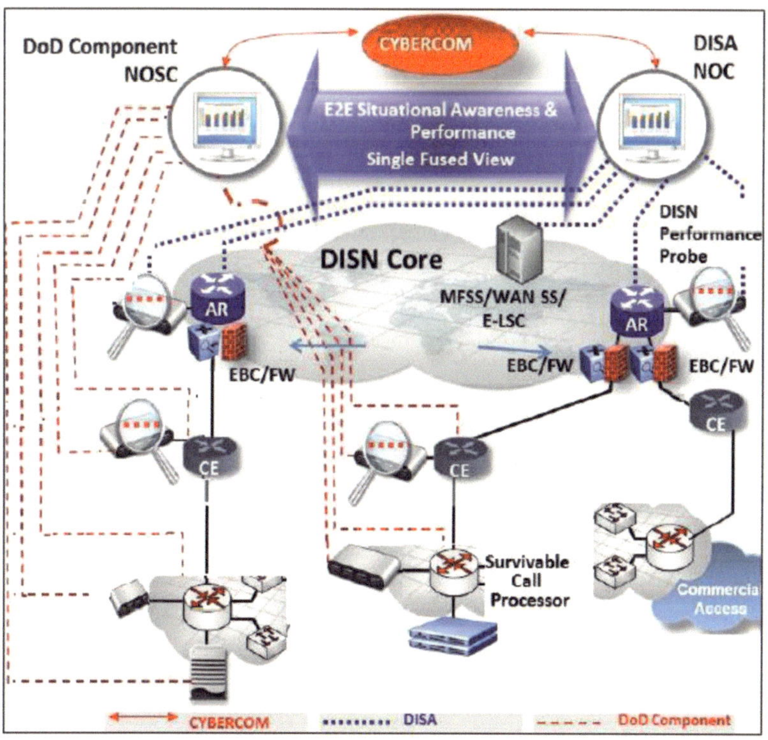


**Figure 8.**
*Operational construct for unified capabilities network operations [12].*

## 5. Joint regional security stacks

The essence of the Joint Information Environment concept is to create a common military infrastructure, provide corporate services and a unified security architecture. The very concept of JIE is extremely complex, and the requirements of cybersecurity make it even more difficult. According to SSA, Joint regional security stacks (JRSS) are the main components of the JIE environment providing a unified approach to the structure of cybersecurity as well as protecting computers and information networks everywhere in military organizations.

JRSS performs many functions as a typical IP-router providing cybersecurity: firewall functions, intrusion detection and prevention, and a lot other network security capabilities. JRSS equipment contains a complex set of cyber-protection software. For example, the typical NIPR JRSS stack is comprised physically of as many as 20 racks containing cyber-protection software and in real time testing information streams. Currently, JRSS stacks have installed for the NIPRNet (Non-classified Internet Protocol Router Network). It has planned also to install the stacks for the SIPRNet (Secret Internet Protocol Router Network). In 2014, 11 JRSS stacks had installed in the United States, 3 stacks in the Middle East and one in Germany. The total amount of works includes the installation of 23 JRSS stacks on the NIPRNet service network and 25 JRSS stacks on the secret SIPRNet network (**Figure 9**). By 2019, it has planned to transfer to these stacks all cybersecurity programs. In nowadays, these programs are located in more than 400 places over the world [13].

The DISN and DoD Component enclaves provide the two main network transport elements of the DODIN (Department of Defense Information Network) with the interconnecting JRSS role as shown in **Figure 10**.

### 5.1 Shortcoming with the GSM-O project

On June 2012, Lockheed Martin won the largest tender for managing the DISN network - Global Services Management-Operations (GSM-O) project. The essence of the GSM-O contract was to modernize DISN management system taking into account the USCYBERCOM security requirements. The cost of work was 4.6 billion dollars for 7 years.

In 2013, the GSM-O team began to study the current state of the DISN management. There are four management centers: two centers in the US - at the AB Scott (Illinois) and Hickam (Hawaii) and two more - in Bahrain and Germany. They are responsible for the maintenance and uninterrupted operation of all Pentagon computer networks. The work is very laborious: there are 8100 computer systems in more than 460 locations in the world, which in turn have

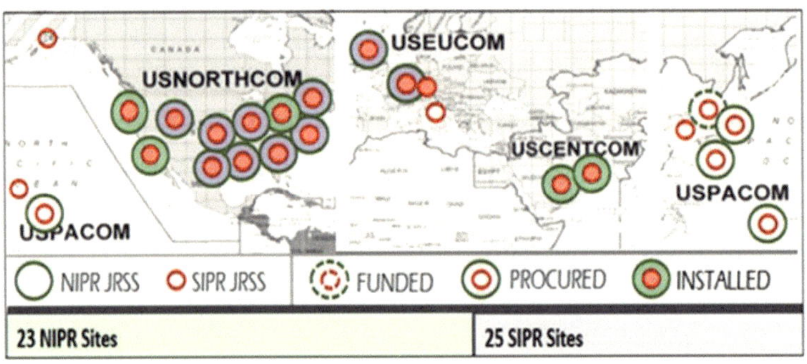


**Figure 9.**
*JRSS current and planned deployments [14].*

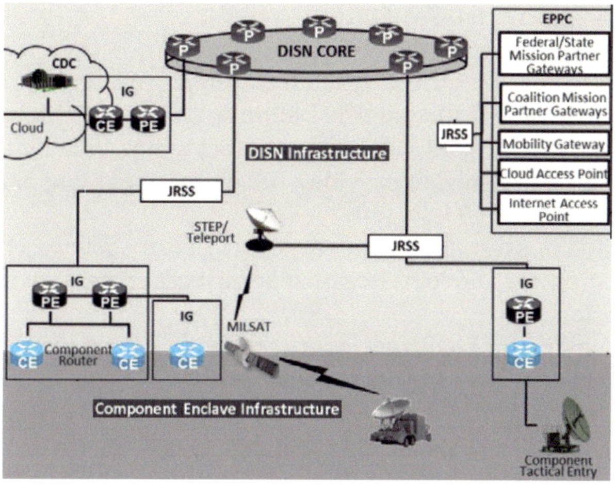


**Figure 10.**
*The leading role of JRSS in DODIN transport [15].*

connected by 46,000 cables. The first deal was to consolidate the operating centers - from four to two, namely, to expand the US centers by closing the centers in Bahrain and Germany.

In 2015, the telecommunications world had shocked by the news: Lockheed Martin is not coping with GSM-O project, not able to upgrade of the DISN network management. Lockheed Martin has sold its division "LM Information and Global Solutions" to the competing firm Leidos. One can assume that the failure of the work was most likely due to the inability to recruit developers. New generation of software makers are not familiar with the 'old' circuit switching equipment and are not capable to combine it with the latest packet switching systems. The more, they should take into account the never cybersecurity requirements [16].

## 5.2 The crucial JRSS failure

This failure is much more scandalous. During several last years, the GAO criticized Pentagon's budget, particularly paying attention to JRSS budget. Many tests regarding JRSS effectiveness were unsuccessful, they were not able to reduce the number of cyber threats [17].

Despite the strong GAO critics, DoD continues the JRSS initiative. DOD stood up 14 of the 25 security stacks planned across the network in the U.S., Europe, and Pacific and southwest regions in Asia. The final security stack has planned for completing by the end of 2019 [18].

Could be fulfilled this Pentagon's grandiose JRSS plan? The complexity of the task, in particular, characterizes the set of requirements for potential JRSS developers, named in the invitations to work for Leidos. The requirement list includes work experience of 12–14 years and knowledge of at least two or more products from ArcSight, TippingPoint, Sourcefire, Argus, Bro, Fidelis XPS, and other companies. In reality, it is extremely hard work to combine all these software complexes for cyber defense. The more, these high-level software developers should work in top-secret environment.

It turned out that the project has a significant critical flaw: JRSS equipment is too S-L-O-W, the time for information stream processing is too long. It sounds like a sentence on the fate of the JRSS project [19]. Despite of that, the JRSS is going on.

### 5.3 Could Leidos cope with GSM-O II?

On October 2018, the Defense Information Systems Agency has released a final solicitation for the potential 10-year 6.52 billion dollars project Global Solutions Management-Operations (GSM-O II). The contract winner is Leidos. GSM-O II is a single award contract designed to provide a full global operations and sustainment solution to support DODIN/DISN [20].

The key GSM-O II attributes include the cybersecurity defense of the DISA enterprise infrastructure and Joint Regional Security Stacks aids in the support to enhance the mission (?).

Now we are looking for Leidos success (or failure). It is yet unclear and 10-year period, of course, is a rather long time. Could Leidos cope with GSM-O II?

## 6. On JEDI cloud strategy and artificial intelligence initiative

The Defense Department's never initiative concerns the cloud strategy. The foundation of cloud initiative is the general-purpose Joint Enterprise Defense Infrastructure (JEDI) [21]. The strategy emphasizes a cloud hierarchy at DOD, with JEDI on top. Many fit-for-purpose military clouds, which include MilCloud 2.0 run by DISA, will be secondary to the JEDI general-purpose cloud.

On April 10, 2019, the Department of Defense confirms that Amazon and Microsoft are the cloud contract winners. The competitors Oracle and IBM are officially out of the race for a key 10 billion dollars defense cloud contract.

Could be the JEDI Cloud Strategy successful? A key technological difficulty for the JEDI project is interoperability of clouds (**Figure 11**). The Pentagon's JEDI cloud strategy leaves a series of unanswered questions that could be reasons for disasters in the future [22].

For internal interoperability, the strategy lays out the correct goal, common data and application standards. There are the 500+ clouds already used within the Pentagon. They have own data formats. Now they need to migrate and interoperate onto the unique JEDI platform.

The next unanswered question regards the JEDI cloud's external interoperability. It concerns a future conflict situation. Would America's allies need to use the same cloud provider (e.g., Microsoft) and the same data-formatting practices as the DoD? The strategy does not discuss these long-term issues.

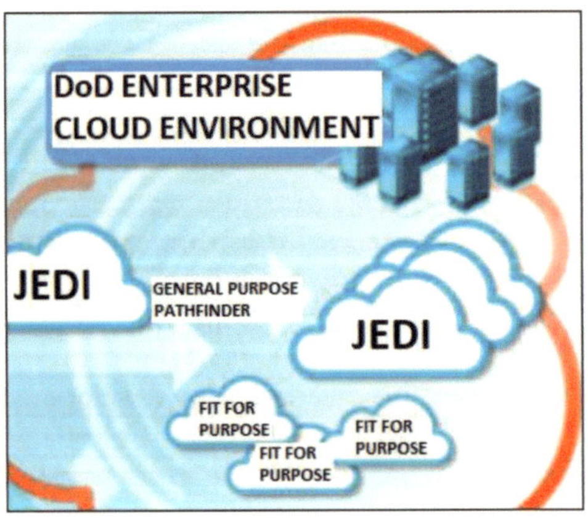


**Figure 11.**
*DoD pathfinder to hybrid cloud environments [21].*

The cloud strategy has started in 2015 by establishing the Defense Innovation Unit (DIU). This DoD organization has founded to help the US military make easier and faster use of innovative commercial technologies. The organization has headquartered in Silicon Valley (California) with offices in Boston, Austin, and some more. The next step – the establishing of Joint Artificial Intelligence Center as a focal point of the DoD Artificial Intelligence Strategy [23].

Taking into account the potential magnitude of Artificial Intelligence's impact on the whole of society, and the urgency of this emerging technology international race, President Trump signed the executive order "Maintaining American Leadership in Artificial Intelligence" on February 11, 2019. That document has launched the American AI Initiative. This was immediately followed by the release of DoD's first-ever AI strategy [24].

Artificial intelligence - this is really one great idea, if it happens be successful. Could it have more success than JRSS initiative?

## 7. Conclusion: do not touch what works

US Army Regulator fights for IP technology but, honesty speaking, unsuccessfully. The Army regulator recognizes in 2017 [25] that there is 'old' equipment on the network: time-division multiplex equipment, integrated services digital networking, channel switching video telecommunication services. According to the document [25], all these services will use IP technology, at least, in the nearest future. As an example, name the instructive claim regarding DRSN:

4–2.d. Commands that have requirements to purchase or replace existing Multilevel Secure Voice (previously known as Defense Red Switched Network (DRSN)) switches will provide a detailed justification and impact statement to the CIO/G–6 review authority.

In conditions of cyberwar, no reason to be surprised that the Defense Red Switch Network (DRSN) will use 40 years old ISDN technology for long time yet, the more – in conditions of cyberwar. DRSN is a dedicated telephone network, which provides global secure communication services for the command and control structure of both the United States Armed Forces and the NATO Allies (**Figure 12**). The network has maintained by DISA and has secured for communications up to the level of Top Secret.

"Red Phone" (Secure Terminal Equipment, STE) uses ISDN line for connections to the network. "Red Phone" operates at a speed of 128 kbps. There is the slot at the

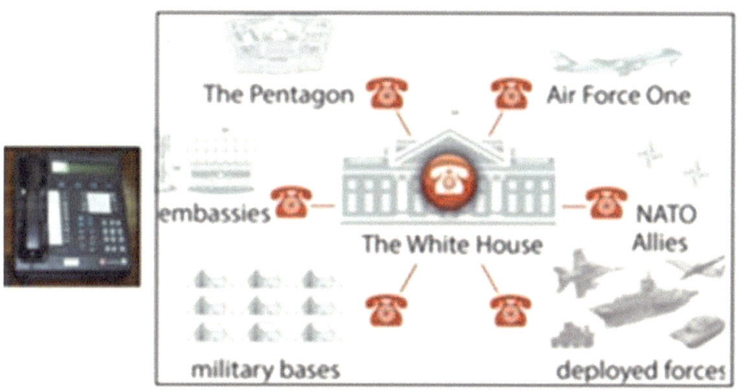


**Figure 12.**
*Secure terminal equipment; note slot in front for crypto PC card (left). The DRSN architecture (right) [25].*

bottom right serving for a crypto-card and four buttons at the top - to select the priority of communications. The STE is the primary device for enabling security. It may be used for secure voice, data, video, or facsimile services.

As we have mentioned above citing the AT&T view [1], the DoD today still has analog, fixed, premises-based, time-division multiplexing and seems could remain for unpredictable period according to the well-known software developers slogan: "Don't touch what works". In conditions of cyberwar, the very transition to internet technologies in telecommunications seems doubtful. Thus, we conclude that the long-term channel-packet coexistence seems inevitable, especially in the face of growing cyber threats.

## Abbreviations

| | |
|---|---|
| AI | artificial intelligence |
| AIN | advanced intelligent network |
| AS-SIP | assured services session initiation protocol |
| CS | capability set |
| DISA | defense information systems agency |
| DISN | defense information systems network |
| DoD | department of defense |
| DODIN | department of defense information network |
| DRSN | defense red switched network |
| GAO | Government Accounting Office |
| IP | internet protocol |
| ISDN | integrated services digital network |
| JEDI | joint enterprise defense infrastructure |
| JIE | joint information environment |
| JRSS | joint regional security stack |
| MFS | multifunctional switch |
| MFSS | multifunctional softswich |
| MG | media gateway |
| MGC | media gateway control |
| NIPRNet | non-classified internet protocol router network |
| RFC | request for comments |
| SIP | session initiation protocol |
| SIPRNet | secret internet protocol router network |
| SS7 | signaling system protocol #7 |
| SSA | single security architecture |
| UC | unified capabilities |
| TDM | time division multiplexing |

## Author details

Manfred Sneps-Sneppe
Ventspils International Radio-astronomy Centre, Ventspils University of Applied Sciences, Ventspils, Latvia

*Address all correspondence to: manfreds.sneps@gmail.com

## References

[1] The Defense Network of Tomorrow—Today. An AT&T Whitepaper. 2018

[2] GAO-19-128. Weapon Systems Cybersecurity. DOD Just Beginning to Grapple with Scale of Vulnerabilities. Report to the Committee on Armed Services, U.S. Senate. United States Government Accountability Office. October 2018

[3] Osborn Ch. Defense Information Systems Network (DISN). An Essential Weapon for the Nation's Defense. Infrastructure Directorate. 16 May 2018. [Internet]. Available from: http://www.disa.mil› Symposium/ [Accessed: 2020-10-14]

[4] Doctrine for Command, Control, Communications, and Computer (C4) Systems Support to Joint Operations. 30 May 1995. [Internet]. Available from: http://waffenexporte.de/NRANEU/others/jp-doctrine/jp6_0(95).pdf/ [Accessed: 2020-10-14]

[5] Defense Networks. Management Information Shortfalls Hinder Defense Efforts to Meet DISN Goals. US General Accounting Office. GAO/AIMD-98-202 July 30, 1998.

[6] Chao W. W. Emerging Advanced Intelligent Network (AIN) For 21st Century Warfighters. In: Proceedings of MILICOM, 1999. IEEE.

[7] DISA. Special Interoperability Test Certification of Avaya S8300D with Gateway 450 (G450). Joint Interoperability Test Command (JITC), 17 Apr 2012.

[8] U.S. Department of Defense. Global Information Grid. Architectural Vision, Version 1.0. June 2007

[9] U.S. Army Unified Capabilities (UC) Reference Architecture (RA). Version 1.0. 11 October 2013.

[10] U.S. Department of Defense. Assured Services (AS) Session Initiation Protocol (SIP). Errata-1, July 2013 [Internet]. Available from: http://www.defense.gov/news/newsarticle.aspx?id=122949/ [Accessed: 2020-10-14]

[11] U.S. Department of Defense. Unified Capabilities Master Plan (UC MP), October 2011.

[12] U.S. Department of Defense. Information Enterprise Architecture Unified Capabilities. Reference Architecture. Version 1.0 January 2013

[13] Metz D. Joint Information Environment Single Security Architecture (JIE SSA). DISA. 12 May 2014. [Internet]. Available from: http://www.esd.whs.mil/Portals/54/Documents/DD/issuances/dodi/801001p.pdf?ver=2018-09-10-082254-477/ [Accessed: 2020-10-14]

[14] JRSS Deployments [Internet]. Available from: https://c.ymcdn.com/sites/alamoace.site-ym.com/resource/resmgr/2017_ace/2017_speakers/2017_AACE_Keynote_Presentations/doc_keynote_Yee.pdf / [Accessed: 2020-10-14]

[15] DoD Instruction 8010.01. Department of Defense Information Network (DODIN) Transport. September 10, 2018. [Internet]. Available from: http://www.esd.whs.mil/Portals/54/Documents/DD/issuances/dodi/801001p.pdf?ver=2018-09-10-082254-477/ [Accessed: 2020-10-14]

[16] Corrin A. Leidos-Lockheed merger changes the face of federal IT. Federal Times. February 5, 2016. [Internet]. Available from: https://www.federaltimes.com/it-networks/2016/02/05/

leidos-lockheed-merger-changes-the-face-of-federal-it/

[17] Cyberscoop. Available from: https://www.cyberscoop.com/audit-warns-of-poor-planning-onvast-pentagon-it-plan/ [Accessed: 2020-10-14]

[18] Williams L.C. DOD CIO: JRSS set for 2019 completion. Mar 05, 2018. Available from: https://fcw.com/articles/2018/03/05/jrss-completionmiller. aspx/ [Accessed: 2020-10-14]

[19] Williams L. C. Is it time to rethink JRSS? Feb 01, 2019. Available from: https://defensesystems.com/articles/2019/02/01/jrss-pause-report-williams.aspx/ [Accessed: 2020-10-14]

[20] Edwards J. DISA Issues Final RFP for $6.5B GSM-O IT Telecom Support Recomplete Contract. October 16, 2018. Available from: https://www.govconwire.com/2018/10/disa-issues-final-rfp-for-6-5b-gsm-o-it-telecom-support-recompete-contract/ [Accessed: 2020-10-14]

[21] Williams L. C. DOD cloud strategy puts JEDI at the center. Feb 05, 2019. Available from: https://defensesystems.com/articles/2019/02/06/dod-cloud-strategy.aspx/ [Accessed: 2020-10-14]

[22] Keelan F. The Pentagon's JEDI cloud strategy is ambitious, but can it work? March 21 2019. Available from: https://www.c4isrnet.com/opinion/2019/03/21/the-pentagons-jedi-cloud-strategy-is-ambitious-but-can-it-work/ [Accessed: 2020-10-14]

[23] Department of Defense. DoD Cloud Strategy Readiness for Artificial Intelligence (Al). December 2018.

[24] U.S. Department of Defense. Summary of the 2018 Department of Defense Artificial Intelligence Strategy: Harnessing AI to Advance Our Security and Prosperity, February 12, 2019. Available from: https://media.defense.gov/2019/Feb/12/2002088963/-1/-1/1/summary-of-dod-ai-strategy.pdf/ [Accessed: 2020-10-14]

[25] Army Regulation 25-13 Information Management. Army Telecommunications and Unified Capabilities. Headquarters Department of the Army Washington, DC. May 11, 2017.

Chapter 9

# Private Investigation and Open Source INTelligence (OSINT)

*Francisco José Cesteros García*

## Abstract

Social Networks has changed the way of developing an investigation as far as people use to explain, graph, show and give details about their life. It is so because people need to communicate and need to share feelings and passionate life. Based on these facts, private investigation uses the information in public databases to make an approach to people, their facts and their details that they publically expose to the rest of the world. So, this chapter explains how to use the OSINT (Open Source INTelligence) methodology for legally become part of the steps on a private investigation. The information is growing up and people expose their images, comment and reference to other ones so it facilities the investigation of getting results. Actually OSINT is the first step that private investigation must consider and this chapter covers and explains why and how to do this.

**Keywords:** OSINT, investigation, social networks, private investigation, private detective

## 1. Introduction

In the age of technology, obtaining information is basically a matter of managing search engines, having a working methodology, knowing how to correlate data and later, drawing conclusions [1].

It is obvious that the information circulates and is not always true, has biases and must be analyzed with prudence and know-how. Anyway, fake news is part of our life, up to day.

Therefore, in the discipline of intelligence analysis, there are multiple methodologies to generate information products with which to make decisions in personal and business life.

One of the mechanisms is what we call "the use of open sources", or in other words, using Open Source INTelligence (OSINT) [1], which becomes a basic part of the research, which must be carried out with care and methodology, avoiding biases and finally verify the information in the field.

Undoubtedly, OSINT is an essential element in the investigation, both previously, to be able to "get an idea", and to go deeper into fundamental aspects of the person or company investigated.

However, the belief that the information is free is not the case and the use of the following premises should be considered in an OSINT analysis [2]:

- Free information sources.
- Sources of payment information.

- Information sources with annual subscription.
- Time spent in the search, analysis and generation of the final product.
- Time spent verifying or biasing the information obtained.

Therefore, far from being a low-cost, low-profile intelligence product, OSINT research requires professionalization of the investigator and:

- Investigator's training.
- Identify sources of use and use credibility, bias and veracity of the information.
- Annual subscriptions with the implicit cost.
- Work methodology.
- Computer tools for the correct analysis, data correlation and generation of the final product [3].
- Research discipline.

Intelligence is the base of success in all fields. Intelligence is used for the military, political, business, and of course private level and investigation. Currently, all organizations and companies, of a certain level, use Intelligence to start, develop, and succeed [4].

If a supermarket wants to expand and locate in another country, it will first have to obtain all the legal, economic, structural, and competitive data, in order to make a decision. In this way it can decide the most suitable country for its investment. We can imagine any other type of business that wants to develop internationally, and it will have to follow the same steps.

Intelligence is used practically since human existence. But, obviously, the OSINT is much more current, since the new technologies have allowed this type of research in Open Sources [5]. And there are more and more research possibilities in this regard, because there is more and more public information available to everyone.

That is why it is essential in the process of obtaining information, to take the utmost care not to leave a trace, since if not, we will go from being analysts to being objects of investigation.

The basis of the Intelligence process is obtaining information. And the first step to obtain information is to search in Open Sources, known as OSINT.

The basis of the private investigation is getting the proof, based on experience, know-how, methodology, sources, man in the field and legal process [6]. So, we are moving on a briefly discovery of these elements and processes on this chapter.

## 2. Searching information in open sources

During the process of the investigation we will always find two different handicaps that should be taken in consideration:

- Amount of information: Need to be limited.

- Quality of information: Data that are not relevant and should be classified.

As in any research process, it is necessary to follow a methodology to obtain results. The OSINT intelligence cycle follows the same methodology as the intelligence cycle, but using Open Source Research tools.

This is the OSINT process [5] we follow in a private investigation:

1. Requirements: Determine which ones are the objectives to investigate. What information is needed to obtain.

2. Information Sources: Establish the information sources that will be needed to obtain the information and, if payment information is required, take into account the cost involved.

3. Acquisition of Information: Search for information in established sources.

4. Processing: With the information obtained, the necessary reports will be made, extracting the useful data for the pursued objectives, and with the same rule of the 3 "C's" that is used for Press News:

   Information needs to be:

   - Clear

   - Concise, and

   - Concrete

5. Analysis: Once the reports are completed, the information obtained will be analyzed, giving meaning to the data found. What they mean for our interests.

6. Intelligence: The analysis will determine the actions that we must carry out based on the information obtained.

We have to give answers to the following questions:

- Who?

- When?

- Where?
- How?
- Why?
- What?

Some of the answers are gotten from the OSINT investigation [5] and traces the way for the field investigation, but, we have always to consider the credibility of the source and the reliability of it.

The information is coming from different sources (with its own reliability and credibility) and should be checked and not taken as valid information [7]. Disinformation is part of what people and companies usually do.

Because of it, the OSINT process has to consider this classification methodology (see **Table 1** below).

As a result, each piece of information is classified and evaluate, answering the big "W's" as follow:

Example: Evaluation of the source: B/2, A/1, C/3... [8].

### 2.1 Type of open sources (for OSINT)

Once we have written about open sources, let us explain the reader where we can search and make the investigation, as an example, but it is not limited to these sources [9]:

- Internet search engines [10] (most used search engines: Google, Bing, Yahoo, DuckDuckGo, Ecosia, IxQuick, Ask, Lycos, Yandex, Dogpile, Startpage, Peekier, Webcrawler, Yippy, Exalead, Factibites, Wayback Machine, Gibiru, Siri, Alexa, etc.) and using the logical operators they have.
    - Google Dorks and its Boolean operators, symbols and commands can be used for explicit and specific search.

        1. AND, OR, NOT, XOR: (example: thread AND jihadism)

        2. (): (example: (thread OR terrorism) AND (islamism OR jihadism)

        3. Operators: *, #, ¿, $, €, "", for example

        4. Symbols: <, >, =, <>, <=, >=

| Reliability | Credibility |
|---|---|
| A – Completely reliable | 1 – Confirmed by other sources |
| B – Generally reliable | 2 – Probably |
| C – Reliable enough | 3 – Possibly true |
| D – Generally unreliable | 4 – Doubtful |
| E – Unreliable | 5 – Unlikely |
| F – Cannot appreciate reliability | 6 – Credibility cannot be appreciated |

**Table 1.**
*Reliability and Credibility of information sources.*

5. Commands: define: term; filetype: term; site: site/domain; link: url, etc.

6. And many others operators of each engine.

- Websites, Forums and Blogs from different countries and languages based on the information we are looking for, the people, the specific information and themes.

- IP [11] and Device locators (networks, open ports, webcams, printer and many other IP devices): Shodan.io, Myip.es, Ip-address.com, Iplocation,net, Httrack.com, Pastebin.com, Whois.com, Robtex.com, IANA, RIPE, etc.).

- Social Networks [12] (Youtube, Vimeo, Instagram, Twitter, Facebook, Pinterest, Reddit, Vkontakte, Tumblr, Linkedin, Infojobs, Snapchat, and so many others including those for Contacts and Couples like Meetic, eDarling, Badoo, etc.).

- Maps (internet) and Geolocation of data (Iplocation.net, Coordenadas-gps.com, Mapsdirections.info, Mapscoordinates.net, etc.).

- Magazines (different languages, countries and specific search engines based on the information and goals we are following).

- Newspapers (exactly the same as before).

- Conferences where people could participate, even in academic, public or private that are published in corporate webs.

- Radio and Television broadcasts

- Official Gazettes and Registration: Civil Registration, Penalties Fee Registration, Property Registration, Commercial Registration, etc.

- Organizations: Professional Associations, Professional Colleges, NGOs, etc.

- Mobile applications: WhasApp, Skype, Telegram, Signal, etc.

- Emails pages that we can use them for generating a temporal email [13] or for looking in case the accounts could be hacked (Pastebin.com, Haveibeenpwned.com, Shodan.io, Verifyemailaddress.org, Mxtoolbox.com, Toolbox.googleapps.com, Mailnator.com, Guerrillamail.com, Temp-mail.org, Correotemporal.org, Throwawaymail.com, Maildrop.cc, Mailnator.com, etc.).

- Images scanning: By looking for images in internet and checking the metadata and location or even a possible fake image of a profile (Google Images, Bing, Tineye, Yandex, Revimage.com, Pictriev.com, Exiftool, Fotoforensics.com, Photo-forensics, etc.).

These sources of information can be classified into:

- Free databases and registers
- Free databases but profile requirement
- Free databases but real profile and request (for example a death certificate)
- Payment sources

And many others tools that frequently appears and disappears in the internet world [14]. Basically talking, we are opening a tremendous world of investigation where, as talked before, know-how, experience, technical knowledge and legal procedures must be under consideration.

As the reader can image, the gather of information is a tough procedure that requires different use of tools, technical background and methodology for the identification, analysis and classification of the information.

And this is part of the education and training that private detective should get as part of the evolution, the state of the art and the success of the private investigation agency (so, the business itself).

But, who can we work for getting the information without been discovered? This is part of the next point.

## 3. Secure investigation using legal tools

Social Networks (SN) are an unimaginable source of information [15] and that makes them an ideal place to locate relevant information on the topics to be investigated.

However, not everything that is on social networks, not even what each company or each person puts is real. Various considerations:

- Each one says what he wants for personal interests.
- Not everything that is said is true and must be checked.
- They have a bias based on who the information is directed to.
- They can also be forwarded fake news.

Therefore, as a premise, and highlighting what we have already been exposing to the reader throughout the chapter, the sources, in this case, social networks (SN), must be:

- Evaluated
- Classified
- Collated

And this is the relevance of having a research, evaluation, classification and methodology for investigating inside the sources.

Many photos, videos and texts are posted that, at first glance, seem real and interesting, but when it is necessary to analyze to make a report, it is convenient to check because if not the credibility of the analyst, remains low if the information has not been verified, and may have financial and legal consequences within an investigation.

Once we have put these premises ahead, we must also remember a legal aspect [16] that is more than important, the usurpation of identity.

> *"Identity theft, also called the crime of usurpation of marital status or identity, consists of the action of appropriating a person of the identity of another, posing as her to access resources and benefits, acting in legal traffic pretending to be the person impersonated. The action described in the criminal type is to usurp the civil status of another".*

Because of this penal action [17], the way remains to build ad-hoc profiles for research. And this is part of the investigation process, methodology, time and technical resources.

On the other hand, the creation of profiles must meet clear objectives:

- Be according to the goal to be investigated.
- Do not use copyrighted or other people's photos.
- Take specific photos and edit them so that they are consistent with the case and can reflect interest for the person or company to investigate.
- Profiles are created, fed and populated and when done they are simply dropped.
- Research profiles are not recyclable. They should not be used in other investigations.
- They must be created in safe places or with non-traceable media.
- They have to show relevant information for the investigation and reliable content for the investigation.
- When you do not reach people directly, you have to look for an alternative route through friends or interests, you have to build the necessary coverage.
- The coverage, direct or indirect, must also be attractive to the goal of the investigation.
- The profiles to be created and the names to be used must be in the language, culture and form of expression of the group, person or sector of the company. You have to take care of the contents and make them credible, including other languages.
- And assign specific cellular phones to the investigation and contact.

Once you decide to undertake an investigation obtaining information from social networks, you must consider:

- What SNs are the appropriate ones for this type of investigation, since Facebook is not the same as LinkedIn, Twitter or Instagram, but there are many as we have introduced early before.

- Consider the ages of the people to be investigated and their origins, since ages mark one or another SN and cultural origins as well.

- The profiles can use the same name in all of them, but perhaps it is worth reflecting on whether for a specific investigation, it is better to use different names in different SNs in order to complement information or avoid blocking.

So with these working premises, and knowing that creating the profiles, feeding them and having them ready to work takes a long time, it is good to consider and keep in mind that:

- Investigations into SN sources take a long time.

- They require prepared profiles, which take time to create and provide adequate content.

- They are not fast.

Some recommendations to be considered:

- It is used to create emails and profiles on social networks when you are traveling, because with them created and saved, they are from different cities or non-native countries and are very useful for investigations and traces of them.

- Provide the profiles that you create with certain information of interest so when the operation of investigation is launched, takes less time and reflects more seniority in the profile.

- Manage information in the profile according to the name, interest and content with which we want to use it later.

The usual formulas to obtain information in SN are:

- Use previously created profiles that have content according to the topic to be investigated.

- Contact the people or companies to investigate using these profiles created ad-hoc.

- Use safe navigation and if possible outside the home.

- If necessary, purchase operator cards and use your mobile for internet connection instead of ADSL at home/office.

- Extreme security measures in communications and traces, firewall, incognito and secure browsing, do not leave traces in search engines or even use a cyber coffee or telephone booth.

- Make friends with the person or company and also seek common interests, common friends and provide credibility and a high number of friends and common acquaintances.

- If possible, illustrate with edited photos the contents of the profile to give it greater credibility and seriousness.

- If it is not possible to get a friendship directly, you have to think about:

    - Go through other friends, family, etc.

    - Have topics of interest to this person and express it so that they accept.

    - Refine the profile created with aspects of interest to your contacts in such a way that they are the ones who introduce us.

So with these recommendations and advises, let us talk something about three other secure things to consider:

- Internet Address (IP) and Virtual Private Networks (VPNs)

- Secure browsing

- Email creation

### 3.1 Internet address and virtual private networks (VPNs)

Another aspect that should be exposed and that says a lot in the investigation of open sources and the obtaining of information, is to obtain the IP [18], or at least, to know from where the entries can be produced, not always easy, and much less when try to follow criminals.

Although obtaining the IP of the people to investigate is difficult, our IP could be also traced and the relevance of the investigation is the security of the agent.

For that reason, we must protect our IP address using different methods:

- Using SIM cards and mobiles that we can throw (at least the SIM card) when we have finished the investigation. This SIM card must be "not traceable" or at least not our name or agency registered.

- Using Virtual Private Networks (VPNs) [19], technology that (free or payable) allows us to connect to internet using a tunnel where our IP original is converted to another, protecting in this way, our location and identity.

- Using TOR (dark web browser), which uses a VPN and relays to jump between one to another node in the internet world.

As per using one or several of these mechanisms we can make the investigation by securing our access and blocking our connection, direction, and location to others. This is the first step, to protect our location and work on locate the investigated people.

As we have briefly explained in point 2.1. of this chapter there are different tools for executing the IP investigation and there are different tools of VPN software for laptop and mobile to protect ours.

### 3.2 Secure browsing

The software mostly used for this kind of investigation is TOR browser, which refers to The Onion Router (TOR) Project [20].

TorProject.org

This navigation is what we call, *The Dark Web [21]*.

A part of the deep web consists of internal networks of scientific and academic institutions that form the *Academic Invisible Web*, which refers to databases that contain technological advances, scientific publications, and academic material.

But there are more services published in this dark web:

- Financial services: bitcoin laundering, stolen PayPal accounts, cloned credit cards, banknote counterfeiting, anonymous money wallets, etc.

- Commercial services: sexual exploitation and black market, stolen gadgets, weapons and ammunition, false documentation and drugs.

- Anonymity and security: instructions to enforce privacy in TOR, especially for a sale or in bitcoin transactions.

- Hosting services: web hosting and image storage where privacy comes first. Some prohibit uploading illegal files and others have no restrictions.

- Blogs, forums and image boards: apart from those related to buying and selling services, two frequent categories of this type of community are hacking and the exchange of images of all kinds.

- Mail and messaging services: some email addresses are free (generally they only offer webmail) and others are paid, with SSL and IMAP support.

- Hacking services: of websites, emails and paid.

- Political activism: censored file sharing, hacktivism, and even a page to organize "mass-funded assassinations." Anarchy is the predominant ideology on the deep web.

- State Secrets: There is a copy of WikiLeaks on the deep web, and several pages where to publish secrets with little activity.

- Books: virtual libraries that measure several gigabytes and contain thousands of ebooks in different formats. Many of them are free of copyright and others are illegally distributed in direct download.

- Erotic pages: paid and free access. The subcategories are diverse and without any moral limit.

Investigations not always require getting into the deep web to look for information, but at least require protecting ourselves from being located. Using the protection of the IP and using an incognito browsing and VPN (TOR for example) we use a double layer of protection who isolate us from being detected and pursue.

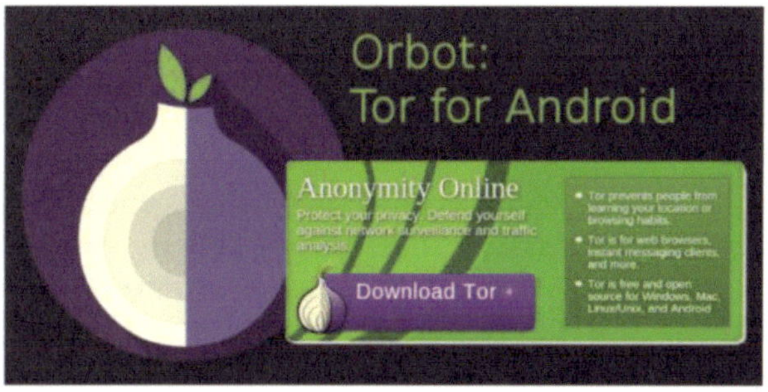


In this moment of the lecture, we have enough information to understand risks of the investigation, technical knowledge we require and evaluate the investigation as a professional way of working, not for amateurs and with time to be paid for.

### 3.3 Email creation

Adding to the previous point, not enough as many webs and search process require an email address; we have to mention something like the creation of emails accordingly, again, with the goal of the investigation.

The registration to create a social network profile requires an email address, and perhaps, depends on the SN, a mobile number.

¡Never use your personal profile or cellular number!

The creation of an email, some years ago, was tremendously easy and limited, not today that we have a lot of services for creating temporal emails or real email for working alone.

But, again, to create an email account, we need an internet connection, so please, remember the previous recommendation, ¡protect your IP! by using the recommendations.

You cannot create a profile in social network using TOR, you cannot create an email account using TOR, but you can protect your IP address by using any other technologies (VPN for example), or using a cyber coffee or when traveling, creating the email account from the hotel. In this way you preserve your home/office IP address.

Once you are sure that your IP address is not conducting to your real IP, then you can use the temporal email accounts creation we have exposure in the point 2.1 of this chapter or you can use the Google, Hotmail, Yahoo, etc. services for it.

The goal is to create a secure email for using temporally to create the SN profile, or not so temporal, to be used contacting with the investigate people or company so it can be left when finished.

However the creation of an email account is very simple, keep in mind what you need for your investigation:

- Email account to be used only for SN profile creation.
- Email account to contact with the investigated.
- Email temporally account.
- Email of a known service provider to give some more credibility.
- Email with a specific goal in mind.

## 4. 360° surveillance

It is very clear, in this page of the chapter, that we are generating digital tracks continuously and because of that, we are creating a digital footprint [22].

Once again, to follow up the footprint of a person requires methodology, knowledge and technical resources for the investigator.

360° surveillance consists in monitoring the footprint that a person, profile, email, etc. (all of them resources of the internet world) are leaving while writing, browsing, using internet from any device.

People use mobile phones, tablets and laptops for accessing resources, services and use the internet applications so the device is another footprint.

It means that the device has an operating system, a geolocation, a camera, a timetable of use and so many characteristics.

Monitoring with methodology we can use the information of the footprint to determine, for example, but not only:

- Where the investigated people are.
- How is using the SN profiles
- When they are mostly connected.
- Which device is mostly used.
- Some characteristics and operating system of the device.
- Sometime way tracking to office.
- Habits and mostly frequently zones or restaurants.
- Comments they write in Blogs and shopping references.
- Determine the style of life.
- Determine if they are always in the same location or move during the weekend and where.
- When they write, where are they writing.
- Etc.

A lot of information is part of this footprint that can be follow up with specific tools and because of the device connection to internet.

360° surveillance is not only monitoring the people investigated and can be done for monitoring family members also, so it creates a big hole for VIP people.

If someone wants to track and monitor the life style or life of an executive, for example, can be done by contacting directly with them or through different profiles, including their children or friends.

Because of public profiles of executives and VIP people in SN, they are exposed to be monitor by any people, with or without a real profile. Part of the investigation that private detective can do is the counter surveillance.

Counter surveillance looks for monitor who is accessing specific profiles, claim for friendship and contact with their victims.

The 360° surveillance can be executed by any person, with good or bad intentions, for example to discover habits, where the person is, life style, if they are at home or vacation, or used for making some scratches, strikes, disturbances, etc. against the company, the executive or to follow up a singer, a football player or disturb them at a disco.

These are some examples, but we leave the reader imagine what can a person do with information of other, for good or bad things.

Based on the reality of the digital footprint, the counter surveillance looks for a protection of the person and their family in order to continuously monitor their network activity, search for any news and alerts, and protect the digital image, the physical person and guarantee the integrity of the information, the person, the family and the corporate image.

360° surveillance and counter surveillance is intended to protect people and companies from scams, scratches, damage to the image reputation, and of course to protect their exposure perimeter.

Open sources, company's news, blogs, social networks, emails, etc. are part of the sources that give a lot of information to others, including criminals, and private detective try to protect their clients of all these risks, not only on the field, either in the digital field.

We are always leaving digital tracks to other by:

- Using different communication channels through internet services.
- Actors that interact with our profiles.
- Activity we realize on internet by purchasing, navigation, cookies, profiles, alerts, etc.
- Blogs, Chats, Recommendations we leave.
- Contents we visit.
- And do not forget that you mobile continuously interact with Google (Android account, Samsung Account) or Apple (iCloud).
- Using cloud storage (Google Drive, iCloud, Dropbox, etc.)
- Sharing images of vacation, for example.
- Sharing the training routes and records.

- Using Youtube.
- Using Google account by default without blocking some services.
- Etc.

Hopefully for the reader, the private investigator has the knowledge to protect companies and private persons, family and friends also and to train, investigate and offer security once analyzed the exposure perimeter, the risk and the goals of the people/family or company.

Private investigation agencies are focused on exactly that, protect and investigate their customer, and in this technological times, digital tracks are part of the protection and investigation that is mostly required.

## 5. Conclusions

After reading this chapter we expect that the reader has a very clear knowledge of what a private investigation agency can do for their security and what is the way of working for getting the information through the internet services and methodology for searching, before going to the field and certify the information gotten.

It is obvious, after reading the chapter, that everyone is having a digital track at least for having a mobile phone connected to internet and this digital connection generates a risk.

The risk is part of the evolution and it is part of the technology. Nothing is 100% secured but we can and we must put the resources to protect ourselves and our family.

WiFi (Wireless Fidelity) at home is another hole of security, especially as most of the routers installed have not changed the password and default passwords are on public technical webs.

By accessing the WiFi at home, every single device connected to it can be hacked and of course information of the devices, stolen.

Profiles, passwords, emails, and devices are objects of desire for criminals and private investigation agencies should improve their investments and knowledge to adapt their detectives to new technologies and methods.

Private Detectives are used to work on the field but in this times, the first thing should be look for information by using OSINT techniques, analyze the information and then verify this on the field. It gives the detective a better understanding of the information and investigation and allow them to be cheaper and more professional.

Of course, OSINT is not the only way of working as many people do not have profiles or share information or do not like to navigate, but OSINT should be the first step in any investigation to have any more information, even the lack of information is, of course, information.

Detectives need to recycle and clients need to understand that OSINT investigation takes a lot of time and should pay for it. It is a mix between working in an office and working on the field. The time required for each kind of investigation need to be considered, evaluated and put in place while preparing the offering to the client.

Open Source INTelligence and Private Investigation have a lot of things in common and both are part of the world of getting information, complementing each other.

It requires methodology, technical resources, education, time and experience to move on private investigation without trespassing laws and be able to add value to a field investigation and success of the customer on a trail.

## Acknowledgements

The author declares no conflict of interest.

Special thanks to my family, colleagues and company that give me some time to write and develop the chapter.

It took some personal time for structuring, develop and write it and this time has been stolen to all of them.

Thanks to the editor for allowing me to write an specific chapter of private investigation and how it can help people and companies to success and follow up situation of conflicts and negotiations.

From the private investigation sight, I wanted to explain the methodology, steps and legal process in order to let readers know that the investigation is something serious, professional and it is far from movies and amateurs who makes things happen for entertainment or for getting some illegal money with criminal offenses.

## Author details

Francisco José Cesteros García
Cuzco Detectives, Madrid, Spain

*Address all correspondence to: fjcesteros@cuzcodetectives.com

## References

[1] INTelligence. Open Source Intelligence. 2010. Available from: https://www.cia.gov/news-information/featured-story-archive/2010-featured-story-archive/open-source-intelligence.html [2020-11-28]

[2] OSINT, the power of the information. 2014. Available from: https://www.incibe-cert.es/blog/osint-la-informacion-es-poder [2020-11-28]

[3] Practical Open Source Intelligence methodology. 2012. Available from: https://medium.com/seconset/practical-open-source-intelligence-methodology-4ddc57eac917 [2020-11-28]

[4] Ciclo de Inteligencia. CNI. Available from: https://www.cni.es/es/queescni/ciclo/#:~:text=Se%20entiende%20por%20Ciclo%20de,%2C%20Obtenci%C3%B3n%2C%20Elaboraci%C3%B3n%20y%20Difusi%C3%B3n. [2020-12-30]

[5] Defining second generation Open Source Intelligence. 2018. Available from: https://www.rand.org/content/dam/rand/pubs/research_reports/RR1900/RR1964/RAND_RR1964.pdf [2020-12-30]

[6] Servicios de Investigación privada. Derechos y obligaciones. 2020. Available from: https://cuzcodetectives.com/servicios-de-investigacion-privada-derechos-y-obligaciones/ [2020-12-30]

[7] ¿Qué son y para qué sirven las fuentes de información OSINT? 2020. Available from: https://papelesdeinteligencia.com/que-son-fuentes-de-informacion-osint/ [2020-12-28]

[8] Source evaluation and information reliability. 2015. Available from: https://www.first.org/global/sigs/cti/curriculum/source-evaluation [2020-11-28]

[9] "Must have" Free resources for Open-Source Intel (OSINT). 2020. Available from: https://www.sans.org/blog/-must-have-free-resources-for-open-source-intelligence-osint-/ [2020-11-28]

[10] Top 12 best search engines in the world. 2016. Available from: https://www.inspire.scot/blog/2016/11/11/top-12-best-search-engines-in-the-world238 [2020-11-28]

[11] IP Location. 2020. Available from: https://iplocation.com/ [2020-11-28]

[12] 95+ Social networking sites you need to know. 2021. [2021-01-05]

[13] 7 servicios de email temporalis. 2016. Available from: https://www.genbeta.com/correo/7-servicios-de-email-temporales-para-evitar-spam-y-otros-problemas [2020-11-28]

[14] OSINT Framework. 2020. Available from: https://osintframework.com/ [2020-11-28]

[15] Las redes sociales como Fuente de información. 2012. Available from: http://portal.uned.es/pls/portal/docs/PAGE/UNED_MAIN/LAUNIVERSIDAD/VICERRECTORADOS/GERENCIA/IUISI/COLABORACIONES/076%20DOC_ISE_08_2012.PDF [2020-11-28]

[16] La usurpación de identidad. 2015. Available from: https://www.legalitas.com/pymes-autonomos/actualidad/articulos-juridicos/contenidos/La-usurpacion-de-identidad [2020-11-28]

[17] Suplantación de identidad, tipos y causas. 2019. Available from: https://protecciondatos-lopd.com/empresas/suplantacion-de-identidad/ [2020-11-28]

[18] IP Address. WhatIsMyIP. 2020. Available from: https://www.

whatismyip.com/ip-address-lookup/ [2020-11-28]

[19] ¿Qué es una VPN? 2020. Available from: https://www.xataka.com/basics/que-es-una-conexion-vpn-para-que-sirve-y-que-ventajas-tiene [2020-12-30]

[20] TOR Project. 2020. Available from: https://www.torproject.org/ [2020-11-28]

[21] Qué es la Dark Web, en qué se diferencia de la Deep Web y como puedes navegar por ella 2020. Available from: https://www.xataka.com/basics/que-dark-web-que-se-diferencia-deep-web-como-puedes-navegar-ella [2020-12-30]

[22] Your digital footprint: What is it and how can you manage it?. 2018. Available from: https://www.rasmussen.edu/student-experience/college-life/what-is-digital-footprint/ [2020-11-28]

Chapter 10

# Bibliometric Analysis of Cyber Threat and Cyber Attack Literature: Exploring the Higher Education Context

*Nazahah Rahim*


## Abstract

In nearly all procedures involving students and faculty, higher education organizations make substantial use of computers and the internet. Little is known on the progress and development of literature on cyber threats and cyber attacks in this sector. This chapter fills this gap by examining the trends of literature on cyber threats and cyber attacks focusing on the higher education. Bibliometric analysis through Scopus database was employed to offer research ideas and trigger debates. Analyzed parameters include the number of document types, publications, authorship, citation, and subject areas, as well as the topographical dispersion of published research. The earliest publication could be seen in the year 2003, and since then 606 papers were published. The majority of publications were conference papers but merely 8.42% of those were open access. The results indicate that publications hit a plateau in 2018, with English becoming the main publication language. The most prominent country that has contributed to the literature is the United States. Nonetheless, the majority of the publications were contained by the subject area of Computer Science, hence it is relatively challenging to trace the progress in education context. This chapter presents a groundwork providing insights for others to probe into the topic further.


**Keywords:** bibliometric, cyber attack, cyber threat, higher education, university

## 1. Introduction

The global population exceeds seven billion humans, and as of February 2019, there were over four billion internet users worldwide (Internet World Stats). Asia accounts for almost two billion of these internet users. From 2000 to 2018, internet use in Asian countries increased at a pace of 1,704% (Internet World Stats). Malaysia, for example, a nation in the Asian region, experienced 880 percent rise from 2006 to 2017, as well as a rise in the number of internet users from 2.5 million to 24.5 million citizens [1]. This trend shows that people across the globe are widely accessing internet capabilities in their everyday lives; as more and more people invest in cyber space to conduct their daily activities, cyber protection is critical.

One aspect adding to this effect is the advancement in information and communication technology (ICT), which provides consumers with unique resources and possibilities. Although ICT and its technology have made substantial strides, the cyber space is still far from protected, as it is prone to cyber breaches and cyber-attacks. For example, despite Malaysia's strong commitment to cyber protection and ranking third among 193 countries worldwide, there were 6,274 cases of cyber-attacks reported in 2017 [2]. This demonstrates that cyberspace cannot be completely protected; therefore, concern regarding cyber protection is critical given the increasing dependency on information systems and the internet. Again, considering Malaysia as an example, a report by Microsoft, an acclaimed technology firm, revealed that the possible economic loss due to cyber threats would reach a stunning USD12.2 billion, which is equal to more than 4 percent of Malaysia's total GDP of USD296 billion [3]. Additionally, the analysis discovered that a large-sized organization in Malaysia would suffer a USD22.8 million economic loss, which is 630 times greater than the average economic loss for a medium-sized organization [3]. While cyber protection is a serious concern, a massive amount of information and information is still exchanged globally through the cyber space. This is true not just for companies, but also for other industries, such as higher education.

Cyber protection is an appealing concern due to the supremacy and rapid development of computing systems and internet capabilities. Higher education is one of the industries under pressure. There have been reports of universities being subjected to cyber assaults in which their data are hacked. Users in institutions of higher education access information through portable devices that enable them to be highly mobile. This familiarity with networking enables them to connect to the network at any time and from any platform. As a consequence of the tradition of transparency and having free access to data and documents, security breaches and cyber-attacks at institutions of higher education are highly challenging to protect [4, 5].

Inadequate computer defense exposes higher education to risks, and the abundance of scholarly study data has transformed educational institutions into an enticing destination for cyber criminals [6]. This demonstrates that institutions of higher education, such as colleges and universities, are increasingly vulnerable to cyber security threats. They become insecure as a result of the open access and information-sharing ethos prevalent in the majority of universities. This is concerning for the higher education industry, as cyber-attacks such as hacking have the potential to halt research operations. Hackers distribute valuable knowledge obtained from universities, and hackers may quickly exchange data when it becomes an asset [6]. Universities' online systems are a prime subject for cyber security attacks like hacking [6]. It is because the network in operation at universities includes highly confidential personal details for students and faculty, as well as a wealth of scholarly intellectual property. The university community's tradition of accessible dialog and teamwork, which includes faculty, administrative personnel, researchers, and study organizations, makes the system much more susceptible to threats and assaults.

Higher education institutions make full use of information technology and the internet in nearly all of their operations. Higher education networks are linked to the virtual realm, but the cyber space remains insecure as a result of fraud and misconduct, posing cyber security risks. Cyber security refers to the process of safeguarding computer-related systems, such as software, hardware and electronic data, from fraud, destruction, disturbance, or subterfuge. Prior research has addressed a variety of topics associated with data security in general, though not directly to cyber-attacks and network security. Only recently have scholars recognized the importance of this problem in an educational or academic environment, particularly when universities begin to adopt online learning. As such, this chapter would examine the pattern of research undertaken in the field of cyber challenges and cyber-attacks in higher education. Its aim is to investigate what is currently available and to explain the history of the literature, as well as to make recommendations for potential study.

This chapter is divided into the following sections: The following segment would discuss the literature review, accompanied by the methodology. The methodology segment details the methodology followed, including the source, dataset, data collection, and major research components. The results and discussion segment includes an overview of the data produced by the bibliometric studies, as well as a summary of the findings. Finally, the conclusion segment discusses the study's shortcomings, makes recommendations for potential studies, and makes several closing remarks.

## 2. Literature review

Cyber threats are the chances of malicious attempts to damage or disrupt a computer network or system and are called cyber-attacks when these possibilities turn into a genuine effort [7]. A cyber-attack can be initiated through viruses, worms, Trojan horses, rootkit, botnet, or spyware that interrupt the online system [8]. These attacks are executed to acquire unauthorized access to personal data, to destroy and steal sensitive information [9]. The terms cyber threat and cyber attack are often used interchangeably in the literature; however, the main difference between these two terms is like intention and actions. When a malicious program is developed with an intention to breach cyber security is called a cyber threat and when it is actually used for intrusion into the system is become the potential attack [10].

Cyber threats have mainly three types, i.e. malware, distributed denial of service (DDoS) attacks, and ransom-ware. Firstly, malware is the most common type of malicious program that can attack a computer system, but the victim must have to click on the link provided. This link is given on an email or web page, and hackers usually place this link under some attractive statement or image that forces the victim to click on it. Upon clicking, the malware downloads into the computer and accesses the system, after which it can delete important files and leak sensitive information [8]. Secondly, Secondly, Ransomware resembles malware in nature, but they do not need to click on a link to download it to the system but are automatically downloaded from an email or website. The ability to auto-download makes it more powerful and dangerous as compared to malware (Russell, 2017). Finally, DDoS attacks are not intended to gain access to the computer system, but to overload web traffic. This causes the website to temporarily shut down, and the company may be facing loss in terms of revenues and consumers [9].

With the robust increase in online activities in the last decade, many virtual networks are exposed to cyber-threats [11]. In this regard, mostly prior studies focused the banking and defense systems, but a little is known about the intensity of cyber threats and attacks in the context of higher education [10, 11]. Higher education institutions are increasingly using web-based portals, where all their educational resources and information (including academic results, students' personal records and e-library) are available [12]. Therefore, higher educational institutions are exposed to cyber-attacks due to the availability of sensitive information and data [13].

Mostly, past studies explored the recent digitization and development of web-based educational management systems in higher education institutes to gain ICT competence [14]. Utilization of cyber services not only develop a knowledge management system of higher educational institutes but also enhance their performance

[15]. This growing trend in e-learning systems adopted by higher education institutions highlights the serious concern for cyber security [16]. In line with this, [17, 18] highlighted the gaps in cyber security and stressed the development automated threat modeling system. Therefore, it is required to develop an effective cyber security system that can detect and prevent cyber-threats and attacks.

Specifically, in the context of cyber security, most of the research in higher education has been done in risk management frameworks and standards whereas, the least focus is given to the governance and cultural awareness [19]. Due to which cyber security has not been implemented in higher education institutions in its true spirit. In line with this, [18], highlighted that generally higher education institutions do not have independent central security services due to lack of resources. As a result, they have to out-source these services, which are insufficient for cyber security [19]. The main reason for this inadequacy is the unique nature of educational institutions' security systems, which is radically different from other institutions' security systems [20].

In addition, [21] argued that linking with a countywide firewall; the institutions can prevent cyber-attacks more effectively. When a network is linked to a national firewall, it filters all the incoming network stream that prevents cyber threats and attacks. One possible drawback of this process is that it reduces the pace of data transmission within the networks that cause in a long delay in system response and sometimes declines the request [22]. In order to smooth and quick data transmission, the threat modeling approach is preferred for cyber-attack prevention, that models the independent and exclusive security framework for a specific system [17]. But this is not possible without the special attention of the administration as it requires considerable resources in the form of a dedicated workforce and system [18].

Furthermore, [23] noted that awareness of the information security of higher education institution members (students, faculty, and employees) could play a vital in the prevention of cyber-attacks. They also assessed the information security awareness among the members of middle-east higher education institutes and found a low level of awareness among them. Similarly, [24] analyzed cyber security behavior among Malaysian students of higher education institutes and also found a low level of understanding about the subject among them. The findings of both studies are similar that indicate the need for a comprehensive training program of higher education institution members to enhance their understanding of information security [23].

## 3. Methodology

A bibliometric analysis was conducted to ascertain the developments in the literature on cyber risks and cyber assaults. Due to the exploratory aspect of this research, bibliometric analysis is an efficient tool for detecting and examining the development of this research field. Although this research offers a foundational analysis, it adds to awareness and experience by being one of the first to analyze literature on cyber vulnerability and cyber assault in higher education since 2004. As of 25 July 2019, the list of publications was retrieved using the Scopus database search engine. Scopus (scopus.com) is an online library that stores the world's biggest collection of abstracts and citations to peer-reviewed literature. The index contains 1.4 billion citations extending all the way back to the 1970s and is an often-referenced source of other bibliometric research studies. Numerous forms of recorded evidence and articles were analyzed, including scientific journals, articles, books, and conference proceedings. Due to the chapter's primary emphasis on cyber threat and attack, the following search words were used: cyber threat*, cyberthreat*, cyber-threat*, cyber attack*, cyberattack*, and cyber-attack*. The index was checked using these words in the following areas: title, keywords, and abstract. The online searching of these words resulted in 606 datasets, which were then analyzed further. The findings were then classified according to the number of articles, document formats, subject fields, authorship, and geographical distribution of countries contributing to the literature. The subsequent section discusses the analysis's findings, which are represented graphically and in organized views of the cited studies.

## 4. Results and discussion

This segment addresses the different methods of access and the amount of publications over time, the text types, the subject fields in which the papers were written, the most influential contributors, the countries where the study was conducted or the regional distribution of the articles, as well as the languages used.

### 4.1 Access types and number of publications

The data was initially analyzed depending on the type of access and the amount of publications. According to **Table 1**, 8.42 percent of documents released on the subject of cyber threats and cyber attacks were open access. This implies that it would be difficult for researchers to obtain and access materials, data, and information from sources such as journal articles, conference papers, and theses, so study outputs are not often freely available online. It is clear that the previous publications occurred in 2003 with two publications and remained a relatively unpublished subject until 2010, when the number of publications increased from fewer than ten per year to fourteen per year. Following the year, there is a reasonably constant growth in the number of publications. This may be due to increased interest in the topic. The most productive year was 2018, with a record of 144 (23.76 percent). **Table 2** and **Figure 1** outline the detailed statistics on the amount of literature written. Nevertheless, further examination of the papers, especially the title, demonstrated that very little research on higher education has been conducted.

### 4.2 Document types

**Table 3** summarizes the document forms, with conference papers accounted for the bulk (54.29% of documents written before 2020), journal articles accounted for 32.67 percent, and book chapters accounting for 6.93 percent. The remaining documents included conference reviews, book reviews, articles in press, brief essays, editorials, notices, and erratum. Over a 17-year span, 329 conference papers on the subject of cyber threat and cyber attack have been published mostly as proceedings

| Access type | Frequency | % (N = 606) |
|---|---|---|
| Open access | 51 | 8.42 |
| Other (non-open access) | 555 | 91.58 |
| Total | 606 | 100% |

**Table 1.**
*Access type.*

| Publication Year | Frequency | % (N = 606) |
|---|---|---|
| 2020 | 2 | 0.33 |
| 2019 | 65 | 10.73 |
| 2018 | 144 | 23.76 |
| 2017 | 99 | 16.34 |
| 2016 | 66 | 10.89 |
| 2015 | 47 | 7.76 |
| 2014 | 41 | 6.77 |
| 2013 | 51 | 8.42 |
| 2012 | 33 | 5.45 |
| 2011 | 17 | 2.81 |
| 2010 | 14 | 2.31 |
| 2009 | 8 | 1.32 |
| 2008 | 7 | 1.16 |
| 2007 | 2 | 0.33 |
| 2006 | 4 | 0.66 |
| 2005 | 3 | 0.50 |
| 2004 | 1 | 0.17 |
| 2003 | 2 | 0.33 |
| Total | 606 | 100% |

**Table 2.**
*Number of publications according to year.*

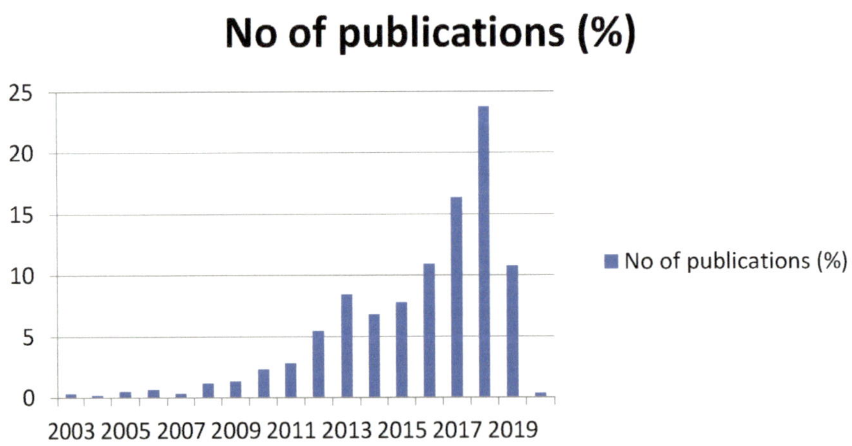


**Figure 1.**
*The trend of publication from 2003 until 2020 (as at 25 July 2019).*

in a variety of venues, including the European Conference On Information Warfare And Security Eccws, the ACM International Conference Proceeding Series, the Proceedings IEEE Military Communications Conference MILCOM, and the Proceedings Of The 12th International Conference On Cyber. Nonetheless, most scholars did not choose to report in specialized publications such as Advances in Intelligent Systems and Computing, Communications in Computer and Information Science, Computers and Security, and Computer Fraud and Security. This may be

| Document Type | Frequency | % (N = 606) |
|---|---|---|
| Conference Paper | 329 | 54.29 |
| Article | 198 | 32.67 |
| Book Chapter | 42 | 6.93 |
| Review | 17 | 2.81 |
| Book | 13 | 2.15 |
| Short Survey | 2 | 0.33 |
| Editorial | 1 | 0.17 |
| Undefined | 4 | 0.66 |
| Total | 606 | 100% |

**Table 3.**
*Document types.*

that proceedings require less time to print than papers. Other variables include the expectations and criteria of journal publishers to ensure that their publications are comparable to existing and high-quality journals.

### 4.3 Subject areas

The subject areas of the publications published between 2003 and 2020 are depicted in **Figure 2** and **Table 4**. As a result of this analysis, 34.91 percent of documents released on cyber threats and cyber attacks fall under the area of Computer Science. This is accompanied by 25% in the field of Engineering and 7.19 percent in the field of Mathematics. Previous authors' works are also available in the fields of Social Sciences, Decision Science, and Energy. This indicates that the difficulty and multidisciplinary existence of the problem are important in a variety of fields. This is significant because the topic of cyber threats and attacks encompasses many subject fields, not just computer science, which examines the philosophy, experimentation, software, and engineering involved in the design and usage of machines, but also social sciences and humanities. This, though, makes it more difficult for prospective scholars to conduct literature searches centered on the education system.

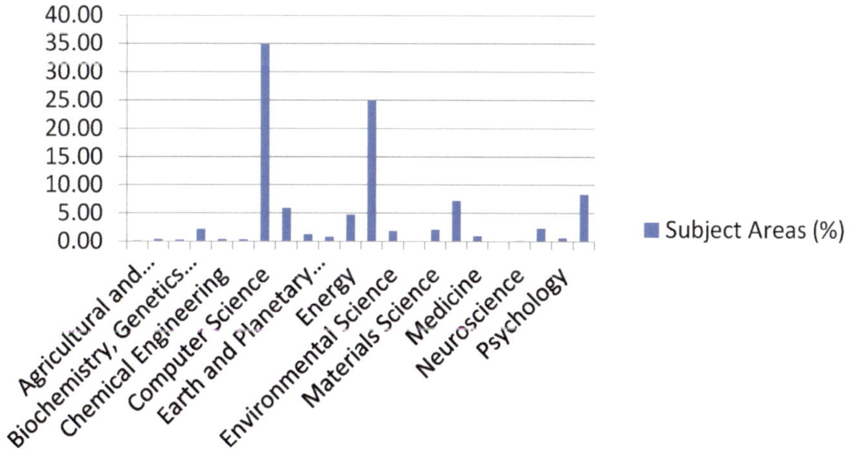


**Figure 2.**
*Subject areas.*

| Document Type | Frequency* | % (N = 1140) |
|---|---|---|
| Agricultural and Biological Sciences | 2 | 0.18 |
| Arts and Humanities | 5 | 0.44 |
| Biochemistry, Genetics and Molecular Biology | 3 | 0.26 |
| Business, Management and Accounting | 25 | 2.19 |
| Chemical Engineering | 5 | 0.44 |
| Chemistry | 4 | 0.35 |
| Computer Science | 398 | 34.91 |
| Decision Sciences | 67 | 5.88 |
| Earth and Planetary Sciences | 14 | 1.23 |
| Economics, Econometrics and Finance | 9 | 0.79 |
| Energy | 53 | 4.65 |
| Engineering | 285 | 25.00 |
| Environmental Science | 21 | 1.84 |
| Health Professions | 1 | 0.09 |
| Materials Science | 24 | 2.11 |
| Mathematics | 82 | 7.19 |
| Medicine | 11 | 0.96 |
| Multidisciplinary | 1 | 0.09 |
| Neuroscience | 2 | 0.18 |
| Physics and Astronomy | 26 | 2.28 |
| Psychology | 7 | 0.61 |
| Social Sciences | 95 | 8.33 |
| Total | 1140 | 100% |

**Some documents were categorized under more than one subject area.*

**Table 4.**
*Subject areas.*

## 4.4 Authorship

The data collection method resulted in the development of 606 datasets, each of which was registered and published by 160 distinct writers. The datasets revealed information about the most prolific writers who have authored several research papers. According to the analysis in **Table 5**, there were two productive scholars who both reported six publications on cyber threats and cyber attacks. Bella Genge of Targu Mures University of Medicine, Pharmacy, Sciences, and Technology in

| Author Name | Frequency |
|---|---|
| Genge, B. | 6 |
| Sengupta, S. | 6 |
| Chen, H. | 5 |
| Cho, H. | 5 |
| Haller, P. | 5 |
| Lakhno, V. | 5 |
| Samtani, S. | 5 |
| Debbabi, M. | 4 |

| Author Name | Frequency |
|---|---|
| Govindarasu, M. | 4 |
| Hwang, I. | 4 |
| Kim, N. | 4 |
| Kiss, I. | 4 |
| Lee, S. | 4 |
| Lehto, M. | 4 |
| Nunes, E. | 4 |
| Shakarian, P. | 4 |
| Ban, T. | 3 |
| Bou-Harb, E. | 3 |
| Chu, B. | 3 |
| Dolan, A.M. | 3 |
| Dondossola, G. | 3 |
| Eto, M. | 3 |
| Fergus, P. | 3 |
| Geers, K. | 3 |
| Graf, R. | 3 |
| Hurst, W. | 3 |
| Husari, G. | 3 |
| Joshi, A. | 3 |
| Kam, A. | 3 |
| Kamhoua, C.A. | 3 |
| Khanna, K. | 3 |
| Kiesling, T. | 3 |
| Kshetri, N. | 3 |
| Kwon, C. | 3 |
| Levy, Y. | 3 |
| Liu, E.C. | 3 |
| Merabti, M. | 3 |
| Panigrahi, B.K. | 3 |
| Ruane, K.A. | 3 |
| Simari, G.I. | 3 |
| Skopik, F. | 3 |
| Stevens, G. | 3 |
| Thompson, R.M. | 3 |
| Akhgar, B. | 2 |
| Al Hamar, J. | 2 |
| Al-Shaer, E. | 2 |
| Al-Shaer, E. | 2 |
| Alves, T. | 2 |
| Anwar, Z. | 2 |
| Arimatsu, T. | 2 |
| Ashok, A. | 2 |
| Assi, C. | 2 |
| Astatke, Y. | 2 |
| Au, H. | 2 |
| Awan, I. | 2 |
| Aydin, F. | 2 |
| Bagrodia, R. | 2 |
| Balitanas, M.O. | 2 |
| Betser, J. | 2 |
| Bracho, A. | 2 |
| Brenner, S.W. | 2 |
| Brooks, T. | 2 |
| Buch, J.P. | 2 |
| Campbell, R.J. | 2 |
| Canzian, L. | 2 |
| Castiglione, A. | 2 |
| Cheung-Blunden, V. | 2 |
| Choi, M.S. | 2 |
| Choo, K.K.R. | 2 |

| Author Name | Frequency |
|---|---|
| Choraś, M. | 2 |
| Chowdhury, A. | 2 |
| Ciancamerla, E. | 2 |
| Clark, R.M. | 2 |
| Cole, D.G. | 2 |
| Conti, M. | 2 |
| Dargahi, T. | 2 |
| Das, R. | 2 |
| Dawson, M. | 2 |
| Dean, R. | 2 |
| Dutt, V. | 2 |
| Dwivedi, A. | 2 |
| Ekstedt, M. | 2 |
| Eldridge, J. | 2 |
| Elliott, D. | 2 |
| Ewart, R. | 2 |
| Gamba, G. | 2 |
| Goncharova, L.L. | 2 |
| Grobler, M. | 2 |
| Ha, B.N. | 2 |
| Hassan, A. | 2 |
| Hein, C. | 2 |
| Henning, A.C. | 2 |
| Holsopple, J. | 2 |
| Hu, J. | 2 |
| Inoue, D. | 2 |
| Jalal, I. | 2 |
| Jaquire, V. | 2 |
| Jun, M.S. | 2 |
| Kalogeraki, E.M. | 2 |
| Kamhoua, C. | 2 |
| Kim, B. | 2 |
| Kim, K. | 2 |
| Kim, T.H. | 2 |
| Koike, H. | 2 |
| Kovacevic, A. | 2 |
| Kozik, R. | 2 |
| Kwiat, K. | 2 |
| Kwiat, K.A. | 2 |
| Lee, K. | 2 |
| Lee, K. | 2 |
| Lee, S.J. | 2 |
| Lee, S.W. | 2 |
| Lee, W. | 2 |
| Lee, Y. | 2 |
| Lim, I.H. | 2 |
| Linkov, I. | 2 |
| Liu, W. | 2 |
| Loukas, G. | 2 |
| Ma, Z. | 2 |
| Maccarone, L.T. | 2 |
| Magalhães, J.P. | 2 |
| McLorn, G.W. | 2 |
| Merino, X. | 2 |
| Minichino, M. | 2 |
| Moazzami, F. | 2 |
| Mokhtar, M.R. | 2 |
| Morris, T. | 2 |
| Musliner, D.J. | 2 |
| Nakao, K. | 2 |
| Nazir, S. | 2 |

| Author Name | Frequency |
|---|---|
| Niederl, J. | 2 |
| Nikolic, D. | 2 |
| Niu, X. | 2 |
| Nobles, C. | 2 |
| Noor, U. | 2 |
| Oksiuk, A. | 2 |
| Olsberg, R. | 2 |
| Omar, M. | 2 |
| Otero, C. | 2 |
| Palmieri, S. | 2 |
| Palomar, E. | 2 |
| Panguluri, S. | 2 |
| Papastergiou, S. | 2 |
| Park, J. | 2 |
| Park, M. | 2 |
| Patel, D. | 2 |
| Patel, S. | 2 |
| Patton, M. | 2 |
| Pena, J. | 2 |
| Polemi, N. | 2 |
| Pota, H.R. | 2 |
| Pourmirza, Z. | 2 |
| Pournouri, S. | 2 |
| Pozzobon, O. | 2 |
| Rahman, M.A. | 2 |
| Rahman, M.S. | 2 |
| Ramim, M. | 2 |
| Ridley, M. | 2 |
| Rob, R. | 2 |
| Undefined | 1 |

**Table 5.**
*Authors and their publications.*

Romania and Sudipta Sengupta of Microsoft Research in Redmond, Washington, USA were the writers. Both scholars have amassed thousands of citations worldwide. Their research made significant contributions to information, experience, and philosophy, especially in the sense of cyber security concerns, but they remain underrepresented in the higher education sector.

### 4.5 Geographical distribution of publications

This division indicates the amount or percentage of papers written by writers from a certain region. The growing proportion of a country's international journals generates fresh opportunities for papers from that country to be seen by other scholars worldwide. Geographically, the bulk of publications (29.45%) originated in the United States of America. This may be attributed to the United States' plethora of resources and experience in the cyber threat and cyber assault domains. The United Kingdom comes in second with 6.69 percent and South Korea comes in third with 5.83 percent. As seen in **Table 6**, the majority of publications (600 papers) were written in English, while two were written in Ukrainian and the remaining in Polish, Russian, Portuguese, French, and Turkish. This specifically shows that writers from different countries have taken an interest in the research on cyber - attacks and cyber threats. Since 2003, researchers and scholars from more than 70 different nations have added to the body of knowledge on cyberattacks and cyber threats. **Table 7** lists all countries that led to the productivity of publications. The

| Language | Frequency* | % (N = 607) |
|---|---|---|
| English | 600 | 98.85 |
| Ukraine | 2 | 0.33 |
| French | 1 | 0.16 |
| Polish | 1 | 0.16 |
| Portuguese | 1 | 0.16 |
| Russian | 1 | 0.16 |
| Turkish | 1 | 0.16 |
| Total | 607 | 100% |

**One paper has been published in dual language.*

**Table 6.**
*Language used in the publications.*

| Publishing country | Frequency* | % (N = 703) |
|---|---|---|
| United States | 207 | 29.45 |
| United Kingdom | 47 | 6.69 |
| South Korea | 41 | 5.83 |
| India | 35 | 4.98 |
| Italy | 21 | 2.99 |
| Japan | 21 | 2.99 |
| China | 18 | 2.56 |
| Australia | 16 | 2.28 |
| Germany | 16 | 2.28 |
| France | 14 | 1.99 |
| Poland | 14 | 1.99 |
| Ukraine | 14 | 1.99 |
| Malaysia | 13 | 1.85 |
| South Africa | 11 | 1.56 |
| Canada | 10 | 1.42 |
| Finland | 9 | 1.28 |
| Russian Federation | 9 | 1.28 |
| Turkey | 9 | 1.28 |
| Pakistan | 8 | 1.14 |
| Saudi Arabia | 8 | 1.14 |
| Romania | 7 | 1.00 |
| Spain | 7 | 1.00 |
| Austria | 6 | 0.85 |
| Estonia | 6 | 0.85 |
| Portugal | 6 | 0.85 |
| Singapore | 6 | 0.85 |
| Israel | 5 | 0.71 |
| Netherlands | 5 | 0.71 |
| Denmark | 4 | 0.57 |
| Sweden | 4 | 0.57 |
| United Arab Emirates | 4 | 0.57 |
| Argentina | 3 | 0.43 |
| Greece | 3 | 0.43 |
| Ireland | 3 | 0.43 |
| Jordan | 3 | 0.43 |
| Kazakhstan | 3 | 0.43 |
| Norway | 3 | 0.43 |
| Qatar | 3 | 0.43 |
| Switzerland | 3 | 0.43 |
| Belgium | 2 | 0.28 |
| Bulgaria | 2 | 0.28 |
| Croatia | 2 | 0.28 |
| Hungary | 2 | 0.28 |
| Iraq | 2 | 0.28 |

| Publishing country | Frequency* | % (N = 703) |
|---|---|---|
| Montenegro | 2 | 0.28 |
| New Zealand | 2 | 0.28 |
| Serbia | 2 | 0.28 |
| Bahrain | 1 | 0.14 |
| Bangladesh | 1 | 0.14 |
| Bhutan | 1 | 0.14 |
| Botswana | 1 | 0.14 |
| Brazil | 1 | 0.14 |
| Colombia | 1 | 0.14 |
| Cyprus | 1 | 0.14 |
| Czech Republic | 1 | 0.14 |
| Ecuador | 1 | 0.14 |
| Hong Kong | 1 | 0.14 |
| Indonesia | 1 | 0.14 |
| Iran | 1 | 0.14 |
| Kuwait | 1 | 0.14 |
| Latvia | 1 | 0.14 |
| Lithuania | 1 | 0.14 |
| Macedonia | 1 | 0.14 |
| Malta | 1 | 0.14 |
| Mexico | 1 | 0.14 |
| Morocco | 1 | 0.14 |
| Nigeria | 1 | 0.14 |
| Slovenia | 1 | 0.14 |
| Taiwan | 1 | 0.14 |
| Viet Nam | 1 | 0.14 |
| Undefined | 39 | 5.55 |
| Total | 703* | 100% |

**Table 7.**
*Countries contributed to the publication.*

**Some papers were published by more than one author.*

United States of America (USA) came in first place with 207 (29.45 percent) documents, led by the United Kingdom (UK) with 47 (6.69%) documents and South Korea with 41 documents (5.83%).

The bibliometric analysis suggests that publications from more than 70 countries around the globe have contributed to the area. Researchers, including scholars from developed and developing countries, demonstrated an appetite and zeal for generating literature in the area of cyber attack and cyber threat.

## 5. Conclusions

The analysis provided in this chapter is aimed at increasing public awareness and interest in cyber threats and cyber attacks studies, especially among higher education institutions. Its aim is to investigate what is available and to explain its evolution over time, with the goal of igniting additional debates on the subject. As a result of the findings above, it is evident that there is a dearth of literature on cyber vulnerabilities and cyber attacks affecting higher education. Thus, much effort should be exerted in terms of this study, such as undertaking studies within the framework of higher education itself, as the effect of cybersecurity is felt worldwide, not only in one area, but in a variety of industries, including higher education. While the authorship and global distribution of the literature on cyber attacks and cyber threats indicate that the United States has the most publications and impact in terms of authorship, research focused on developing countries remain scarce. The majority of writers in this field come from developed countries such as the United Kingdom and South Korea. This means that additional research from researchers and scholars in developing countries is needed.

A further consequence is the usability problem, in which it is difficult to access information or literature pertaining to research on cyberattacks and cyber threats, given that the majority of published works are password-protected (non-open access). The majority of highly published articles were conference papers, such as proceedings, which lack the depth of data and facts included in complete papers. Additional investigation through prolonged study projects is necessary to fully comprehend the reasoning behind this problem and to comfortably apply it to related studies.

This paper was inspired by two observations: first, cyber attacks and cyber threats challenges have remained a contentious subject in the literature in recent years but are still uncommon in higher education; and second, handling this challenge in the higher education sector is difficult. Despite this, there is no consensus in the literature regarding progress in this field, particularly in higher education. This chapter began by indicating that there was a lack of clarification about the current extent of improvement achieved in the area of cyber threats and cyber attacks on higher education.

The aim of this paper is to examine the patterns and advances in this field using bibliometric analysis of written documents accessed from an online database. This article conducts a bibliometric analysis in order to achieve a better understanding of the cyber attack and cyber threats literature's dynamics, historical review, predictions, and contributions. The findings indicate that the literature on this subject began in 2003 and has continued to grow, with the peak of publications occurring in 2018 with a total of 144 publications, up from 99 in 2017. It is estimated that the overall number of publications will rise in 2021, since there are publications that have not yet been indexed by Scopus and therefore are not included in the datasets for this analysis as of 25 July 2019. However, there is also a lack of understanding about the patterns and advancements in the field of higher education.

This analysis has some drawbacks due to the database used. Thus, prospective scholars should be aware of these limits. To begin, even though Scopus is one of the largest directories, it does not archive all journals and names, and so publications in these journals might have been overlooked. Second, this review narrows the attention on malware attacks and cyber challenges based on the titles, abstracts, and keywords of the documents. Thus, all other elements of the literature that are relevant to the subject but are not specifically classified under these requirements were omitted, including the journal title, abstract, and keywords. Thirdly, since the database is continuously modified, the cumulative number of publications and other details collected are only accurate at the time of the scan. The data collection phase began on 25 July 2019, and as a result, the data used in subsequent evaluations were focused on this date.

Amid these drawbacks, this research is one of the first to analyze a variety of bibliometric indices of literature in the field of cyber threats and cyber attacks. This research aims to lay the foundation for future discussions on the subject of handling cyber threats and cyber attacks in higher education. The results should be able to inform future researchers on how to expand the subject. Future scholars are encouraged to pursue textual study, which would undoubtedly uncover additional and important results. It is because this research used basic search terms, including article titles, abstracts, and keywords, which are all accessible electronically via the Scopus website, rather than searching through entire articles or complete records. The data is gathered using a single database - Scopus. Although Scopus is the largest abstract and citation archive for peer-reviewed literature, including scientific journals, books, and conference proceedings, prospective research could include additional databases to obtain full and detailed findings on the published works of writers worldwide on the subject of cyber attacks and cyber threats. Comparative studies are often recommended in order to ascertain the parallels and discrepancies between findings obtained from various databases. Additionally, future studies may wish to use a range of research techniques, such as interviews, group discussions, surveys, or other approaches, in order to gather evidence and obtain rich information.

## Acknowledgements

The author wishes to thank the Ministry of Education Malaysia for funding this study. The grant is coded as 13598.

## Author details

Nazahah Rahim
Othman Yeop Abdullah Graduate School of Business (OYAGSB), Universiti Utara Malaysia, Malaysia

*Address all correspondence to: nazahah@uum.edu.my

## References

[1] Povera, A. 2018. Internet users in Malaysia up from 2.5mil in 2006 to 24.5mil in 2017. Available at https://www.nst.com.my/news/nation/2018/02/331284/internet-users-malaysia-25mil-2006-245mil-2017

[2] Aruna, P. 2017. Combating cyber crimes. Available at https://www.thestar.com.my/business/business-news/2017/11/18/combating-cyber-crimes/

[3] Paramasivam, S. 2018. Cybersecurity threats to cost organizations in Malaysia US$12.2 billion in economic losses. Available at https://news.microsoft.com/en-my/2018/07/12/cybersecurity-threats-to-cost-organizations-in-malaysia-us12-2-billion-in-economic-losses/

[4] Ramim, M., and Y. Levy. 2006. Securing e-learning systems: a case of insider cyber attacks and novice IT management in a small university. Journal of Cases on Information Technology (JCIT). 8(4): 24–34.

[5] Davidson, P., and K. Hasledalen. 2014. Cyber threats to online education: a Delphi study. In ICMLG2014 Proceedings of the 2nd International Conference on Management, Leadership and Governance: ICMLG 2014 (p. 68). Academic Conferences Limited.

[6] Chabrow, E. 2015. China blamed for Penn State breach: Hackers remained undetected for more than two years. Available at http://www.databreachtoday.com/china-blamed-for-penn-state-breach-a-8230

[7] Abomhara, M. (2015). Cyber security and the internet of things: vulnerabilities, threats, intruders and attacks. Journal of Cyber Security and Mobility, 4(1), 65–88.

[8] Abraham, S., & Chengalur-Smith, I. (2010). An overview of social engineering malware: Trends, tactics, and implications. Technology in Society, 32(3), 183–196.

[9] Singh, R., Kumar, H., Singla, R. K., & Ketti, R. R. (2017). Internet attacks and intrusion detection system. Online Information Review, 41(2), 171–184. https://doi.org/10.1108/oir-12-2015-0394

[10] Awan, J. H., Memon, S., Memon, S., Pathan, K. T., & Arijo, N. H. (2018). Cyber Threats/Attacks and a Defensive Model to Mitigate Cyber Activities. Mehran University Research Journal of Engineering and Technology, 37(2), 359–366. https://doi.org/10.22581/muet1982.1802.12

[11] Loukas, G., Gan, D., & Vuong, T. (2013). A review of cyber threats and defence approaches in emergency management. Future Internet, 5(2), 205–236. https://doi.org/10.3390/fi5020205

[12] Pattanayak, S., Mohapatra, S., Mohanty, S., & Choudhury, T. (2019). Empowering of ICT-Based Education System Using Cloud Computing. Innovations in Computer Science and Engineering, 32, 113–120.

[13] Baygin, M., Yetis, H., Karakose, M., & Akin, E. (2016). An effect analysis of industry 4.0 to higher education. In 15th International Conference on Information Technology Based Higher Education and Training (ITHET) (pp. 1–4). IEEE. https://doi.org/10.1109/ITHET.2016.7760744

[14] Khwaldeh, S. M., Al-Hadid, I., Masa'deh, R., & Alrowwad, A. (2017). The Association between E-Services Web Portals Information Quality and ICT Competence in the Jordanian Universities. Asian Social Science, 13(3), 156. https://doi.org/10.5539/ass.v13n3p156

[15] Aulawi, H., Ramdhani, M. A., & Slamet, C. (2017). Functional Need Analysis of Knowledge Portal Design in Higher Education Institution. International Journal of Soft Computing, 12(2), 132–141.

[16] Arlitsch, K., & Edelman, A. (2014). Staying Safe: Cyber Security for People and Organizations. Journal of Library Administration, 54(1), 46–56. https://doi.org/10.1080/01930826.2014.893116

[17] Xiong, W., & Lagerström, R. (2019). Threat modeling – A systematic literature review. Computers and Security, 84, 53–69. https://doi.org/10.1016/j.cose.2019.03.010

[18] Chapman, J. (2019). HEPI Policy Note 12 - How safe is your data? Cyber-security in higher education. London, UK.

[19] Bongiovanni, I. (2019). The least secure places in the universe? A systematic literature review on information security management in higher education. Computers and Security, 86, 350–357. https://doi.org/10.1016/j.cose.2019.07.003

[20] Doherty, N. F., Anastasakis, L., & Fulford, H. (2009). The information security policy unpacked: A critical study of the content of university policies. International Journal of Information Management, 29(6), 449–457. https://doi.org/10.1016/j.ijinfomgt.2010.06.001

[21] Sari, A. (2019). Turkish national cyber-firewall to mitigate countrywide cyber-attacks. Computers and Electrical Engineering, 73, 128–144. https://doi.org/10.1016/j.compeleceng.2018.11.008

[22] Russell, G. (2017). Resisting the persistent threat of cyber-attacks. Computer Fraud & Security, 2017(12), 7–11. https://doi.org/10.1016/S1361-3723(17)30107-0

[23] Al-Janabi, S., & Al-Shourbaji, I. (2016). A Study of Cyber Security Awareness in Educational Environment in the Middle East. Journal of Information & Knowledge Management, 15(1), 1–30.

[24] Muniandy, L., Muniandy, B., & Samsudin, Z. (2017). Cyber Security Behaviour among Higher Education Students in Malaysia. Journal of Information Assurance & Cybersecurity, 2017, 1–13. https://doi.org/10.5171/2017.800299